W9-CAH-512

# PRAISE FOR STEVE JACKSON'S
## *NO STONE UNTURNED*

"Jackson's sharp eye misses nothing in the painstakingly rendered details. A must-have for true crime fans."—*Publishers Weekly*

"Jackson takes readers on an often shocking journey into a realm of crime investigation few people know about."—*Law Enforcement Technology*

"This is a must-have for mystery lovers who need to know the real-life investigations that make today's fiction so compelling."—*St. Petersburg, Florida, Times*

"A treasure. It's a well-written, fast-paced ride along with gifted [forensic] investigators."—Carleton Stowers, best-selling author of the Edgar Award–winning *Careless Whispers*

"[An] inside view of crime, science and the unrelenting hunt for evil . . . remarkable and stunning."—Gregg Olsen, best-selling author of *Starvation Heights*

"A fascinating journey into the trenches of crime [investigation]."—Lowell Cauffiel, *New York Times* best-selling author of *House of Secrets*

"Well-written, well-paced . . . Jackson did his homework. A must read for true crime enthusiasts."—Philip Carlo, best-selling author of *The Night Stalker*

"Gives a true and accurate insight into how the scientific world, outside the 'crime lab,' can impact a criminal case." —Michael "Coach" Schmitz, Divisional Tactical Advisor (ATF), interagency team on the Christine Elkins case

"Steve Jackson introduces the hard-working professionals [of Necrosearch International] and their methods to anyone who has not had the privilege of working with them as I have." —Kathy Young, lead detective on the Michelle Wallace case

# <u>BOOK YOUR PLACE ON OUR WEBSITE</u> AND MAKE THE <u>READING CONNECTION!</u>

We've created a customized website just for our very special readers, where you can get the inside scoop on everything that's going on with Zebra, Pinnacle and Kensington books.

When you come online, you'll have the exciting opportunity to:

- View covers of upcoming books
- Read sample chapters
- Learn about our future publishing schedule (listed by publication month *and author*)
- Find out when your favorite authors will be visiting a city near you
- Search for and order backlist books from our online catalog
- Check out author bios and background information
- Send e-mail to your favorite authors
- Meet the Kensington staff online
- Join us in weekly chats with authors, readers and other guests
- Get writing guidelines
- AND MUCH MORE!

**Visit our website at**
**http://www.kensingtonbooks.com**

# PARTNERS IN EVIL

## STEVE JACKSON

**PINNACLE BOOKS**
Kensington Publishing Corp.
http://www.kensingtonbooks.com

# ACKNOWLEDGMENTS

The author would like to thank the usual suspects: editor-in-chief Michaela Hamilton and senior editor Johnny Crime at Kensington Publishing Corp. for their patience; my wonderful agent, Mike Hamilburg of the Mitchell J. Hamilburg Agency, and his consigliere, Joanie Kern, for their hard work and friendship. Also, I could not do what I do without my friends and my family; with all my heart I thank them for their love and support.

Most of all the author would like to thank Peggy and Bob Luiszer, who have suffered the most horrible ordeal that can happen to parents and done so with nobility and courage. There are no words to ease the pain, no time that can pass that will make it better, nothing that can—or should—be done to help you "get over it." There is no getting over the loss of Jacine for her family or friends. I can only hope that there will come a time when you'll find yourselves again basking in the light and warmth of her smile and love.

The books owes portions of its text to a variety of sources including court transcripts, notes, interviews, and a number of media outlets. At certain points, the media were as much part of this story as they were later an information source for the author. In part their reaction was used herein to illustrate the impact of such a crime on the media of a midsized city and in turn, the media's impact on the justice system.

In instances where comments were made to the media in

general (such as a press conference), that's how they are attributed in the text; otherwise the author endeavored to credit the specific source in the attribution of the text. Some aspects of this book originally appeared in June 2001 as work done by the author for *Westword* newspaper in Denver, Colorado. Otherwise, the author would like to credit the work during the three and a half years of hearings, trials, and sentencing of: KCNC-Channel 4, KUSA-Channel 9, KRDO-Channel 12, the *Denver Post*, the *Rocky Mountain News*, the Colorado Springs *Independent*, the *Littleton Observer*, and most of all the *Gazette* in Colorado Springs and the writing of then-Metro Editor Valerie Wigglesworth, columnist Ralph Routon, and reporters John Diedrich, Debra Franco, Ardy Friedberg, Jennifer Hamilton, Bill Hethcock, Bill McKeown, Jeremy Meyer, Danielle Nieves, and Erin Randolph. The author would like to thank in particular from the *Gazette*: *Gazette* cartoonist Chuck Asay for the cartoons that appear in this book, as well as his insights into the community he loves, and Creators Syndicate for allowing his work to appear here, as well as photographer Jay Janner for his assistance.

Also the author thanks the staff of the Fourth Judicial District Attorneys Office, in particular Gordon Denison, Dan Zook, and David Young, who knew the truth and proved it.

# CONTENTS

# PART I

## WOUND UP
## BY THE DEVIL

*If one can only perform good or only perform evil, then he is a clockwork orange—meaning that he has the appearance of an organism lovely with colour and juice, but is in fact only a clockwork toy to be wound up by God or the Devil or (since this is increasingly replacing both) the Almighty State.*

—Anthony Burgess, from the introduction to his 1962 novel *A Clockwork Orange*

# PROLOGUE

## A LITTLE OF
## THE OL' IN-OUT

*March 1997*
*Colorado Springs, Colorado*

The light from the television flickered hypnotically in the darkened living room of the small apartment where George Woldt and his best friend, Lucas Salmon, had settled in to watch a movie. Woldt's wife, Bonnie, seven months pregnant, joined them, though she was the outsider in that company.

A face appeared on the screen. Eyes blue and chill as ice, one adorned with makeup and false lashes, looked out from beneath a bowler. They belonged to the film's narrator and protagonist, Alex, who smirked all predatory and cunning-like as his working-class British voice cut in:

ALEX: There was me, that is Alex, and my three droogs, that is Pete, Georgie Boy and Dim. And we sat in the Korova Milk Bar trying to make up our rassoodocks what to do with the evening.

The camera angle widened to reveal Alex and three

other young men—all dressed alike in what appeared to be white long underwear with protective codpieces worn on the outside, as well as bowlers and black Doc Marten boots—drinking milk (laced with drugs) on a nightclub couch.

ALEX: The Korova Milk Bar sold milk plus— milk plus vellocet or synthemesc or drencrom, which is what we were drinking. This would sharpen you up and make you ready for a bit of the old ultra-violence.

Both thin and of average height, George Woldt and Lucas Salmon were an unlikely pair: the big-talking, pornography-loving ladies' man and the quiet, God-fearing missionary. One was the leader and the other the follower, but it's doubtful that either would have had the nerve to do alone what they would do together.

Woldt had seen the 1971 film *A Clockwork Orange* many times; it was one of his favorites, but tonight he had an ulterior motive for renting it. Call it the next step in his plan to seduce Salmon into helping him realize the fantasy he nurtured. He'd tried to recruit other friends in the past, but when they realized that he wasn't just kidding, they'd distanced themselves from his "demented" ideas. But Salmon was different—weaker, socially inept, a twenty-one-year-old virgin, and willing to do almost anything to keep Woldt's friendship. The perfect droog, to use the movie's vernacular.

He looked over to see if Salmon was paying attention. The dialogue in the movie could be hard to understand with its futuristic slang and British accents. But the script wasn't what really mattered to his plan.

The tone began with the Korova Milk Bar where the glass tops of the tables were supported by alabaster statues of nude women, faceup and braced on their hands and feet, breasts and pelvises thrusting up, white legs akimbo and genitalia exposed. But that was just scenery, a taste of what was to come. Woldt was anticipating his friend's reaction to what Alex called *"the ol' ultra-violence"* . . . and especially *"the ol' in-out."*

The film quickly shifted to a scene of a drunk lying in the gutter of an alley, singing with his hand on a paper bag containing a bottle. Trouble appeared in the form of four dark figures wearing bowlers and carrying sticks, silhouetted against the glare of a streetlight. The drunk stopped singing at the approach of the smiling Alex and his gang. He smiled back and held out his hand.

With the suddenness of a cobra, Alex struck his cane hard into the gut of the old man, who cried out.

With that, the four hoodlums set upon the old man with their clubs and chains, kicking his prone body with their big, black boots as they shrieked like delighted apes. Granted, nearly thirty years after the film was released, the savagery of the attack was somewhat tame and not as graphic as were current movies, but there was still something about the randomness and conscienceless implementation of the "ol' ultra-violence" that appealed to Woldt.

The narrator, Alex, continued his monologue as the camera shifted to a trashed stage in an abandoned theatre where a young woman was being stripped and ravaged by a different gang of young men dressed in various pieces of World War II German uniforms. As though in a dance performance, the assault was set to classical music and carefully choreographed. The victim even pointed her toes like a ballerina as she struggled to get away from her attackers, only to be carried to a mattress on the stage floor where the gang prepared to rape her, or as they called it, "a little of the ol' in-out, in-out."

The rape was interrupted by the appearance of Alex and his gang. The young woman escaped as the two groups of young men clashed with knives and clubs. Again, the violence was set to music and performed with a comic flare.

After the gang rumble, Alex and his droogs drove out into the countryside where they rampaged through the home of a writer and his wife, who let them into the house when Alex said that there'd been a traffic accident and he needed to use the telephone. While Alex sang and danced, the writer was stomped, bound, and gagged, and then forced to watch as his wife was cut from her clothing with a pair of scissors and then raped.

All of this had occurred in the first half hour of the film, and that was enough for Bonnie Woldt. "This is sick," she said. "I'm going to bed." With a baby due in May, she was getting a little fed up with having Lucas Salmon as a constant houseguest. He'd moved in shortly after she and George got married in February and didn't appear to be leaving any time soon.

Moreover, Salmon had changed since she'd first met him in 1995. Back then he'd been a shy but intelligent and well-mannered young man who talked a lot about God and how he and his father and brothers were active with their church. His particular brand of Christianity was strict; he did not drink alcohol or smoke cigarettes, and he was still a virgin—a fact her husband was constantly giving him a hard time about, not that she had been above joining in the teasing.

Initially, she'd hoped that some of Salmon's better traits would rub off on her husband, but the effect had been just the opposite. Now, Salmon was foul-mouthed and coarse. He drank several beers a night, smoked cigarettes as if making up for lost time, and was preoccupied with sex and his lack of conquests.

After several unsuccessful attempts to set Salmon up with young women friends, she wondered if he was a homosexual. He wasn't bad-looking—just geeky and plain with his thick lips, slightly bulbous nose, and pronounced male-pattern baldness; his hazel eyes protruded a little, giving him a deer-in-the-headlights expression, especially in the company of girls.

There was no denying that her husband was a bad influence on Salmon. George was a womanizer before she met him and, she suspected, was still on the prowl, especially with her being pregnant. Her husband was obsessive about his appearance; even at home while he was relaxing in front of the television with his friend and wife, his dark hair was exquisitely combed, his fingernails immaculate at the end of his carefully scrubbed hands. There were stranger aspects, too. He insisted on symmetry when it came to his appearance—his hair was split straight down the middle, not an extra strand to left or right; and if he wore a Band-Aid on one part of his body, he put another on the opposite side. He also had an almost absentminded habit of sniffing everything he came into contact with, including other people, while at the same time his omnipresent cologne hung in the air like a bad dream.

If he was slavish about his appearance, he was even more obsessed with sex, the rougher and kinkier the better. He liked to watch pornography—especially the kind that depicted rape or some other sort of violent acts—and his favorite time to have sex was after they fought. It seemed that the anger and even the occasional bit of physical violence between them aroused him.

She wasn't surprised that *A Clockwork Orange* with all its beatings and rapes fascinated George and probably turned him on. But it was obvious, tonight anyway, that he was less interested in her than Salmon, whose pious personality seemed to be getting further submerged, like a drowning man going under for the third time. So she waddled off to bed.

As for Woldt and Salmon, they'd certainly seen more graphic and violent sex acts in vivid pounding detail in other films they watched. But again, there was something about the almost comical portrayal of the rape scenes in

*A Clockwork Orange* that seemed to blur the line between fantasy and reality. The movie made rape look like a fun outing in the park.

Many lines were blurring for Salmon, especially between the teachings of his church and what he knew to be sinful. He'd told friends before that Woldt was "bad news," and yet he wanted nothing so much than to be like him, even if George didn't always treat him well.

So what if George made fun of him in front of other people, especially about his virginity? And so what if every time George wanted something or felt he should punish Salmon for some transgression—real or imagined—he only had to say "we're not friends anymore" and Lucas had to crawl to get back in his good graces? The fact remained that he'd asked him, Lucas Salmon, to be the best man at his wedding.

So what if George had strange, sinful fantasies? That he liked to talk about sexually assaulting and sodomizing women? Or that he'd even suggested that they rape a woman when they were in Delaware for the wedding? After all, George smiled when he said those things so that Lucas would know that he was "just kidding."

Anyway, Salmon found all the talk about sex—even about forcing himself on a woman—exciting. Every day that passed in the company of Woldt made it easier to ignore the voice of his conscience complaining that even thinking about such things wasn't right. Indeed, he had a few dark secrets of his own that he hadn't shared with his "best friend" George.

Woldt had taught him a lot, exposed him to a world he would have otherwise never known. Such as the film they were watching that ended with Alex imagining having sex in the snow with a beautiful young woman, who was obviously enjoying the event, while spectators on either side of the couple clapped in appreciation of the performance.

As the two young men concentrated on the women's

breasts and pubic regions, neither of them understood—or they chose to ignore—that the film and the 1962 novel upon which it was based was a satire about the aestheticism of violence and the objectifying of women. Lost in their heated brains was the movie's pointed commentary about the politics of a justice system that couldn't decide whether its purpose was to punish or rehabilitate. Nor when it was over did they debate the film's ultimate question of whether moral choice could exist without both good and evil in the world.

The rapes and violence fed Woldt's fantasy, whetted his appetite for blood, or what Alex referred to as *"the old red red vino."* But he wanted an accomplice, someone with whom to share the excitement, as well as the risks, of his fantasy.

Salmon imagined himself in place of Alex—the happy woman, the applause . . . his friend would have to stop teasing him about being a virgin. He felt himself slipping further into the dark places of his mind. He was still resisting but every day he spent with George, it became easier to disregard the voice that warned him about the wages of sin.

Life was imitating art. George Woldt and his droog, Lucas Salmon, were clockwork oranges. Outwardly they were just two rather ordinary young men, working menial jobs but with their whole lives ahead of them. Internally, however, they were wound up like toys and set in motion toward a monstrous act of evil. An act George Woldt now innocently couched as a way to solve his friend's dilemma about still being a virgin.

"We need to get you one," he said, smiling, "for a little of the ol' in-out."

Salmon smiled back. He was thinking along the same lines, but leave it to George to put the fantasy into words. Of course, Lucas knew that his best friend was still just kidding.

# ONE

# "DID SHE SUFFER?"

*April 29, 1997*
*Littleton, Colorado*

For whatever reason, the first time someone tried to call about their daughter Jacine that night, the telephone didn't ring in the bedroom where Peggy Luiszer and her husband, Bob, were sleeping. But Bob heard the answering machine go off in the kitchen and got up to see who would be calling at 11:30 at night.

He was surprised to hear the voice of Jacine's former boyfriend, Marvin Lee, a police officer in the town where she had attended junior college before transferring to the University of Colorado's campus in Colorado Springs. "Have you been contacted by anyone in Colorado Springs about Jacine?"

"Who's calling?" Peggy wandered into the kitchen. "What's the matter?" It had been a long day. After she got off work at a child-care center, she and Bob drove to a local hospital to visit one of his coworkers who had just had a baby girl. Returning home from the hospital, they'd stayed up long enough to watch the ten o'clock news and then turned in for the night.

As they closed their eyes and fell asleep, they were just

a nice, middle-class couple, living a quiet life in a pleasant neighborhood of tree-lined streets, well-groomed lawns, and small, ranch-style homes. There was nothing out of the ordinary about their lives. She worked at the child-care center and he as a project planner for a company that made aerial lift trucks, the sort with a bucket or cherry picker on the end of a boom.

Every year, they spent their summer vacation visiting a friend who lived in San Diego, stopping at sites like the Grand Canyon along the way. The most extravagant trip had been the week they spent in Jamaica when Jacine, or "Jace" as she was known to family and friends, was twelve. Otherwise, like any other average American family, they worked during the week and looked forward to the weekends, especially during football season when they gathered on Sundays to watch their beloved Denver Broncos play and hoped for the day when star quarterback John Elway would finally win a Super Bowl.

Together they'd raised Peggy's daughter from a previous marriage, Jacine Gielinski, since she was two. Twenty years later, they were both looking forward to the day she would marry and to the happy years beyond.

At the hospital that evening, Peggy had held the other woman's infant—inhaling the sweet and sour baby smells, all of them good—and envisioned Jacine making her a grandmother. She hoped that her daughter would live nearby so that her grandchild could walk to Highlands Elementary School—just a few blocks from her home in Littleton, a small city grafted onto the southern end of Denver—as Jacine had done.

Of course, the thought of twenty-two year-old Jacine brought its worries, too. Peggy was concerned about her daughter's health, which had been on a downhill spiral for months. Jacine was only just recovering from a bout of mononucleosis, but her troubles weren't just physical. She also seemed to be suffering from depression over her failed relationship with Marvin Lee, as well as the death of her biological father, Jake Gielinski. The latter distressed her so much that Jacine recently confided that she believed that Jake was visiting her from beyond the grave.

Having the doldrums was unlike Jacine, who had always been such a strong, confident, enthusiastic bundle of energy and joy. Peggy put the onus of Jacine's problems, physical and mental, on Lee. He had, in Peggy's estimation, taken advantage of her daughter financially and emotionally, as well as directly causing some of her health problems.

Peggy also blamed him for the rift that had come between herself and Jacine. She and her daughter had always been honest with each other, but when Peggy said she thought that Lee was using her, she and Jacine had fought. Her daughter stopped calling as often, and the conversations they did have were strained. Peggy got the feeling her daughter was hiding things from her, something she never would have done in the past.

It was the first thing that had ever really come between them, and Peggy had hated Lee for it. So Peggy had been overjoyed when Jace announced in January that she wasn't seeing Lee anymore. Only recently had mother and daughter patched the quilt of their relationship and started talking frequently again on the telephone.

Considering Peggy's well-known animosity toward Lee, it had been a surprise to hear his voice on the answering machine. But the surprise gave way to fear. Lee said he'd heard something on his police scanner about the Colorado Springs police looking for Jacine. He left the name and telephone number of a detective in "the Springs."

Colorado Springs was where Jacine had moved after receiving her associate's degree at the junior college in 1995. She'd been offered a volleyball scholarship at the University of Colorado and went to pursue her bachelor's degree in communications. The move was welcomed by the

Luiszers, as Colorado Springs was only an hour's drive south of Littleton, compared to the five-hour drive to the junior college. They did not care for the city's conservative Christian fundamentalist politics, but there was no reason to believe that their daughter would not be safe there.

Bob Luiszer called the telephone number that Lee left, as Peggy hovered next to him. He was connected to a detective who told them that the police had received a report of a woman being abducted from an apartment complex parking lot by two men. The detective said there'd been a number of witnesses to the alleged abduction. Someone even had the presence of mind to take down the license plate number of the car used by the men to take their victim. A purse had been found in the parking lot containing a driver's license belonging to Jacine Gielinski.

The Luiszers asked if they should get in their car and drive to Colorado Springs. "No, just stay put until we find out more what's going on," the detective said.

So began a vigil of sitting at the small table in the kitchen, waiting for updates from the police. Not knowing what else to do, Peggy called her friend and neighbor, Cathy, who rushed right over, assuring her that it was all "probably just a prank."

At some point, Peggy got up from the kitchen table and wandered into Jacine's bedroom. The walls were painted lilac, purple being her daughter's favorite color, and the room reflected Jace's personality clearly. It was filled with trophies and stuffed animals—especially lions, the mascot of her alma mater Littleton High School—and peopled with photographs of her family and friends.

The room offered little except to remind Peggy that its owner was missing. So she left and went back to the kitchen to wait. Every so often, the telephone would ring with a new update from the Colorado Springs police, none of them good.

There was a call to say that the police had learned the

identity of the man suspected of driving the getaway car. They needed to ask a few questions. Did Jacine know anyone named Lucas Salmon? A friend or, perhaps, someone she might have met high school?

The Luiszers said they'd never heard the name, but they looked through Jacine's high school yearbook just in case. There was no Lucas Salmon. She had a cousin named Luke who lived in Arizona, they told the detective, but they knew of no one with that last name.

More time passed, and the dark outside pressed in against the windows. Then the ringing of the telephone slapped them out of their private thoughts. It was the police again. They'd located the car outside an apartment building and were talking to two male suspects. Another question: Did the name "George Woldt" ring a bell? No, they replied, he and Salmon were strangers to them and, as far as they knew, to Jacine.

The Luiszers held on to a ray of hope, but their grip slipped with each telephone call. The next one informed them that the suspects' car had been searched. Several items had been found in it smeared with what appeared to be blood. That was when Bob knew it was hopeless. The tears welled in his eyes as he recalled the last conversation he'd had with Jacine. She'd been talking about her dead father, but she stopped to reassure him of his place in her life, as she always had when there might be some question. "He was my father," she said, "but you'll always be my dad. You'll be the one who'll be walking me down the aisle someday." The words echoed in his mind now as the tears rolled down his cheeks. He knew there would be no marriage, no tears of joy. But he tried to stay strong for his wife.

Peggy was a wreck, weeping, staring with fear at the telephone every time it rang. She kept hoping that she was about to wake up and find out it was all a dream. *Wake up, wake up,* she told herself. But the nightmare kept unfold-

ing telephone call by telephone call. She took down a photograph of her daughter taken that previous Christmas that
had been on the mantel above the fireplace. Jacine smiled
at her in that way she had that made anyone who saw it
smile back. She was so pretty—blond curls to her shoulders, blue-eyed—yet she was no porcelain doll. Her beauty
was enhanced by the aura of an accomplished athlete.

Suddenly it struck her, there was no more pretending.
Peggy knew when she looked at the photograph that her
only child was dead. *Murdered.* The word infested her
mind like a cancer, eating up everything around it until
there was nothing else but the blackness it left behind.
*Murdered, but why? Who would want to kill such a lovely
young woman?* Her daughter got along with everyone; she
had friends in all walks of life, many of them since childhood. Peggy had never once heard her daughter say that
she hated anyone, or that anyone hated her. What could she
have done now that someone would want to kill her?

The Luiszers knew she was gone and yet they didn't
know, so they waited as the minutes dragged on beneath
the harsh fluorescent light in the kitchen. The telephone
rang again at 2:30 A.M. "This is the hardest thing I have to
do as a police officer," began the detective on the other end
of the line.

Peggy never heard the rest. She began to scream. "They
killed her!" she yelled and wept at the same time. "What
did they do to her?" She reeled as if mortally wounded, as
though she felt her daughter's torment.

Bob Luiszer watched his wife, helpless to do anything
for her. He wanted to break down himself, but he remained
on the line to listen to the last thing he would ever have expected to hear.

The detective said that they'd located Jacine's body. She
had been murdered. The two suspects had confessed and
took the police to the scene of the crime. Lucas Salmon
and George Woldt were under arrest and being questioned

further. There wasn't much else, he said, that he could tell them until after the autopsy later that day. "I'm sorry," he added.

Crying without reservation now, Bob wanted to ask one more question, but he was afraid of the answer. At the last moment, he mustered the courage. "Did she . . . did she suffer?"

There was a pause. Then, softly, the detective answered, "Yes, she suffered."

# TWO

# ". . . PRETTY STRANGE IDEAS."

*February 1997*
*Wilmington, Delaware*

The young woman turned the key in her car's ignition. The engine chugged a couple of times and then gave up. She tried again with the same results. Getting out of the car, she heard a man's voice from the yard next door.

"Need some help?" George Woldt called over to her. He and his friend, Lucas Salmon, were staying in the house next to where the young woman lived. They were awaiting Woldt's marriage the next day to his pregnant girlfriend, Bonnie.

Neither he nor Salmon, who was standing next to him, knew much about cars. But that didn't matter; he'd noticed that the woman was attractive and figured her troubles were a good excuse to introduce his best man to a little fantasy he nurtured.

The woman shook her head as she headed back into her house. "No, thanks," she called back and smiled.

Woldt nudged his friend and nodded toward where the woman had disappeared. "Let's go inside and rape her," he said. He laughed at the look on Salmon's face, but noticed how his friend's eyes had followed the woman with something akin to hunger.

Woldt had been born November 8, 1976, in South Korea, near the U.S. Army base where his father, Bill, was stationed. His mother, Song-Hui, was a local girl and eight months pregnant with George before Bill felt obligated to marry her. Part of his hesitation had to do with the erratic, emotional outbursts exhibited by Song-Hui and the other women in her family.

Song-Hui doted on George, who for his first five years was primarily raised by the Korean side of his family. In fact, he did not start speaking English until he entered school. He was a healthy, attractive boy, whose mother dressed him effeminately and entered him in children's beauty contests, several of which he won.

Another son, Eric, was born into the Woldt household two years later while they still lived in Korea, but Song-Hui's attention was focused on her eldest child. She was obsessed with his appearance—every hair had to be in place, his hands scrubbed, his clothes immaculate. He didn't even eat the same meals she cooked for his father and brother; instead, she made special foods for him.

However, being the prodigal son was not always a good thing. Song-Hui was prone to extreme mood swings and bouts of delusional ranting that, his being the one closest to her, were often directed at young George. Song-Hui ascribed her temperment to being "nervous." But her son never knew when she might scream at him and try to hit him over some small transgression, or hold him tight, cooing what a perfect child he was.

There was only one thing that marred his physical perfection. When he was five years old, George's index finger on his left hand got caught in a bread-making machine,

tearing it off near the second joint. Throughout his childhood, he wore a Band-Aid on the injured finger, though it
wasn't needed, and also wore one on the index finger of
his other hand.

The family eventually moved out of Korea as Bill Woldt
was transferred to other bases in Germany, then Indiana,
and finally the Fort Carson army base south of Colorado
Springs, Colorado. Being separated from her home and
family did nothing to improve Song-Hui's mental stability.
She believed that other people, especially the police, were
following her, intending to do her harm. She was convinced that their neighbors plotted against her, and she
accused her husband of having affairs.

In 1991, the psychosis was so severe that she was in-
voluntarily committed to a psychiatric unit, diagnosed as
suffering from depression "with psychotic features." The
psychotropic drug Haldol helped, but as soon as she was
released from the hospital she stopped taking the medica-
tion because "it hurt."

Her husband tried taking her to a psychiatrist as an out-
patient. However, the paranoid delusions continued
unabated—only now she thought that her husband was
having an affair with the psychiatrist, who was female, and
that the two were colluding against her. She refused to go
back for follow-up treatment. Instead, she accused her
husband of trying to get rid of her by "locking me up."

As he grew older, George Woldt's peculiarities picked
up where his mother's left off. As a teenager, he spent
hours in front of mirrors making sure that his hair was just
so, and that his fingernails were clean and well trimmed
with the ever-present nail clippers he carried in his pocket.
Perhaps as a lingering manifestation from the traumatic
experience of losing a finger, he developed a fascination
with Band-Aids, wearing them stuck to his clothes and
body regardless of whether they were needed. Afraid of
germs, he wouldn't eat off of plates that he suspected—

whatever their appearance—of being less than sterile. And he sniffed things he came into contact with, as though always trying to locate the source of some odd smell.

No matter what he did to make himself presentable, it was rarely good enough for his mother. She got on him about his skin, his hairstyle, his clothing, and the way he stood or sat. If he did not meet her criteria, she lashed out with her tongue. However, at the age of ten, he laughed if she hit him and infuriated her by saying, "It doesn't hurt." The balance of power in their relationship was beginning to shift.

The treatment he received from his father wasn't any better. Unhappy in his marriage, Bill Woldt thought of his wife's side of the family as "crazy" and "overemotional." But it wasn't as if his family had a clean bill of mental health, as there were branches of schizophrenia and alcoholism in the family tree.

Bill drowned his sorrows by going to bars every night after work with his army buddies. Then he'd come home drunk, angry and explosive. He never hit his wife, but he certainly had no such compunctions about his sons. Twice the army's child protective services agency investigated allegations of abuse, but both parents denied that there was a problem.

The Woldts transferred to Colorado Springs just prior to George's senior year in high school. He didn't like the move, and it seemed to exacerbate his destructive fits of rage and the frequent screaming matches with his parents.

George complained to friends, as well as teachers and employers, that his father beat him. One day when he was seventeen, he left the house and found a police officer to whom he complained that his father had assaulted him. The officer followed George home and asked about the boy's allegations. Bill Woldt admitted that he'd struck his son in the past, but denied the current allegation. The matter was dropped.

Shortly thereafter, George moved out of his parents' house and in with his pregnant girlfriend, Becky. She saw her boyfriend as someone who desperately needed the attention and affection that he didn't get from his parents. But she discovered, as would many others, that there were two different sides to George Woldt.

At times, he could be outgoing and charming, a popular student at Harrison High School. Intelligence tests placed him in the exceptionally bright range, and he'd done fairly well academically in high school until his final semester as a senior, when his grades fell noticeably. He was far more interested in being the center of attention, and was as slick around young women as the pomade he used in his hair. He bragged to his friends that he'd had sex with more than two dozen young women. Then again, he also claimed to have been a contract killer and, noting his Korean heritage, a tae kwan do martial arts expert. Not that anyone could remember him ever getting into a fight—at least not with anybody his own size.

Woldt's charisma did not work on everyone. One of his teachers later described his behavior in school as "sporadic and bizarre." He and others noted that sometimes when they spoke to Woldt he was unresponsive and would stare right through them as though they didn't exist. It was like he had some internal light switch on his personality that he turned on and off depending on his mood. But Harrison High had a reputation in the city for gangs, violence and drugs—teachers complained that they spent more time disciplining students than instructing them—and so one more troubled youth like Woldt did not stand out among the many others.

While he often turned on the charm with women, Woldt talked a different story when he was around his male friends. Females, he said, were all "bitches" and good for one thing—sex. He'd started watching pornographic films he took from his father's collection as a young teenager.

Girlfriends like Becky learned that the charm he used to woo them disappeared after he had them hooked. The worst of his misogyny he reserved for his mother. His friends were often surprised by the vehemence he sometimes turned on Song-Hui. He seemed to enjoy goading her into screaming matches, and friends stood slack-jawed as he would curse at her or slam doors in her face. Sometimes she would curse him back and leave. Other times she'd meekly obey when he'd order her to perform some service, such as taking him and his friends to lunch.

Becky was no stranger to his violent outbursts, either. She even tried to get him to go to counseling to deal with his anger, but he wouldn't. Instead, she learned to do what he said or suffer the consequences. He was a master manipulator, threatening to leave to get his way, and he was not above getting rough with her. In fact, he seemed to enjoy it.

Woldt's desire to control others didn't stop with women. Many of his male friends were strong enough to laugh off his manipulations, but there were others who fell into his snares, especially Lucas Salmon.

The two met in April 1994 when Woldt got a job with Future Call, a telemarketing firm where Lucas was already working. Woldt took it upon himself to educate the Bible-quoting, shy Salmon, who was nine months older, about women. He invited him over to smoke pot, drink beer, and watch pornographic films. Bragging about his sexual conquests, he constantly teased his new friend about being a virgin.

The sex-education classes continued after they graduated from high school in June 1994, when Salmon moved in with Woldt and Becky. He was planning on attending a small Christian college in southern California that fall, but in the meantime, he was learning all he could from the more worldly George Woldt.

When not teasing Salmon about his sexuality, Woldt seemed determined to assist him in finding a woman to sleep with. He and Becky even tried to set Salmon up with one of her friends, Angela. The stage was set for Salmon's deflowering when the four went out of town one weekend and rented a hotel room with two double beds.

After a few beers, Woldt got on one of the beds with Becky and the two began to have sex. They only paused long enough to suggest that Salmon and Angela do the same on the bed next to them. Angela was willing, but Salmon left the room. When he returned later, he slept on the floor, leaving Angela alone in the bed. He later explained that he didn't believe in premarital sex; that was pretty much it for Angela, who decided that while he was okay looking, he was "too nice" for her tastes.

After the incident, Woldt had given him a hard time. He acted like he was angry with Salmon after all Woldt had tried to do for him, but he then came around and resumed the usual "good-natured" teasing about his friend's virginity.

In the fall, Salmon left for California to attend school, but he was back in Colorado Springs that next summer. He again moved in with Woldt, Becky, and the couple's newborn son. However, Becky and her child soon moved out. She'd learned that her boyfriend was seeing other women.

Woldt told Salmon that she left because Salmon had left the toilet seat up. Making his friend feel guilty about imaginary transgressions was a typical example of how Woldt manipulated Salmon. One minute he'd tell Salmon they were best friends, the next he'd be making fun of the size of his penis or his virginity in front of others.

Sometimes Salmon didn't know which way to flip. After

Becky left, Woldt would dance around the apartment in his bikini underwear and demand that his friend look at him. If Salmon gave in, Woldt would then accuse him of being "a faggot." Sometimes out of the blue Woldt would declare that they weren't friends anymore, then delight in making Lucas find ways to crawl back into his good graces.

Salmon still went to church regularly and tried to get his friend to go with him, with no luck. Woldt didn't like the rules of the church, and he was also afraid of Salmon's father, Robert, who regarded him as a bad influence on his son.

Woldt seemed determined to shape Salmon in his own image. After an evening of watching pornographic films together, he'd declare that it was time they got Salmon laid, despite his friend's protests that he didn't want to have sex before marriage.

In August 1995, Woldt was dating a young woman named Karen, and he talked her into bringing a friend, Allison, over to the apartment to introduce to Salmon. When the girls arrived, Woldt announced that he had something special planned for the evening: a game of strip poker in the bedroom.

Woldt had no compunction about cheating at poker, and soon both young women were naked. Karen thought it was strange that her boyfriend seemed to be making a point of showing off her body to his friend, though she didn't resist when Woldt pulled her onto the bed and they began to have sex in front of Salmon and Allison. Again, Salmon turned down the opportunity.

Karen thought Salmon was strange. It wasn't so much his rejecting Allison, but the way he clung to Woldt. One evening she and Woldt got into an argument that had nothing to do with Salmon. He'd remained quiet through the discussion, but all of a sudden Salmon scowled and yelled at her, "Bitch!" The remark surprised both her and Woldt, but Salmon went back to sitting quietly as if nothing had happened.

For all of Woldt's self-assured behavior in most situations, there were some who thought it was all a front. Coworkers at Future Call noticed that when someone got the best of him teasing, he'd slip into some fantasy character out of a movie or a television show. One of his acts was doing a routine with Salmon modeled on *Beavis and Butthead*—an MTV cartoon about two "loser" adolescent males who spent most of their time parked on a couch in front of a television making wisecracks about other people, especially women.

There were other times when the veneer cracked entirely. One day a supervisor at work, Johnny Lopez, noticed that Woldt had come to work with a split lip and marks on his face. When Lopez inquired about the injuries, Woldt burst into tears and blurted out that his father had struck him during an argument at his parents' house.

Others, however, wondered if even those emotions were real or just another way Woldt had of manipulating others. There were times, especially when talking to women, when he would get tears in his eyes as he spoke about his "mean" former girlfriend who'd left him and wouldn't let him see his son. But the next minute, he'd be flirting or suggesting that he and the female object of his attention get together some time.

There was also a streak of meanness in him that, at times, he couldn't seem to control long enough to consider the consequences. One day one of his managers, Yusef Cinlemis, received an anonymous telephone call in which the caller said, "Fuck you, Yusef, I'm going to kill you," and then hung up. However, Cinlemis pressed star 69 and was told the telephone number of the caller, which he turned over to the police along with a report on the threat. The number turned out to be Woldt's, who at first denied making the call, then finally admitted it. He was fired. But he told Salmon he was dismissed because he'd had sex with Cinlemis's wife and got caught.

In the fall of 1995, Salmon returned to California to go back to school. So Woldt turned to new friends. One of them was James Wilson, whom he met in September.

When he first met Woldt, Wilson thought his new friend was quiet and shy, but he soon learned that a different personality lurked beneath the surface. For one thing, Woldt bragged a lot. One story was that he'd been awarded a million dollars because of the injury to his finger, but that the money was in a trust and his parents were stealing it. He also claimed that his former girlfriend, Becky, had taken $60,000 from a joint account they shared.

Sometimes in public, Woldt would pretend to be a homosexual—stereotypically mincing his walk, talking effeminately, and even grabbing Wilson's buttocks. It was all an attempt to embarrass Wilson, who mostly just laughed it off and told him to quit.

Woldt told Wilson that he was his "best friend." But Wilson knew that Woldt, who was his roommate from December 1995 to March 1996, had a habit of backstabbing his "friends." Sometimes he spoke fondly of another pal, Lucas Salmon, who was living in California, but other times laughed about him, calling Salmon a "bum" and "a loser."

Wilson also learned that beneath the kidding, fun-loving exterior, Woldt had a darker side. In addition to rape-oriented pornographic films, Woldt liked obscure, violent movies and introduced Wilson to his favorites. One was *Faces of Death,* a documentary depicting a variety of dead and dying animals and people, including the assassination of a French politician. Most of the "eyewitness" deaths of humans were staged, but the film was full of bodies from airline crashes and drownings.

Woldt's favorite, however, which he insisted on watching repeatedly until he knew every line, was *A Clockwork Orange,* the disturbing 1971 Stanley Kubrick film version of the 1962 novel by Anthony Burgess. Although the film seemed to have a message about moral choices, on the surface it was about Alex, the leader of a gang of thugs who spent their evenings assaulting people, "ultra-violence," and raping women or, as Woldt gleefully recited, "the old in-out, in-out."

The films seemed to inspire Woldt. He was always talking about sex, especially anal sex. And he did more than talk. Several times Wilson watched as Woldt wrestled with his current girlfriend, Jessica, pinning her down or twisting an arm until she cried out in pain. He'd only let up if she begged him to use his "big dick" to have anal sex with her.

Woldt also had a fantasy that went beyond tormenting his girlfriends. One night in 1995, he and Wilson were at a nightclub when Woldt nodded toward an attractive young woman and suggested that they kidnap and rape her.

Wilson didn't take him seriously that night. However, Woldt kept bringing up the subject and Wilson began to wonder whether he was kidding or not. After a while, every night they went out, his friend would point out some attractive young woman, especially blondes, and say something to the effect of, "What do you think about raping that girl?"

Male friends weren't the only ones exposed to Woldt's weird views on sex. A young woman, Mandy, began hanging out with Woldt in late 1995. She fell in love with him, but while she was more than willing, they had sex only once. The strange thing to her was that they would lie on the couch and watch pornographic films together three or four times a week. She was sexually aroused by the movies, but Woldt would get bored after a bit and simply turn off the television and go bed. Sometimes he let her stay in his bed but, except on the one occasion, wasn't interested in having sex with her.

Woldt's lack of sexual interest in Mandy might have been that she was too willing. He told a friend that he preferred sex with women who would "put up a fight" and that "it's no fun getting it from somebody who will just give it up." But when the disappointed Mandy asked why he wasn't interested, he told her a sob story about wanting to get back with his former girlfriend, Becky, because he missed his son.

However by the spring of 1996, Woldt was living with another young woman, Lori, in a trailer with Lori's sister, Lisa, and mother, Samantha. Sifting for weaknesses, Woldt knew how to pick his victims. Lori had been raped when she was fifteen years old, and he came on initially as the champion who would protect her from all harm. He'd charmed her, took her places, and bought her things. Only after she fell in love did he begin to change for the worse.

Woldt frequently criticized and humiliated her in front of others, including her family and friends, for her looks or things she said. He was very controlling—getting angry and accusing her of sleeping around if she went out with her girlfriends for an evening—even though he frequently went out without her. Her friends noticed that he treated her like his property. He even insisted that she dress like him when they went out together, which meant nearly always wearing white shirts and black slacks. And those were just the things that other people noticed.

Privately, Woldt was even worse. He insisted that if she loved him, she had to submit to whatever his sexual desires of the moment were, including anal sex. She also noticed that he got sexually aroused on the few occasions when she stood up for herself. That's when he wanted sex . . . hard, angry sex.

It wasn't any consolation, but Lori noted that he reserved the worst of his temper for his mother. He told her and other friends that he wished she was dead and that he'd considered killing her. Once he and Lori were riding with Song-Hui in her car when mother and son got into a screaming match. Song-Hui stopped the car and ordered him to get out. He did, dragging Lori with him, but not before spitting in his mother's face. Then, as they stood on the sidewalk, he blamed Lori for the fight.

Woldt met his next "best friend" when Lori's sister, Lisa, introduced him to her boyfriend, Derrick Ayers. For a period of two months, the two young men were nearly inseparable. They smoked a lot of pot, watched pornographic and violent movies, and went out nearly every night, often to play pool at a place called Corner Pocket Billiards.

Lisa was jealous of how much time Ayers was spending with Woldt. But she had other reasons to dislike her sister's boyfriend—not only did he mistreat Lori, but one day he'd suggested that Lisa should come to his apartment, alone. She turned him down, and in fact thought there was something wrong with him. When he wanted to go out with Ayers, he'd say something like, "Let's go beat up some punks and rape some chicks." He always said it with a smile, but there was something in his undertone that wasn't joking.

After a while, Ayers also started to get uncomfortable with Woldt's views about women. They were all "bitches" and whores, and then Woldt told Ayers that he preferred women who fought his sexual advances. Soon Woldt began asking if Ayers had ever thought about what it would be like to abduct and rape a woman. Then he upped the ante.

One evening, they went for a drive in the mountains west of Colorado Springs. Woldt was behind the steering wheel of Lisa's car because Ayers's license had been revoked. He headed for an area overlooking the city below that was famous for couples parking to neck.

As they cruised the gravel roads that wound along the forested mountainsides, Woldt talked about finding a couple parked at some desolate spot and attacking them. He said they'd rape the woman in front of the man, and then kill them both with large rocks.

Again, Ayers thought it was just more Woldt fantasy until his friend stopped the car, got out, and picked up two large rocks, which he put in the vehicle. The rocks would be their murder weapons, he said with a smile.

Ayers looked at his friend. Woldt had to be kidding, he thought. He was just trying to yank his chain. But a little farther down the road, they came upon a couple in a red sports car parked at one of the overlooks.

Woldt pulled in a few spaces from the couple in their car. This was perfect, he said. They'd drag the man out of the car and subdue him. Then they'd rape the woman and when they finished, kill them both, and throw their bodies off the cliff.

Now, Ayers was frightened. Woldt was smiling, but there was something else in his eyes. Hunger. Anger. Something. Whatever it was, Ayers didn't want to see it anymore and insisted that they drive home. Woldt laughed. Of course, he was just kidding, he said. He just wanted to see Ayers's reaction.

The next day, Lisa asked Ayers what the large rocks were doing in her car. He gave her a story about wanting to build a rock garden. But he also started to pull away from Woldt. His friend was weird, and he wasn't at all sure that he was kidding.

Several weeks after the incident in the mountains, Ayers warned Lisa to get her sister away from Woldt. "He has some pretty strange ideas," he said.

When Lisa insisted that he explain what he meant, Ayers asked if she remembered the rocks she'd found in the car. "They weren't for any rock garden," he said and told her about Woldt's fantasy.

Without being specific—because she knew that Lori would never believe it—Lisa tried to steer her sister away from Woldt. But Lori insisted that she loved him and couldn't live without him.

In the summer of 1996, one of Woldt's friends, Lucas Salmon, returned to Colorado Springs from California and stayed with Lori and Woldt in an apartment they were renting. Lori thought it was cruel the way her boyfriend constantly teased Salmon about being a virgin. Crueler still was when Woldt suggested that she have sex with his friend to remedy the situation. It hurt that her boyfriend seemed to view her as his property to be handed out like candy. But he would soon hurt her worse when she found out that he was seeing another woman: Bonnie, the divorced mother of a two-year-old boy.

When Woldt left Lori a short time later and moved in with Bonnie, Lori tried to kill herself by taking an overdose of pills. The only thing that saved her was Lucas Salmon arriving at the apartment with his father and rushing her to the hospital.

The suicide attempt didn't appear to trouble Woldt. However, he tried to use it to his advantage with his boss at the perfume store where he was working. His supervisor, Angela King, thought he was a good employee, except for his frequent absences from work. After yet another "no call, no show" she telephoned Woldt and said she had no choice but to fire him. He begged her for another chance, saying he'd been having a rough time because his girlfriend had killed herself.

By the end of 1996, Woldt was disappointed that his fantasy was no closer to reality. He'd tried with Wilson and Ayers to recruit an accomplice, but he was unable to bring them into his fold. He needed someone he could control and manipulate. He needed Lucas Salmon.

In January 1997, Woldt wrote to Salmon, who had been expelled from college for academic deficiencies, encouraging him to return to Colorado. Salmon had resisted, saying he had a job and was living with friends, even playing in a rock and roll band. But then Woldt played his trump card.

Bonnie was pregnant with his baby, and he'd given in to her suggestions that they get married. Her family lived back in Delaware, and that's where they decided to go for the ceremony.

As he made plans, Woldt had first asked Wilson to be his best man. But when Wilson said he couldn't make it, Woldt angrily said he was going to have to ask a "loser," Lucas Salmon, to stand up for him. He did not, however, couch the invitation to Salmon like that. Instead he asked his "best friend" to be his best man.

Salmon agreed and arrived in Colorado on February 20. A few days later, the two young men flew back to Delaware. After his initial disappointment with Wilson's rejection, Woldt was actually pleased by how things were turning out. Not so much for the sake of the wedding, but toward the implementation of his fantasy.

It was going to take a little work to wean Salmon away from all that church stuff, but he'd already seen signs that it was possible. Woldt began by suggesting they follow the young woman with the car troubles. "Let's go in . . ."

# THREE

# "MY BEST FRIEND"

". . . and rape her."

Tearing his eyes away from where the woman had disappeared into her house, Salmon looked back to Woldt. His friend was smiling, like it was all a big joke. But there was something else in his eyes, and it wasn't humor. More like hunger.

Salmon understood the hunger, although at this point it still troubled him, gnawing at his psyche like a trapped rodent. Or as though he were in the television cartoon with an angel—the voice of his conscience—speaking in one ear and a little devil perched on his shoulder whispering in the other. Only the devil sounded a lot like George Woldt.

Yet Woldt was his closest friend. He'd invited Lucas to be the best man at his wedding.

Lucas Salmon was the middle child born to Robert and Gail Salmon in a small town in northern California. His parents had married young and immediately began producing a brood—five children in six years—raising them in a fundamentalist Christian church after coming from dysfunctional families themselves.

Gail had been an only child and, as she'd later tell psychologists trying to understand why her son did what he did, that made her the only witness when her father would beat her mother. Her mother had been raped when she was a teenager and after that considered "damaged goods" by her family until she got married to a man who treated her like property. Life actually improved when Gail's father abandoned his wife and child.

Bob's early circumstances weren't any better. His father was a stern disciplinarian, a believer in the Biblical admonishment and didn't spare the rod when dealing with his children. Bob would later confide to the same psychologists who talked to Gail that during his childhood, his family "operated on guilt."

His father taught him to "put women on a pedestal," but several times his mother left the family for extended periods. She would eventually return, and the family would go on as if nothing had happened. Young Bob got the impression that part of the marital discord stemmed from his mother not being interested in having sex with his father.

Bob began dating Gail in 1968 when he was eighteen and she was sixteen. It wasn't long before she wanted to get married. He said he wasn't ready, but when she started dating someone else, he decided that he better give in or lose her.

Once married, the couple wasted no time producing offspring. The young couple had emerged from the difficulties of their early lives with strong Christian faiths and named the children after characters in the Bible, including Lucas, who was born February 9, 1976.

Lucas's older brother, Daniel, would tell the psychologists that his parents were anxious that they be perceived as the perfect family in public, especially in front of church members. Infractions of the rules outside the home were later disciplined with a paddle. But there were secrets in the Salmon household that had nothing to do with the children misbehaving. Bob, then 28, became involved with the family's fifteen-year-old baby-sitter. The scandal was followed by another involving a different baby-sitter.

Despite the transgressions, it was Bob who left Gail. He chose Valentine's Day, after giving her a bouquet of flowers, to tell her that he wanted a divorce. Gail was devastated and believed that the reason was that he was having an affair with another woman.

However, Bob was still interested in keeping up appearances. According to Daniel, for a time after he left the family, his father came home on weekends and attended church with them so that the rest of the congregation wouldn't know.

In 1984, Bob Salmon married Nancy Smith and the two moved up to Bend, Oregon, a booming town on the east side of the Cascades near the Mt. Bachelor Ski Area. Smith would later tell investigators that the move wasn't entirely by choice; a woman had accused Bob of sexual harassment and, given the nature of a small town, it was better that they leave.


After her marriage collapsed, Gail was often depressed and emotionally unavailable. Lucas, who was in the third grade when his father left, coped by creating an imaginary friend. He learned to enjoy being by himself and drawing. Even when his parents had been together, he was the proverbial middle child—Daniel was his father's favorite and his mother doted on the youngest—quiet and sweet-natured.

When Lucas was twelve, his mother announced that she was sending him to live with his father for a while. Lucas actually welcomed the idea. He thought that it would be fun to be the only child in his father's house. Therefore, he was disappointed when Daniel decided at the last moment to go, too.

Slight of stature and shy, Lucas was the target of bullies

in his new school, and was generally teased by other students for his haphazard appearance. Although exceptionally bright (his IQ of 134 placed him in the top 10 percent of the population nationally), he was apt to leave the house for school with his shirt inside out or on backward.

Still, it wasn't all bad in Bend for Lucas. He participated on the school's ski team, made friends, and in 1992 went to Germany as an exchange student, returning with a good understanding of the language. However, he was about to be moved again.

Bob Salmon owned a mail-order company called Motorcycle Accessories Warehouse. He began to court a woman who worked for him, Cindy Jones. She wasn't comfortable with his advances while he was still married. But that problem had been rectified in 1991, when Bob had abruptly announced to Nancy that he was filing for divorce. Keeping with his penchant for dramatic gestures at such times, he told Nancy while they were at a hotel celebrating their wedding anniversary.

In 1993, Bob Salmon moved with his girlfriend and two of his sons to Colorado Springs. Again, the decision to move to a new city wasn't entirely without an outside push. Jones would later tell investigators that Bob had been accused of sexual harassment for a second time and he'd opted for a change of scenery. However, Bob said that the move was Cindy's idea and that he'd agreed because he wanted to be near the headquarters for Focus on the Family, a fundamentalist Christian organization that was headquartered in that city.

Located sixty miles south of Denver, "the Springs," as the city was commonly known, sat in the shadow of massive Pike's Peak, the 14,110-foot mountain that had inspired Katherine Lee Bates to write the song "America the Beautiful." In 1859, before there was a city, gold was discovered in the South Park area directly west, farther into the mountains, and "Pike's Peak or Bust" became a popular slogan as vast numbers of fortune seekers poured into the Rocky Mountains. That particular spot was a funnel for all those people because it sat at the foot of Ute Pass on the south side of Pike's Peak, the most accessible route to South Park.

In August 1859, two surveyors from Denver began looking over the bowl-like area in front of the mountain for a town site. While exploring, the surveyors came upon a beautiful, parklike area containing large, stand-alone sandstone formations. The giant, salmon-colored monoliths, some several hundred feet high and etched into convoluted shapes by eons of wind, rain, and snow, had inspired Native Americans to consider the spot to be holy ground. The newcomers were equally impressed.

At the turn of the century, a local railroad magnate deeded the land of the monoliths, known as the Garden of the Gods, to the city of Colorado Springs as a park. The park was only lightly developed, with winding roads and gentle paths. It was popular with bicyclists and joggers, or those out for a quiet drive past acres of scrub oak, spike-leafed yucca, prickly pear cactus, piñon, juniper, and Ponderosa pine trees.

Right up until the early 1970s, Colorado Springs had mostly been contained in the bowl bounded by the Rockies in the west, white sandstone bluffs (the bones of an ancient mountain range older than the Rockies) to the north and northeast, and the wide open prairie to the east and south. Founded as a gold-rush and railroad city, the town's character in the last half of the century changed to that of a military town. Colorado Springs was literally surrounded by Fort Carson, a sprawling Army base, to the south, Peterson Field Air Force Base to the east, and the U.S. Air Force Academy, about twenty miles north of town. The encirclement was completed by the presence of the

North American Air Defense command center, the nerve center for the country's air defenses. It was hidden away in a man-made cavern that had been drilled into the side of Cheyenne Mountain to the southwest.

The presence of these facilities brought nearly thirty thousand active-duty personnel to the area. It was no surprise that many who left the service chose to remain in such a beautiful place, and those who put in enough time to retire could also use the military bases' medical and shopping facilities.

As the city grew, it retained its small-town flavor and look. The tallest building downtown was fifteen stories, and that's the way the city planners liked it. But the population grew quickly beginning in the early seventies, with housing developments spreading out of the bowl that had once contained the city. Developments spread east across the prairie, as well as south and, especially, north along the front range of the Rockies.

There were some holdovers from the glorious past. At the southwest end of town at the base of Cheyenne Mountain was the area known as the Broadmoor. It was graced by large, million-dollar homes, some of them built by those who made their fortune in gold or silver or as railroad potentates. The area was known for its international ice rink, a longtime training area for Olympic stars, as well as the luxurious and pricey Broadmoor Hotel.

Post–high school educational opportunities abounded in the city. In addition to the Air Force Academy, there were two more four-year colleges. One was Colorado College, a small, well-regarded liberal arts school in downtown Colorado Springs that was generally populated by students from wealthy families. The second was the Colorado Springs branch of the University of Colorado, the main campus of which was in Boulder, about a hundred miles to the north on the other side of Denver.

However, at its heart Colorado Springs was a blue-collar

town, a working man's town. Mostly white, mostly conservative, it was a Republican stronghold as epitomized by the fact that the local newspaper, the *Gazette-Telegraph*, had been owned for years by the family of Bill Armstrong, a staunchly right-wing congressman during the seventies and eighties. The paper had been sold and renamed simply the *Gazette,* but it retained its conservative outlook.

Like any mid sized city, the Springs had its troubles with crime. Gangs infested many of the high schools and neighborhoods. Outlaw biker gangs had settled into the area, often making their money by dealing the blue-collar drug of choice, methamphetamines or speed, and bringing a culture of guns and violence. However, in the nineties the city had a lower crime rate than many cities its size. Violent crime, including murders, rarely touched the lives of those citizens outside the subcultures that preyed upon each other.

The city's conservative character attracted an infusion of what could be described as the industry of fundamentalist Christianity. The big mover and shaker in town, however, was Focus on the Family, the organization that in the nineties had coined the phrase "family values," which it defined as traditional morals, and critics described as intolerant and inflexible.

According to the organization's press releases, Focus on the Family had been founded in 1977 by the Rev. James Dobson in response to his "increasing concern for the American family." His internationally syndicated radio program aired daily on more than 3,000 radio stations in twelve languages, broadcast to more than ninety-five countries. Although a nonprofit organization, Focus on the Family generated millions of dollars in yearly donations to support its activities and increasingly large payroll, and to build an immense, multistory office complex just off the interstate north of the city.

Focus on the Family's published mission statement was preaching the Gospel "to as many people as possible." The organization intended to "accomplish that objective by helping to preserve traditional values and the institution of the family . . . drawn from the wisdom of the Bible and the Judeo-Christian ethic, rather than from the humanistic notions of today's theorists." Among the "five pillars" defining the organization's principles was one that the "institution of marriage was intended by God to be a permanent, lifelong relationship between a man and a woman, regardless of trials, sickness, financial reverses or emotional stresses that may ensue." Children were a gift from God, according to the literature, who would hold parents accountable for "raising, shaping and preparing them for a life of service to His kingdom and humanity."

The organization did not limit itself to spiritual aspects, but delved into the politics of the town and the state. Its members served on the Colorado Springs city council, the El Paso County commissioners, and in the state legislature. Its members put pressure on schools and libraries regarding what books they felt constituted "appropriate" literature for schoolchildren. They were vehemently anti-abortion. "Human life is of inestimable worth and significance in all its dimensions, including the unborn, the aged, the widowed, the mentally handicapped, the unattractive, the physically challenged and every other condition in which humanness is expressed from the conception to the grave."

Focus on the Family had jumped into state politics with its backing of a controversial amendment to deny "partner" benefits for gay marriages, homosexuality being one of the great sins in the eyes of the organization. The press releases and seminars were peopled by "former homosexuals" who had seen the error of their ways and had been welcomed back into the fold. As Dobson frequently preached, "God hates the sin but not the sinner."

* * *

Bob Salmon had heard of Focus in the Family and decided that Colorado Springs was his type of community. So he moved his company, two of his sons, and his girlfriend to Colorado Springs, where Lucas was enrolled at Cheyenne Mountain High School for the eleventh grade.

Lucas was unhappy with the decision to move, but he didn't have a choice, especially after his mother and her second husband moved there as well. He was enrolled at one of the city's older but well-regarded high schools, located in the Broadmoor area. Much of the school's student body were the children of wealthy parents.

Although exceptionally intelligent, Salmon was an average student. He was socially immature and again the subject of teasing about his haphazard appearance. He wanted friends, but he also spent a lot of time alone, drawing and playing video games.

Cindy Jones continued to work for Bob and remained his girlfriend for several years, but they never married. She later noted to investigators that her boyfriend treated the two sons living with him differently, as demonstrated by the photographs he had on display in the house. There were many of Daniel throughout the residence, but she said there was none of Lucas. The proverbial middle child, he was described by Cindy as "tenderhearted," but passive, drifting along the path of least resistance.

Lucas participated in church activities with his father and two brothers (after his brother Micah moved to the city). As such, he was well indoctrinated with the prohibitions against smoking, drinking, profanity, pornography, and premarital sex. God hated the sin but not the sinner, and all one had to do was accept Jesus, ask forgiveness, and the slate would be wiped clean. He was taught to believe that every life was predestined, part of God's grand design—even horrible things like fatal car accidents and deadly diseases—and that it wasn't man's place to question the Almighty.

In October 1993, Salmon, now a senior in high school, got a job with the telemarketing firm Future Call. He made a variety of impressions on his bosses and fellow workers. Some thought he was odd, even disquieting, in the way he stared. But most considered him to be a polite and religious young man, a shy loner but a good worker who showed up when he was supposed to and did his job.

In April 1994, he met a new employee—a cocksure, smirking Amerasian named George Woldt. At first Salmon didn't care for Woldt. But Woldt seemed to see something in Salmon that he liked and turned on the charm. A month later when Woldt declared him to be "my best friend," Lucas couldn't have been happier.

Woldt even made him feel safer. His friend claimed to be a martial arts expert and bragged about the fights he'd been in. Salmon was sure that if he had any troubles with bullies at school, his "best friend" would be there to put them in their place.

However, at times, Salmon felt torn by his relationship with Woldt. On one shoulder perched the voice of his religious upbringing, and on the other, the darker, more exciting voice of George Woldt. His friend seemed to have a way with women, bragging about his many conquests. He invited Salmon to watch pornographic films at his place, while they drank beer, smoked cigarettes and marijuana, as well as dabbled in harder drugs like LSD.

Salmon had never been in trouble with the law before. In fact, his career goal when he got through college was to be a police officer. But in July 1994, he joined Woldt throwing rocks through the windshields of cars. They were caught when the owner of one of the vandalized cars took down the license plate number of Salmon's car as he tried to make his getaway. The police showed up and arrested Salmon and Woldt, but they both had clean records and received a fine and probation.

Salmon didn't like it when Woldt teased him about

being a virgin. And it had both embarrassed and excited him when Woldt and Becky tried to set him up with Angela in the motel room.


In the fall of 1984, Salmon left for California to attend college. The time away from Woldt seemed to be good for him. He was still quiet and shy, but once drawn into conversation, other students and teachers found him to be articulate and thoughtful.

When away from George Woldt, the voice of his better side seemed to prevail as he participated in missionary projects with his classmates. He gave haircuts to the homeless and went on two missions to Mexico, where he helped build an orphanage. His fellow students and teachers noted how well he got along with the children. However, Salmon did not apply himself with quite the same fervor to his studies. He was on academic probation by the end of his first semester and dismissed from the school at the completion of his freshman year.

Salmon returned to Colorado Springs that summer, again moving in with Woldt and Becky until she moved out. He noticed that his friend's preoccupation with pornography was changing subtly, as he was gravitating further into films depicting violent rapes, even so-called snuff movies in which the rape victim was purportedly murdered, though it was difficult, if not impossible, to tell if the killings were real or faked.

Woldt had plenty of other strange behaviors. For one thing, he made a game out of trying to catch Salmon masturbating at night. And once he burst into the bathroom to take a photograph of Salmon on the toilet.

Salmon resisted the temptations Woldt placed before him, including declining to have sex with Allison after the strip poker game. Woldt sometimes accused him of being "a faggot," but he was interested in girls. Even then, Woldt sometimes got in the way. There was a girl at Future Call named Jamie, whom Salmon liked, but then Woldt started flirting with her and it was soon clear she preferred him.

While working again at Future Call that summer, he did date another employee, named Jenny. She thought he was nice, "sweet," if somewhat clingy and needy. He was also considerate when she made it clear that she wasn't going to have sex with him and didn't try to push her boundaries.

At the end of August, Salmon returned to California, this time to attend a different college. However, that only lasted a semester after he managed to garner a single C to offset three Fs.

Still, he did not return to Colorado right away. He had friends in California who didn't tease him about his virginity or call him names. He even helped form a rock band and was the lead singer—or more accurately, according to the father of one of the other band members—the lead "grunter."

During this time, he lived with relatives and his friends' families. To support himself, he took a job as a caregiver for a program that worked with autistic adults. His first job paid minimum wage and gave him a place to stay in exchange for providing twenty-four-hour care for a man who was unable to control any of his bodily functions and needed constant supervision. On top of that, the man was verbally and physically abusive. The job ended when Salmon locked himself in a bathroom during one of the man's tirades and was too terrified to come out until his client was removed.

The next client was a young autistic boy. The agency for which he worked thought Salmon did a wonderful job and really seemed to have a knack in working with troubled children. However, he lost that job after three weeks when he had a disagreement with the boy's mother and she asked that he be reassigned.

Salmon still thought about becoming a police officer. In

the summer of 1996, he even took the written exam for the Los Angles County Sheriff's Department and was invited back for an interview. However, he didn't show up.

Instead, Salmon traveled back to Colorado Springs for a week in July, most of which he spent with Woldt and his friend's new girlfriend, Lori. Of course, that meant more teasing about his virginity and even the embarrassment of being offered Woldt's girlfriend for sex. But Salmon had his own little secrets. One was that he'd developed a fetish for women's shoes, especially red ones. He'd taken several boxes of them with him to college and when alone, he masturbated holding the sole of the shoe against his penis. Even worse, he'd started fantasizing about having sex with little girls as young as nine or ten years old.

Yet he could be kind and caring. When Lori learned that Woldt was seeing Bonnie, she called, leaving a garbled message on Woldt's telephone answering machine. Salmon, worried about the jilted girl, called her back, but there was no answer. Fearing the worst, he'd called his father and the two went to her apartment, where they discovered she'd taken an overdose of pills in an effort to commit suicide. They saved her life by rushing her to a hospital.

In the fall, Salmon was back in California, where his friends noticed significant changes in him. He seemed preoccupied with sex, bragging about his friend George's exploits. His language was laced with profanity, and he disparaged women at every turn. They wondered what had come over him.

Salmon returned to Colorado in December for the Christmas holiday. He spent part of it with his family, but most of the time he was with Woldt. He did date Christina Fridenthal. She liked him well enough, but she felt that he just wanted to have a girlfriend so he could be like his friend George Woldt.

Like Jenny before, Salmon didn't try to push Christina's boundaries when it came to sex. She broke the romance off when he announced that he was returning to California, saying she didn't want a long-distance boyfriend.

Salmon was hardly back in California when he began to get letters from Woldt. It seemed that his friend missed him and wanted him to move back to Colorado. Although flattered by the attention, Salmon had his reservations. He told friends in California that he was resisting returning to Colorado Springs because he knew that Woldt was bad news. But then there came an invitation he couldn't refuse. George was getting married to Bonnie in Delaware, and he asked Lucas to be his best man.

Lucas Salmon returned to Colorado Springs on February 20, 1997, and a few days later, he left with Woldt for Delaware. The next day, they were out in the yard of the home where they were staying when they saw the young woman with car troubles.

"Let's go inside and rape her," Woldt said. But then he'd smiled. Partly relieved and yet vaguely disappointed, Salmon realized it was a joke.

The moment passed and George Woldt was married the next day with Lucas Salmon standing proudly at his side. That George, he was always kidding . . . like after the wedding when Salmon gave him a congratulatory hug and George reached down and grabbed Lucas's buttocks with his hands. Embarrassed, Salmon stepped back quickly, turning red as his "best friend" burst into mocking laughter.

# FOUR

# CLOCKWORK ORANGES

*April 29, 1997*
*Colorado Springs*

Lucas Salmon slouched down in the front passenger seat of George Woldt's old green Buick as they cruised slowly past the attractive blond woman jogging along the bicycle path in the Garden of the Gods. Just that day he had shaved his head bald at his friend's suggestion. George told him he would look better that way, and what George said was gospel.

After Woldt's marriage to Bonnie, Salmon had returned to Colorado Springs to live with his brothers, Daniel and Micah, and father, Robert, who hired him to work at his company. Robert Salmon had given his middle son a gray 1985 Ford Thunderbird to drive and registered it to the business address for Motorcycle Accessories Warehouse.

When the Woldts returned to Colorado Springs from their honeymoon in early March, Salmon moved in with them. At first, he slept on a futon in the living room, but had soon moved back into the bedroom with Bonnie's three-year-old son, where he had his own dresser and the bottom bunk.

Salmon repaid the favor by getting Woldt a job at his father's company, which meant they were hardly ever apart. Something in Lucas Salmon was changing, or had been released from whatever place it had been imprisoned. He cursed and drank and smoked; he rarely went to church anymore. Almost overnight, it seemed to others who knew him, he started imitating Woldt—his clothes, his mannerisms and behaviors, and his ladies' man attitude.

At work Salmon began making sexually suggestive remarks to some of his female coworkers, leering when they walked by as if undressing them with those strange hazel-colored eyes. But he was the boss's son, so they ignored most of it.

Salmon's libido heated up when one of the women, a middle-aged, heavyset, married woman, responded positively. At first the woman told him that he should find someone his own age and single, but he countered that he liked older, married women. Before long the two were passing notes. Some of their coworkers, acting as go-betweens, saw the notes and their sexually explicit messages. They also noticed how the object of Salmon's desire had begun dressing provocatively for work.

One of the woman's friends finally asked about the budding relationship and was aghast when the woman said she was considering having an affair with her young suitor. Asked why she would consider such a thing, the woman replied that she felt sorry for Lucas, who despite his playboy facade was obviously inexperienced and maybe even a virgin. Besides, she said, she found his attentions flattering and admitted that several times he'd reached beneath her work desk and touched her suggestively when no one was looking.

When he first started at Motorcycle Accessories Warehouse, Woldt came off as shy and polite, but before long most of his coworkers thought that he was just plain weird.

If he wasn't "on," as in performing or flirting, he had an unnerving way of staring through people who were talking to him as if he couldn't understand what language they were speaking.

Most considered Woldt the leader between the two friends, though others felt that Salmon played up being the boss's son and sometimes took the lead. It was clear that they fed off each other, such as when they would act out scenes from movies.

Some of their coworkers wondered if there was something sexual going on between the two young men. At times the women would nudge each other and nod at the pair who would be staring at each other from across the room as if in a trance.

It wasn't just the workers at Motorcycle Accessories Warehouse who wondered what was going on between the two, if not sexually, then psychologically. Micah Salmon thought of his older brother as kindhearted and immature, and he did not like the influence George Woldt was having on him.

One minute Woldt would be calling Lucas his "best friend," and the next he'd go out of his way to make fun of him in front of other people. Micah thought that Woldt enjoyed making his brother jump through hoops to maintain their friendship, which George threatened to end any number of times. It was obvious to him that his brother was struggling between his religious upbringing and the allure of his friend's worldliness, particularly when it came to Woldt's sexual exploits, which his brother seemed to envy.

Lucas certainly didn't judge his friend, no more than he looked down on their father for his past indiscretions. The Salmon children were all aware of the stories about their father and the baby-sitters, as well as the allegations of sexual harassment. When Micah brought it up to Lucas, wondering if it might be having an effect on his behavior, his brother shrugged and said he wasn't about to cast stones at their father.

Some of the people Lucas knew in California also were worried about the shift in behavior. They'd known a young man who based his social life around the church and its teachings. But in March 1997, he wrote a letter to one of his friends in California. The letter was rife with references to the "bitches" he'd had sex with. "Find them, fuck them, and forget them" was his new motto, he said. He used curse words as often as he used commas and periods, and went on and on about the great times he had with George Woldt . . . drinking and smoking and chasing women.

God, formerly a staple of Salmon's conversations, now seemed to be missing from his life entirely. He obviously knew that what he was doing was wrong when he closed his correspondence, "Don't let your mom read this letter." But the note was so disturbing that the other young man showed it to his parents and then shared it with his church's congregation, asking them to pray for Salmon's soul.

As they drove past the blond jogger, the two decided that she was a good target and sped up to circle around the park and come back for her. Salmon was both excited and frightened now that the moment of truth appeared to be at hand. The game had sped up, too, ever since April 15 when Woldt told him he was going to have to move out of the apartment. Apparently, Bonnie didn't want him living there after the baby arrived in a month.

Salmon began to cajole his friend that they needed to find him someone to have sex with before he had to leave. Living with the Woldts had only added to his sexual frustrations—lying there in the dark on his bed, listening to the loud sounds of their liaisons, or seeing Bonnie wandering around the apartment in her lingerie, or obviously nude beneath a bathrobe. Then there was the pornography that George watched like some people watched sitcoms.

For her part, Bonnie was tired of Salmon being around all the time, and tired that her husband spent more time with his friend than with her. She'd had a hard life—abandoned by her mother at age fourteen, in and out of foster homes. She'd been married once and had a three-year-old son as a result, but that relationship had been marred by violence, some of it instigated by her, and she'd finally been divorced.

Bonnie and George certainly seemed made for each other. She noted to her friends that she'd subscribed to the Playboy Channel and had her own collection of pornographic films before she started seeing Woldt. She confided to those same friends that her sex life with George was kinky and rough, and that her husband preferred anal sex, especially after they got into one of their frequent fights.

Although she sometimes felt sorry for Salmon when her husband ridiculed him for being a virgin, she wasn't above joining in the teasing. One night in March, she and George had her foster sister, Adrianna, come over to the apartment. They told Salmon they were setting the two of them up. Salmon fell for it and clumsily tried to make his move, but Adrianna, who was in on the joke, wasn't the least bit interested and the three all had a good laugh at Lucas's expense.

Sometimes the humiliation of Lucas Salmon was unintentional. Once Bonnie actually did ask her biological sister, Celeste, over to meet him with the hope that the two might hit it off. Salmon was interested, but the girl was not.

Bonnie had noticed that the "nice guy" she'd met when she started seeing George had changed, especially since returning to Colorado for the marriage. Salmon partied a lot now and didn't talk about God anymore—just sex and "bitches." Where he used to be polite and a good houseguest, now he wouldn't help clean up around the apartment and acted like he expected her to wait on him like he was her husband, too. He could be weirdly immature, once getting in a squabble with her three-year-old son and wound up biting the child's thumb hard enough to make him cry.

Soon after she got back from her honeymoon, Salmon and her husband started going out nearly every night—they said to play pool at the Corner Pocket Billiard hall. At first she told her friends that she didn't mind. She wanted George to "get it out of his system" because he was going to have to settle down when the baby arrived in May. But most of the time, George hardly seemed to care that he was about to be a father again. If she complained that he needed to get more involved with the impending arrival, he would stomp off and go somewhere with his friend. She resorted to writing him a letter begging him to go shopping for baby clothes with her as a way to show her he cared. She noted in the letter that they didn't spend much time together anymore. He told her to get over it.

Now, she wanted Salmon out of the apartment and her marriage. Even George's mother was on her side. Song-Hui told her son that Salmon needed to move out and find a place of his own. George had a child coming and needed to settle down.

George's response was to spend even more time with Lucas. Especially after they watched *A Clockwork Orange*. After that, to Bonnie's chagrin, the two men went out every night and often during the days they had off. In fact, they could hardly wolf down dinner and a couple of beers fast enough before they were out the door to "go play pool."

As far as the baby went, George couldn't be troubled. In fact the night of April 28, Bonnie thought she was going into premature labor and called her husband, who was out

with Salmon, to come take her to the hospital. Both he and
Salmon had showed up, looking miffed that their evening
had been interrupted. Her husband got even angrier when
the labor pains turned out to be a false alarm.


Bonnie was right that *A Clockwork Orange* seemed to
have set something in motion. Lightly at first, like a sabo-
teur probing the enemy's defenses, George began to
describe a fantasy to Salmon about abducting and raping
a woman. He said it jokingly, ad-libbing from the movie
about what fun it would be to go get "a little of the ol' in-
out." Then Woldt suggested that, perhaps, it would be a
way to resolve Salmon's dilemma with his virginity. Kidding, of course.

However, it wasn't long before they were talking about
the fantasy five or six times a day, discussing how it could
be pulled off without getting caught. But they added one
more component to the fantasy . . . to avoid capture, they
agreed that they would have to kill their victim.

They began to cruise the nightclubs and city parks looking for a "target," at first treating it like a game, *the game*.
Sighting a potential victim, following her in whichever car
they were driving that night, Woldt's Buick or Salmon's
Thunderbird. Somewhere along the line, the game began
to grow more serious, fantasy began to dissolve into reality. They even considered the potential consequences and
decided that the thrill would be worth the risk. Finally, it
was no longer just Woldt's idea. He might have conceived
of it and lured Salmon as a fly fisherman teases a trout to
the surface, but by the closing days of April they were
equal partners in a conspiracy to rape and murder a young
woman.

Every day they stepped further from thinking about it
and closer to doing it. They often started their evening
hunts by relaxing first at the Corner Pocket before moving

on to scope the nightclubs. Soon they began to hunt during the day as well, driving slowly through neighborhoods and parks.

When they spotted a potential victim, the game would start. A lot of it was big talk, pumping each other up. They'd stalk a young woman, and Woldt would say something like, "You can fuck her pussy. I'll fuck her ass," to which Salmon gleefully assented. But always there would be something that prevented them from taking the final step. Too many witnesses. Or a male would appear on the scene, like a dominant lion, forcing the young hyenas to slink from the scene, their hunt frustrated.

They came close several times. One day, driving through a neighborhood they happened upon a little girl walking on a sidewalk alone. Woldt was driving and pulled over. He called out to the child, who was maybe nine or ten years old, and tried to get her to come over to the car. "Do you need a ride?" he asked nicely.

The child ran off, and Woldt quickly drove from the neighborhood. Excited and appalled at the same time, Salmon asked Woldt what he would have done if the child had complied with his request. "Raped her, of course," Woldt said with a grin.

Woldt gave the same reply several days later, after they offered a woman who appeared to be in her late fifties a ride. She, too, had turned down their offer, never knowing how close she'd come to being the finish line in their game.

Somewhere about the third week of April, the stakes of the game jumped up a couple of notches when they took a steak knife from the Woldts' apartment and placed it in the glove box of the car they were driving. The knife never made it back into the house, but was transferred, almost as a symbol of their commitment, to whichever vehicle they were using.

One of their favorite hunting grounds outside of the nightclubs was the Garden of the Gods. There were a lot of women alone jogging, hiking, or riding their bikes, and even a few places they thought were secluded enough to carry out their plan. They'd formulated a couple of simple strategies. One was to pull up suddenly, grab the woman and force her into the car, beating and threatening her into submission with the overwhelming nature of their attack. Another was to actually bump the victim with their car and then to offer the dazed victim assistance to a hospital or to a telephone—except she would never arrive.

On the afternoon of April 29, 1997, the pair were again cruising the Garden of the Gods. Salmon, with his head shaved, was feeling particularly bitter. His father had recently fired him because several of his female coworkers had complained that he was making sexually inappropriate comments and using crude language. For some time the women had been afraid to do anything because he was the boss's son. However, one day when he thought that they were talking about him behind his back, he stood up and yelled across the room, "I'll have you fat bitches fired!" They decided that it was time they went to his father, who called him in and told him to leave. The worst part was he thought that his father should have fired the women, too. They'd played along, and it wasn't fair.

Lucas was ready to bring the game to a conclusion. But that wasn't to say that his conscience wasn't troubling him. He kept his Bible, embossed on the front cover with his name, in the backseat of his Thunderbird, and it reminded him that God would not be pleased. But it was more important that he do what George Woldt wanted. He'd known before he returned to Colorado that George was dangerous, but he believed that his friend would never do anything to hurt him, and that somehow, even standing on the precipice, his "best friend" would protect him from harm. He envied George Woldt and wanted to be like him—have sex with women and not care what other people thought of him. And he especially wanted George to quit teasing him about being a virgin.

Perhaps to quiet the pleas from his conscience and calm his nerves, he was drinking more (six or seven beers in a night) and chain-smoking. Of course, that just meant the voice of George Woldt grew louder, more commanding. He believed that Woldt had "powers"; his "friend" had convinced Salmon that he could bend spoons with his mind and other feats.

They'd left the house a little before 3 P.M. that day. It was George's idea to hunt in the Garden of the Gods. But it was still just a game until they came up from behind the blond woman jogging along the bicycle path at the side of the road.

Salmon hunkered down in the seat and looked back as they passed. So did George. They figured she was in her late teens and definitely attractive. "She's the one," Woldt announced. They decided to circle around and come up behind her.

Approaching the woman at about fifteen miles an hour, Woldt pulled over into the bicycle lane and struck her. She flew forward and sprawled into the gravel off the side of the road.

Woldt immediately stopped the car and got out. Stunned, Salmon followed more slowly; his friend was already approaching the young woman who had picked herself up off the ground.

"Are you all right?" Woldt asked. The men could see that her knees and an arm were bleeding though she didn't appear to be seriously injured. Her mouth worked just fine, though, as she berated Woldt.

Eighteen-year-old Amber Gonzales was mad as hell. It

wasn't as if she had been out in the road or it was a blind corner. "What the hell were you doing?" she cried.

Woldt ignored her question and kept walking up to her. "Are you all right?" he asked again. Now, he grabbed her forearms as though to comfort her. "Do you need a ride to the hospital?"

Gonzales pulled away from him. Something was wrong with these two—the dark-haired one with the slight grin and his strange-looking bald friend, who stood near the car as if waiting for something else to happen. There was no way she was going to get in a car with them. "My father's the park ranger," she said. If they wanted to do something to help, they could help her find her $170 sunglasses that had flown off when they hit her.

Woldt gave up trying to get her to come with him. He and his friend made a show of looking for the sunglasses, but soon got back in their car and took off.

A few minutes later, Sabrina Bayles and her daughter, who were riding their bicycles on the path, came upon the young woman crying by the side of the road. Amber told them what had happened, which reminded them of the car that had passed them earlier that morning. They'd noticed that the male passenger with the shaved head had tried to hunch down in the seat as though he didn't want to be seen. She'd been smart, they said, not to get in the car.


Meanwhile, Woldt turned on Salmon as they left the park. "Why did you just stand there?" he demanded. "We almost had her!"

Salmon tried to think of something to explain why he froze. He gave a lame excuse about the bushes on the passenger side getting in his way. And he'd stopped to pick up the woman's sunglasses, which he now exhibited like a trophy.

Woldt didn't stay angry for long. There had been too

much traffic on the road anyway, and too many people around if the woman had put up any kind of struggle. Besides, her father was the park ranger, a cop. If he'd spotted them with her, there'd have been hell to pay. But the blood was pumping something fierce. "You excited?" he asked, grinning at his partner.

"Did you see the look on her face?" Salmon responded with a laugh.

They'd drawn first blood in the game. Now they were more determined than ever to finish it.

# PART II

## ACTS OF VIOLENCE

*"It is as inhuman to be totally good as it is to be totally evil. The important thing is moral choice. Evil has to exist along with good, in order that moral choice may operate."*
—Anthony Burgess, from the introduction to his 1962 novel *A Clockwork Orange*

# FIVE

# ALL-AMERICAN GIRL

*April 29, 1997*
*Colorado Springs, Colorado*

Jacine Gielinski didn't look over at the two young men in the Ford Thunderbird who pulled up next to her red Geo Prism at the stoplight. Nor did she notice after the light turned green that they had fallen in behind her, several cars back, and followed her to the apartment complex where her boyfriend was preparing a late dinner for her. As far as she knew, she didn't have an enemy in the world.

Some of that had to do with her upbringing, as her mother had taught her the Golden Rule practically from the moment Jacine could talk: Do unto others as you would have done unto you. Her mother impressed upon her not to judge people by the way they looked, the clothes they wore, how much money they had, or even their pasts. She was told that there was *some* good in everyone.

They were easy lessons to teach "Jace." Being nice just came naturally to the little girl with the golden locks, merry blue eyes, and a smile that made everyone else around her smile back. From early childhood, she demonstrated an empathy for other people that couldn't be taught. One such example occurred in the second grade.

Highlands Elementary was a safe, easy three-block walk along the tree-lined street from her home. However, another little girl in her class lived miles away and sometimes her parents made her trudge to school if she didn't finish her chores in the morning in time to catch the bus. It meant the seven-year-old child had to cross dangerous intersections and navigate heavy traffic on her own, often arriving long after the bell had rung for classes to begin.

Yet there would always be one person waiting outside the school—rain, snow, or shine—to make sure she arrived safely. Jacine insisted on it and her teacher allowed it, recognizing that this wasn't a battle she was going to, or should, win with the strong-willed Gielinski girl.

Jacine never complained about being an only child, but then again, she was rarely alone. Her home was the playhouse for nearly every child close to her age in the neighborhood. Bob and Peggy Luiszer learned to expect three or four other children to be in the house at any given time—and probably at the dinner table, the breakfast table, or both. Jacine was a born leader but not the sort to insist that the others play what she wanted. Whether it was Barbie dolls in her room or hide-and-seek outside, what mattered to her was that she was with her friends, many of whom remained as close as sisters and brothers throughout her life.

If there was one activity she loved more than any other, it was competing at sports. She learned to swim when she was five, and by age seven she had placed second in the breaststroke for her age group at the state meet. If she was not the top athlete in the pool, on the soccer field, or in the gymnasium, then she was one of the best, and she made up for any deficiencies by working harder and playing with more heart than anyone else.

Yet, for all her successes, she was never the sort of athlete who looked down her nose at those less talented. Just the opposite. Jacine was confident enough in her own abilities that she always trying to bring everyone else up to her level. She exhibited this trait at a young age on her soccer team. One of the other players was an overweight child, slow and unskilled. As the worst player on the team, the other girl didn't play much during the games, and she was ignored or teased by the team's star players. But Jacine stayed after practice and games to work with the other girl on her skills and conditioning.

Jacine's childhood personality traits continued as she became a young woman in high school. She'd quickly established herself as an athlete and a leader, twice helping take her team to the Colorado state high-school basketball championship game.

Jacine played her senior year of basketball in pain because of ankle surgery she'd had in the off-season, but she never gave less than everything she had. Her coaches knew that she was the glue that held the teams together. She made them all better as athletes and as people, handing out inspirational quotes she'd written down before the games to every player, no matter if the other girl was a starter or riding the bench. Jacine was always the one who remembered to bring a birthday cake for a friend or teammate when everyone else forgot.

At summer basketball camp before her senior season, the buzz was about a hot freshman player who was thought to be a lock to make the varsity team. Some of the varsity players, apparently fearing that the new girl would usurp their place on the squad, shunned her at the beginning of the first day of practice. But Jacine saw the girl standing by herself and made it a point to walk over and welcome her to the team with a hug. The other girls had no choice but to follow her example and include the new girl.

Jacine didn't limit her friends to the school jocks. Few, if any, could resist her smile and the personality it advertised. She moved easily in all circles—from the heavy-metal head-bangers in their black leather coats and studded dog collars to the artistic types in the drama club and the cheerleaders and football players. It didn't surprise anyone who knew her when she befriended a developmentally disabled girl who otherwise had a lonely existence at the high school.

Academics didn't hold the same fascination for her, but she did well enough in school to get by. In the meantime, she had grown into a beautiful young woman—blond and blue eyed with a cute, athletic figure. There were plenty of boys interested, and there were plenty of dates, though nothing serious. Yet for all the friends and people who felt her touch their lives, if there was one incident that demonstrated the true heart of Jacine Gielinski, it was her reaction to the news in the spring of 1993 that her biological father, Jake Gielinski, had contracted lung cancer and was dying.

Jake Gielinski was Peggy's second husband. Peggy had grown up in the Denver area, mostly in the Littleton neighborhood near the home where Jacine would be raised. All of Peggy's siblings were married before she was, and she was beginning to imagine herself a future as a spinster. So when she was eighteen she married her boyfriend, Richard.

The marriage lasted a year and a half. Richard turned out to be a jealous and controlling husband. Peggy couldn't go to the grocery store without him accusing her of sleeping with other men. He also tried to prevent her from seeing her family and friends, a tactic she only later realized was part of his effort to make her entirely dependent on him.

A year after her divorce, she met Jake Gielinski at a bar where she was working that summer. He lived in Evergreen, a small town in the mountains thirty miles west of Denver. She wasn't looking for another long-term relationship, but he was funny and nice and a few months later, she was married for the second time.

Jake didn't try to control her like Richard. But he had other problems that he kept secret from her until several months after their marriage, the worst being that he was an alcoholic and a drug dealer. He sold speed, a nervous system stimulant he also used to counteract the effects of alcohol. However, some of the side effects of the drug were paranoia, delusions, and irrational, even violent, behavior.

In 1974, after the couple had moved into their house in Littleton, his behavior worsened. One night he called from a pay phone a few blocks from their house saying he was afraid to come home because the disc jockeys from a local radio station were trying to kill him.

When he wasn't drinking or on speed, Jake was his old self, sweet, funny, the nicest person anyone would want to meet. Peggy loved him, but it was becoming harder to deal with his problems, especially because he refused to help himself.

Jake got in trouble with the law several times, including a conviction for forging prescriptions. He was placed on probation with the requirement that he take Anibuse, a drug that makes the user physically ill if combined with alcohol. Only after he was out of her life did Peggy find all of the untouched bottles of Anibuse in a shed in the backyard.

In the midst of these tribulations, Peggy got pregnant. She hoped that the added responsibility of a child would straighten her husband out, but he didn't change. In fact, he only got worse.

One night he came home in a rage and started punching holes in walls. Afraid, Peggy called the police. When they arrived, Jake refused to leave the house and yelled out the window that he was armed. However, he didn't really have a gun. Instead, he painted a banana black with a felt-tip marker. Then with his fruit "gun" and all the kitchen knives he could find, he stepped out of the house to confront the police.

It was obvious to Peggy that he was trying to commit suicide-by-cop and he nearly succeeded. She looked out the window and saw the officers kneeling with their guns drawn and pointed at her husband, who was raving at them from the front doorstep. Peggy knew that if he moved toward the officers, they'd shoot. She pleaded for Jake to stop. At last he put down the banana and the knives and allowed himself to be handcuffed and taken off to jail. Once again, he got probation.

There was one bright spot in all the insanity. On January 16, 1975, Jacine Renee Gielinski was born. But even on that auspicious day, Jake Gielinski could not keep it together. He barely stayed awake to drive Peggy to the hospital, but a few hours later, after she'd delivered their child, he bounced into the room, his eyes wide open and glittering with the effects of speed. He was all smiles, but Peggy's mouth hardened, angry that he couldn't even stay off drugs long enough to greet his daughter.

The marriage lasted another eighteen months. When he was around and sober, he was a good father who enjoyed spending time playing with his infant daughter. But he couldn't, or didn't want to, kick the habits that were destroying his marriage and his health.

Many nights, Peggy lay in bed with her child, afraid to get up when she heard him come home, banging about the house like a madman. One morning she got up and went out to the living room and found that he'd covered all the windows with butcher paper so that no one could see in. Then he'd set up a tent in the room where, he declared, he was going to live.

The final straw for Peggy was the day he ransacked their daughter's room and found a collection of rare, old silver dollars that had been given to Jacine as a birth present. He took the coins, hawked them, and spent the money on drugs. Then he went to the home of Peggy's parents, broke in, and stole their liquor. It was just more proof that there was nothing he wouldn't stoop to in order to feed his addictions. She told him he had to leave their home, and she divorced him shortly afterward.

Peggy wasn't looking for another man in her life when she met Bob Luiszer in 1977. Actually, she remet him, as they'd both belonged to a bowling league the summer before. But they'd also both been married at that time, so nothing had come of it. A year later, they were both divorced and began seeing each other.

Jacine was two and a half at the time, which was about the same age as a son Bob had with his former wife. However, his divorce had been bitter, and she allowed him little contact with the boy. Bob transferred his affection to the little blond girl with the 1,000-watt smile and a personality to match. She was all the more endearing because of a speech impediment that made it difficult for her to pronounce certain hard consonants—she called herself "Day-dine"—and Peggy and Bob were almost sad when speech therapy corrected the problem.

Bob moved into the house in Littleton a year after he and Peggy started dating. He was willing to marry her, but Peggy wasn't interested in a third try at matrimony. Then again, she hadn't counted on Jacine, who in 1982 decided it was time for her mother and Bob to get hitched. The reason was she wanted to be the flower girl in their wedding. The ceremony was held in their backyard in front of family and a few friends. Of course, it was seven-year-old Jacine happily tossing turquoise daisy petals who stole the show.

When it came to male role models, Jacine was fortunate to have Bob Luiszer. He liked to cook and bake—every

Christmas he made on the order of 2,000 cookies from scratch for relatives, friends, and coworkers—and she liked to eat anything he was willing to prepare. He was particularly famous among Jacine's friends for the chocolate-chip pancakes he made without fail the morning after sleep-overs. Jacine would turn eating the pancakes into a contest, like she did with everything else. She always won.

Bob joined Peggy in attending all of Jacine's sporting events: a never-ending procession of swim meets, soccer, basketball and volleyball games. He'd been the one to encourage her to sign up for the basketball and volleyball teams on the first day of high school when she was feeling a little intimidated. He and Peggy were the teams' biggest boosters, helping any way they could, including taking tickets at the door.

Jake Gielinski, on the other hand, had little to do with his daughter after the divorce. And Peggy didn't try to shield her daughter from the truth about him. When Jacine was old enough, Peggy told her about the drugs and alcohol and run-ins with the police. He'd rarely paid the child support he owed, and Peggy told her daughter about that, too. She and her daughter had always been honest with one another, and she saw no reason to hide the fact that Jake Gielinski was a lousy father.

Every so often, they'd hear about his continuing troubles after he moved back to Evergreen. Once there was a call from a concerned driver who'd found him passed out in a car alongside the road and got Peggy's number from his wallet. Another time there was a call from a sheriff's deputy. Apparently, Jake had just had an operation on his arms for carpal tunnel syndrome, then got drunk and decided to go rock climbing. By the time the police got to him, he'd busted out the stitches in his arms; the deputy said his blood alcohol content was so high, Jake was lucky to still be alive.

Jake saw Jacine twice a year, at Peggy's secret insistence: on her birthday and at Christmas. He would spend hundreds of dollars at those times buying Jacine extravagant presents as if making up for the other 363 days of the year. But when Peggy would ask him to spread the money out over more of the year and make more of an effort to see his daughter, he just couldn't seem to find the time.

Peggy knew his apparent indifference hurt Jacine, though her daughter tried not to show it. One incident, however, she could not ignore. In Jacine's senior year her volleyball team was scheduled to travel to play the high-school team in Evergreen where Jake now owned a security-guard company. Peggy had begged him to come to the game, and he'd agreed.

Jacine was surprised and overjoyed when she saw him, wearing his uniform, walk into the gymnasium. He came over to talk to her, but then he dropped the bomb. Something had come up, he said, and he couldn't stay for the game. With that, he turned and left.

Waiting only until he couldn't see her pain, Jacine then flew into a rage. She started throwing balls and crying.

When Peggy learned in the spring of 1993 that Jacine, a senior, had been nominated for Prom Queen, she'd gone to the school counselor and asked to be told beforehand if her daughter was going to be crowned. She explained that if Jacine won, she wanted to make sure that her daughter's father was present. But Jacine was the runner-up, so that moment in her life passed, like all the others, without Jake.

Shortly after, Peggy informed her daughter of Jake Gielinski's illness and prognosis: the doctors were giving him six months. She was surprised by her daughter's reaction. She expected sadness, maybe even bitterness, over the father she hardly knew, but not Jacine's announcement that she was going to "get to know" her father.

Jacine contacted Jake and began to visit him regularly in Evergreen. She spent weekends with him, coming home with stories about how much fun they had, even if it was just watching their favorite cartoon, *Beavis and Butthead.* "You should watch it," Jacine told Peggy. "It's sooooo funny."

After the initial surprise wore off, Peggy realized that Jacine's reaction to her father's illness wasn't so hard to understand. Jacine sometimes described herself as Jake's "caregiver," and if there was one term that fit her daughter, *caregiver*—not just to her father but to the world at large—could have been it.

As Jake's disease progressed, it was clear to Peggy and Bob how much the pain of watching him deteriorate was taking a toll on their daughter.

However, as much as she let her emotions show regarding Jake, Jacine was careful to make sure that Bob Luiszer understood that nothing had changed between the two of them. Jake was her father, she said, and she had learned to love him despite his faults. But Bob would always be "my real dad. . . . You'll be the one who'll walk me down the aisle when I get married." That's okay, he replied, he understood.

Near the end of that summer, Jacine was spending as much time as she could caring for Jake. He had a woman friend in Evergreen who assisted as well, but otherwise, he was too weak to take care of even personal matters on his own. Jacine had to clean him, feed him, and help him with his medications.

The end wasn't pretty. He was taken to a hospital and set up in a hospice room. Although he was medicated for the pain, drugs couldn't mask all of it, nor stop him from coughing up blood. Death, when it finally came, was as merciful for his daughter as for himself.

Even in death, Jake Gielinski didn't change. He'd told Peggy that he'd made arrangements with a mortuary in Evergreen to be cremated. However, she learned that although he'd talked to the mortuary representative, nothing had been paid for and it fell to her and Bob to cover it. He left little behind except more debts, including one with the Internal Revenue Service, which tried to collect from the Luiszers. Other than a few personal effects, there was no sort of inheritance for Jacine. Still, she seemed to have peace of mind that she at least had the time to get to know her father, and the long good-bye had somehow made it easier to accept the inevitable.

Or so her surviving parents believed.

After graduation from high school in June 1993, Jacine was awarded a full volleyball scholarship at a junior college in southern Colorado. While she was a star player on the junior-college team, she was also the one who would decorate the locker room before games, cutting out inspirational sayings to tape to her teammates' lockers.

While at college, Jacine also fell in love with Marvin Lee. He was a police officer with the town department who also helped as an assistant coach for the volleyball team.

The first time Peggy met Lee, she was struck by how much he reminded her of Jake Gielinski. She wondered if that wasn't part of the attraction for Jacine. Maybe even the uniform had reminded her of her father.

Otherwise, Peggy didn't think much of him. At Christmas in 1993, he and Jacine came up to visit and Peggy got a chance to talk to him with one of her friends when Jacine went out on an errand. Most of the time was spent listening to him talk about himself and all the wonderful things he'd done in his life. He said he'd been a professional ski racer and was an army veteran who'd fought in the Desert Storm campaign.

Peggy thought Lee was a liar, and her suspicions seemed confirmed when she called the college he said he'd graduated from and they had no record of him. In that respect, he was a lot like Jake, but there were also some similarities to her first husband, Richard, especially the way he seemed to control Jacine. A red flag went up when she learned that he and Jacine sometimes came to Denver to visit his sister, who lived only a few miles from the Luiszers, but he wouldn't let Jacine call or visit her parents. By now, Peggy knew that separating their girlfriends and wives from family and friends was how guys like Richard and Marvin maintained control over them.

When Peggy mentioned her misgivings to Jacine, her daughter didn't want to hear it. They'd always been more like best friends than mother and daughter, but now Jacine told her to stay out of it.

After Jacine's first year at college ended in May 1994, she decided to stay in town so that she could work and be near her boyfriend. Peggy grew more concerned when she learned that Jacine had been hospitalized for what she later learned were complications from an abortion.

Peggy suspected that Jacine was giving Lee money. She learned that her daughter was working at a pizza joint so she could make payments on a bank loan she'd taken out to buy Lee a jet ski. She pointed out that she thought Lee was just using her, but Jacine grew more distant and stopped calling as frequently. They couldn't talk about Lee at all without angry words and telephone hang-ups.

Peggy blamed the loss of her daughter's affections on Lee and hated him for it. She reacted like a mother bear protecting her cub, so much so that she fantasized about hurting him. One particularly black afternoon, depressed and missing Jacine, she pulled up in front of a pawnshop and considered going inside to purchase a handgun. She sat there imagining what it would be like to drive the five hours to the town where Lee worked and then seeing the look on his face when she shot him.

Of course, she knew that she couldn't act on her urge. She was just venting. The anger, however, remained so strong that she sought counseling. It helped her realize that Jacine was not a child, and she couldn't protect her daughter from all harm anymore.

Peggy hoped that after Jacine graduated and moved away, she'd get over him. The opportunity arose when she was given a volleyball scholarship at the University of Colorado campus in Colorado Springs that would allow her to pursue her bachelor's degree.

Jacine still wasn't sure what she wanted to do with her life. Sometimes she joked about being a "professional beach volleyball player" in California with her high school teammate and best friend, Maggie Bush. But she was a communications major and also talked about becoming a sportswriter, a vocation her mother thought she would excel at.

Jacine had played for the university team for the 1995–96 season, but she quit the next year so she could concentrate on her studies; her maternal grandparents made it easy by paying her rent and tuition. She was renting an apartment with a good friend of Lee's, Allen Crumb, and his girlfriend, Tisha Terrell, but Peggy thought her daughter was through with her old beau. Then Jacine told her that she and Lee were going on a vacation to the Caribbean in January. What's more, Jacine was paying for it.

When Peggy asked why, Jacine sadly told her that Lee had cancer. He had been traveling to the city of Pueblo for treatments, and she wanted to do something nice for him. Something did not seem right to the Luiszers. Coming on the heels of Jake Gielinski's death due to lung cancer, it seemed like he might be manipulating Jacine, knowing how she had responded when her father was dying.

Bob looked into it, calling the American Cancer Society, and learned that the type of cancer Lee professed to have had a 95 percent mortality rate. If Lee did have it, he was almost certain to die.

If so, he wasn't very grateful for Jacine's gesture. She called her mother in tears shortly after they got back and said that they'd hardly stepped off the plane in Denver when he told her to "fuck off" and that he never wanted to see her again.

Jacine was devastated, but at last seemed to be done with him. She began to sound better to Peggy during their weekly telephone calls after she met Tim Ratican through her new job at a local hotel. She said that Ratican was funny and treated her nicely. She told Peggy that she was looking forward to introducing him to her and Bob.

Most of the time, Jacine was Jacine. She'd been assigned a project that winter in one of her classes to study the causes of homelessness, including interviewing homeless people on the streets. She felt so bad after talking to one man that she went home to her apartment, packed a box full of food, grabbed an extra coat and a blanket, and returned to give it to him. Another time she was out with Ratican when she spotted a vagrant who had no socks. That time she made her boyfriend return to his apartment, where she claimed a $15 pair of his best winter socks and drove back to give them to the surprised man.

However, not everything was all right with Jacine. For one thing, she learned she would not be able to graduate from the university that spring, nor was a course she needed going to be offered that summer. She was going to have to wait until the next fall. She felt that she was letting down her grandparents, who were supporting her and telling her how proud they were that she was going to be the first on their side of the family to graduate from college.

She also was not over Lee and would call him dozens of times a day, only to be ignored. She grew depressed and her health deteriorated until she was battling mononucleosis, which left her exhausted and even more down in the dumps. By mid-April, all of it—the postponed graduation, her health, and Lee—was too much for Jacine. She called her mother in tears.

Peggy was disturbed to hear Jacine—once so confident, the picture of health—so down. It got worse when Jacine started talking crazy about her dead father, Jake Gielinski. Jacine said she was certain that his ghost was visiting her when she slept, moving things around in her room.

The conversation alarmed Peggy so much that she was worried her daughter might be contemplating suicide. She called Bob at work and told him to come pick her up. They needed to drive to Colorado Springs as soon as possible.

They arrived at Jacine's apartment with Peggy determined to talk Jacine into moving back to the Denver area. However, Jacine was angry that they'd come. Everything was all right, she said. They should just turn around and go home. But everything was not all right. She looked worn out and cried the entire time, admitting that she was concerned about being infected with HIV.

Jacine repeated that she'd been dreaming a lot about her father lately. He'd been in her room, and she felt that he was nearby for some reason. She was full of tearful questions. "Where do you go when you die?" Was her father trying to communicate with her? Was he watching over her? "Do you think he's in heaven?"

Peggy said she had no explanation. Who knew? What was important to her and Bob was that they wanted her to come back to Littleton with them. She could get her own apartment—heck, her grandparents would probably pay for that, too.

Jacine shook her head. No, she sobbed, she had to stay in Colorado Springs until she graduated. Her grandparents were counting on her.

The Luiszers said that it didn't matter. Her grandparents would be just as proud if she finished her degree at the University of Colorado campus in Denver or Boulder. She could go home, rest, get healthy, and then finish whenever she wanted.

Jacine wouldn't budge. "Don't worry," she said, drying her tears. She was just having a bad day. Her health was improving and besides, she had a new boyfriend, Tim, and she didn't want to leave him.

After a while, Jacine was doing better. She even remembered, for all the talk about Jake Gielinski, to once again remind Bob that he was her "real dad" and the man who would be "walking me down the aisle."

Reluctantly, Peggy and Bob left her in Colorado Springs and went home to Littleton. A week later, after returning to their house from visiting Bob's coworker and her new baby in the maternity ward of the Littleton hospital, they were imagining the day Jacine would marry and make them grandparents. Tired, they watched the late news and then went to bed, just another middle-class American couple.


At about the same time, Jacine Gielinski said good night to her roommate, Tisha Terrell, and left for her boyfriend's apartment. She was still having dreams about her father, but generally was feeling more upbeat than she had in a while. Part of the reason was Tim Ratican, who was at that moment fixing them a late dinner.

Jacine pulled up in the right lane at the stoplight on Austin Bluffs Drive. She didn't turn to look at the two young men—one dark-haired, the other with a shaved head—who were staring at her from the car in the far left lane. Nor did she notice when they followed her to the apartment complex where Ratican lived.

Getting out of her car, Jacine walked toward the security door so she could be buzzed in to the building. She was dressed in a light gray sweatshirt, shorts, and black sandals. Although she was carrying her purse with her credit cards and $157 in cash, she was not concerned about the two men who walked behind her. There were 120 apartments in the complex, and someone was always coming and going.

Then one of the men grabbed her from behind, wrapping his left arm around her waist and placing his right hand over her mouth. He yanked her violently backward toward his companion, who grabbed her legs. Freeing her mouth from her captor's grasp, she began to scream for help.

# SIX

# THE SCENES
# OF THE CRIME

*April 29, 1997*
*Colorado Springs*

Officer Greg Wilhelmi was on routine patrol when the dispatcher sent him to check on the possible abduction of a woman from an apartment complex at the north end of town. He pulled into the complex about 11 P.M., where he was met by a half-dozen people who claimed to have witnessed the crime.

A ten-year veteran of the Colorado Springs Police Department, Wilhelmi had dealt with a lot of different criminals. In this instance, the suspects were either inept or they hadn't cared who saw them.

Although the case would probably be handed over to detectives later, Wilhelmi talked to the witnesses to try to establish exactly what had transpired. If the initial report was correct, a woman was in trouble and time might be of the essence.

Wilhelmi began with four women, Mormon missionaries who'd been in the parking lot of the apartment complex across the street when they heard a woman scream. One of the women, Glenda Hansen, said that when she first heard the woman cry out, "Help me! Help me!" she thought it was one of the teenagers in the neighborhood playing around. But the screams were too real and when she looked across the street, she saw a struggling woman being dragged across the other lot by two white males. Hansen had told her companions to cross the street to see what they could do. In the meantime, she ran to a telephone and dialed 911 to summon the police.

Another of the women, Margaret Zarate, ran across the street. She saw that the victim was a young blond woman and noted that the suspects' car was an older, gray sedan: "I think a Ford Thunderbird."

The two men forced their victim into the backseat of the car, but not without a fight. Zarate said she saw from a distance of about twenty feet that the bald male in the front seat leaned over toward the back, trying to hold the woman down as she screamed and kicked at the roof and windows. The dark-haired suspect, who appeared to be in his twenties, was straddling the woman and punching her in the face.

Zarate estimated that the dark-haired man struck the woman for a full minute before the other man turned around, started the car, and drove off. The car passed close enough that she clearly saw the face of the man in the backseat illuminated by streetlights, three times in fact. The first time he looked up at her, he seemed merely curious as if he couldn't understand what she was doing there. The second time, she thought he seemed scared. But then he glanced down at his victim and when he looked up again, she saw that he was smiling.

The strange thing was that he continued smiling even though he had to have noticed that one of the other women with Zarate, Torina Homer, was writing down the license plate number of the car. It was a Colorado license plate with the green mountains and white numbers and letters: KBN6729.

The Mormon missionaries weren't the only witnesses. Several of the residents in the apartment complex also heard the screaming and came out to see what was going on.

In her third-floor apartment, Linda Glaza had just turned in for the night when a woman's cries made her sit up in bed. She rushed out onto her balcony above the parking lot and saw two men by the rear door on the passenger side of a gray sedan, trying to force a blond woman into the backseat. The woman was putting up a good fight and had gripped the sides of the door frame to prevent them from forcing her inside the car. But one of the men, the bald one, raised his clasped hands above his head and smashed them down on the woman's arms and broke her grip.

Glaza yelled down, demanding that the men let their victim go, but they acted like they never even heard her. When they got the woman in the car, the dark-haired kidnapper crawled into the backseat with her. Meanwhile, the bald one walked quickly around to the driver's side, looked around as if checking for witnesses—of which he had to have seen there were a few, then hopped in the car.

Other residents had appeared on their balconies and yelled at the men. Some emerged from the building to try to help, but they were too late to rescue the woman. All that was left were memories of the terrifying scene, as well as some items left behind by the victim. A pair of black sandals lay on the pavement near the door as if the owner had stepped out of them for a moment and forgotten to come back.

The witnesses also pointed out a woman's black wallet for the officer. It contained a driver's license with a photograph of a young, smiling blond woman by the name of Jacine Renee Gielinski, date of birth January 16, 1975.

When Wilhelmi pulled out the driver's license for a better look, Zarate shouted, "That's her. That's the person who was grabbed." So there was little question it had belonged to the victim.

The wallet also contained a checkbook, a Social Security card, credit cards—all registered to Jacine Gielinski—and $157 in cash. Apparently, the kidnappers weren't after money.

As soon as he got the suspects' license plate number from the witnesses and a description of the car and occupants, Wilhelmi called it in before continuing his investigation. From there, the Colorado Springs Police Department moved quickly—a BOLO (be-on-the-lookout) bulletin was put out on the radios and updated as more information came in—and more officers were dispatched.

The police soon had a telephone number for the address listed on Jacine Gielinski's driver's license and called it. A young man who identified himself as Allen Crumb answered and was joined on the line by Tisha Terrell. They said they were Jacine Gielinski's roommates. They said the last time they saw her was a little after 10:30 P.M., and she was heading out the door to go to her boyfriend's apartment. She drove a red Geo Prism and her boyfriend was Tim Ratican.

Crumb and Terrell were asked if they were aware of any volatile domestic problems Jacine might have been having with a boyfriend or former boyfriend. They said she'd recently broken up with her longtime boyfriend, Marvin Lee, but they knew of no problems. Crumb identified Lee as a police officer and said he was a good friend.

They also said they didn't know of any problems between Jacine and Ratican. She'd experienced some bouts of depression lately having to do with her father's death, they said, but the bouts seemed short-lived and she was otherwise happy and outgoing.

The police asked if Jacine had any identifying marks

and were told she had a small tattoo of the Tasmanian
Devil cartoon character at her bikini line. Otherwise, there
wasn't much they could add except she worked the 3–11
shift at the hotel and before that had worked as a waitress
at a Colorado Springs sports bar.

A detective called Ratican, who, confused, said he was
waiting for his girlfriend, Jacine Gielinski, to show up. He
was asked to go to the parking lot and talk to a police officer there. Ratican and his roommate, Greg Dana, went
outside and spoke to Officer Mark White, who had arrived
on the scene.

Ratican was bewildered. He identified Jacine's car in the
parking lot but hadn't known she'd even arrived.

White asked if he knew of any trouble between Jacine
and her former boyfriend, Marvin Lee. Ratican nodded—
nothing specific, but she was afraid of Lee, he said. Greg
Dana added that in a private conversation he'd had with
Jacine, she also said she was afraid of Lee and that he'd
been "physically abusive." Other than that, the two roommates said, they didn't think Jacine had any enemies.

Meanwhile, Crumb had supplied a telephone number
for the missing woman's parents, Bob and Peggy Luiszer,
who were then called by a detective. All he could tell them
was that their daughter had disappeared under "suspi-
cious" circumstances and that her purse had been found at
the scene. They wanted to drive down to the Springs, but
he advised them to stay put until they knew more.

Sgt. Jerry Steckler, who was heading up the initial response, ran the license plates and found they belonged to
a 1985 Ford Thunderbird registered to Lucas Salmon,
whose date of birth was given as February 9, 1976. The detective quickly ascertained that the address on the
registration was for a business, Motorcycle Accessories
Warehouse. At ten minutes after midnight, Steckler called
the owner of the business, Bob Salmon, at his home and
asked if he knew Lucas Salmon.

"He's my son," Bob said, confirming that Lucas drove a gray Ford Thunderbird. He told Steckler that his son wasn't living with him, but thought he was staying with a friend, George Woldt, and Woldt's wife, Bonnie. He produced a telephone number for the Woldts.

Tracing the number to an apartment at a condominium complex on King Street, Steckler and other officers arrived outside the building. A gray Thunderbird was parked in the driveway. The sergeant looked through the windshield and saw an identification card belonging to Lucas Salmon lying on the dashboard.

Steckler approached the front door while other officers took up positions until they had the place surrounded. Officer Tom Heath crept up to the front window, which had its blinds pulled down, but he could just see under them into the lighted living room. When Steckler rang the doorbell, Heath saw two pairs of feet move to the front door. The sergeant knocked again and shouted, "Police officer!" This time the lights went out and Heath saw the feet walk out of the room.

Getting no answer, Steckler radioed to the dispatcher and asked her to call the apartment and announce his presence. He heard the telephone ring in the apartment, but no one answered it.

At that point, Steckler told Heath to go around to the back of the apartment and break a window to get the suspects' attention. A minute later, there was the sound of shattering glass and Heath shouted that he was a police officer.

At the same time, a frightened voice from within yelled, "Hey!" Then the dead bolt on the front door clicked and the door was opened by a young man with dark hair.

With his gun drawn, Steckler told Woldt to back away from the door. "Are you armed?" the sergeant yelled.

"No," Woldt said. He was wearing a white polo shirt and black slacks, the pockets of which he now emptied at Steckler's command, placing a pager and a silver-colored nail clipper on the table.

Another young man entered the room. His head was shaved and he was wearing a striped shirt and jeans. He was followed by an obviously pregnant woman, who tried with limited success to keep a bathrobe wrapped around her as she kept asking, "What's wrong? What's wrong?"

Steckler immediately had his officers separate the three occupants of the apartment. He told Heath to take the dark-haired suspect, who'd identified himself as George Woldt, outside. The woman—who said she was Woldt's wife, Bonnie—was escorted back into a room where her son was sleeping.

The bald one identified himself as Lucas Salmon. Steckler sat him down on a couch in the living room and told him why there were there. Witnesses had seen a woman assaulted and kidnapped by two men, who'd driven away in a vehicle matching the description of his car and license plate.

Salmon said he had no idea what Steckler was talking about. He and his friend George had been playing pool at the Corner Pocket all night until they came home.

It was a few minutes after 1 A.M., and Steckler asked Salmon if he minded if police officers searched his car. Salmon mumbled something incoherent so the sergeant repeated his question.

Salmon sighed. "Yeah, go ahead. You can search it," he said. He handed the keys to Steckler, who got up and passed them on to Officer Olav Chaney, who'd just arrived from the kidnapping scene.

Chaney and another officer looked first at the interior of the car. There was a Bible on the backseat, but he saw no sign of blood or a struggle. He next proceeded to the trunk to see if the victim had been placed inside. There was no body, living or dead, in the trunk, but what he saw was chilling nonetheless.

Lying inside was a light gray sweatshirt, which was smeared with a dark substance and also a drying red liquid that appeared to be blood. On top of the sweatshirt was a wooden-handled steak knife; the blade of the knife was bent and it, too, was covered with what looked like blood.

Chaney didn't touch the items and closed the trunk of the car. Crime-scene investigators would be called in to carefully document and remove the evidence. He walked back into the apartment and took Steckler aside to tell him what he'd seen.

Steckler nodded and went back to confront Salmon. That's all it took. The young man said matter-of-factly, "We stabbed a girl."

What struck Steckler about the admission was that the way Salmon said it without emotion. He could have been admitting to running a red light.


After hitting the jogger in the Garden of the Gods, Salmon and Woldt had returned to the condominium, where they settled down to a game of Monopoly with Bonnie and one of Bonnie's female friends, Rachel Strattman. A hour earlier, they'd assaulted a woman and come within a hairbreadth of abducting, raping, and killing her. Now they were happily squabbling over imaginary pieces of property, rolling the dice and hoping to avoid the following instructions: Go to Jail. Go Directly to Jail. Do Not Pass Go. Do Not Collect $200.

When the game was over, Strattman announced that she had to go home. George Woldt immediately volunteered to drive her, but she declined his offer. It wasn't that far, she could walk.

Apparently, that wasn't satisfactory to Woldt, who repeated that he and Salmon would take her home. He was clearly agitated when she again said thanks but no, thanks.

A little later, she was outside talking to Bonnie before leaving when she noticed Woldt staring at her as he talked to Salmon. Whatever it was he was saying, she knew it had to do with her, and that he was really angry and not just with her. As he spoke, he nodded his head toward Rachel, but Salmon kept shaking his head no. The conversation between the two men ended with Woldt accusing his friend, loud enough for the women to hear, of being "a faggot."

Strattman left and the two men and Bonnie went inside for dinner. During the meal, Salmon polished off two beers. They then got up, with Woldt announcing they were going to the Corner Pocket.

The pair drove to the pool hall, where they played for a couple of hours. Salmon drank several more beers, but not Woldt, who was not twenty-one yet and could not legally drink. The waitress who brought the beers, Laura Shugart, did not enjoy serving the strange-looking bald one. He made her nervous the way he followed her everywhere with his eyes, as if he were looking beneath her clothes. She was glad when they left.

Although they were using his Thunderbird, Salmon asked Woldt to drive. He didn't want to get pulled over and arrested for drunk driving. As they headed down the road, they started talking about the events of the afternoon and how they'd had their fantasy woman in their grasp. They were ready, Woldt declared, for "a little of the ol' in-out."

They headed for one of the popular nightclubs, determined to make their fantasy a reality. They pulled into the parking lot and went into the club to see if they could spot any likely targets. There were plenty and when one would leave, they'd quickly follow her out the door, stalking their prey toward her car. But every time they started to move in, a car would pull into the parking area or some males would exit the club.

Frustrated, they at last gave up and decided to go back to the Woldts' apartment. Tomorrow would be another day. Tomorrow they would find a victim.

On the way home, they pulled up to the stoplight and looked over at the small red car in the right lane. She was young, maybe late teens or early twenties, blond and attractive. They decided to follow her. "Yeah, we'll get you one," Woldt said.

They trailed her to the apartment complex and pulled into the lot after her, parking near the entrance. Woldt came up with the idea of pretending they were just visiting. They got out of the car and followed the woman toward the security entrance. She was a moment from buzzing to be let in when Woldt grabbed her with one arm around her waist and the other over her mouth; Salmon had then moved in to grab her legs. She screamed as they carried and dragged her to their car, but they were beyond caring.

As soon as Salmon made his confession, Steckler had stopped the conversation and advised him of his Miranda rights. But Salmon waived his rights to have a lawyer present and to remain silent. They'd stabbed the girl, he repeated, and left her beneath a white van "near a park." He didn't think that she was still breathing.

The sergeant, a twenty-year veteran, immediately called for more help and alerted paramedics. There was a chance the girl was still alive, but they had to find her quickly.

The trouble was getting Salmon to recall where he and Woldt left her. It was a dark parking lot surrounded by a fence, he said, but he wasn't from that part of town and wasn't sure where they ended up after leaving the kidnapping scene. He agreed to go with them when Steckler asked him to help to locate the victim.

Salmon was handcuffed and placed in the backseat of

Steckler's vehicle, and they were followed by Chaney. They drove to the general area where Salmon thought he'd been that night. As they checked out different streets, Salmon related bits and pieces of the events leading up to their assault on the girl and then the attack itself.

Salmon said that he and Woldt had been looking for a month for an attractive woman to abduct and rape. After subduing and raping this woman, they'd discussed what to do next and decided to kill her so that she couldn't identify them. As he spoke, Salmon's voice was calm and subdued, a matter-of-fact, monotone recitation of the facts.

At eight minutes after 2 A.M., they drove over a set of speed bumps that Salmon said he remembered. He noted that they were at the right place when they pulled up next to the Foothills Elementary School, about a mile from the apartment complex where they'd kidnapped Jacine.

Steckler pulled into the parking lot and saw a white van. He turned on his car's searchlight and shined it on the vehicle. Even at a distance, it was easy to see there was a nude body lying facedown on the pavement beneath the vehicle.

As he pulled up closer, Steckler looked in the rearview mirror at the suspect. Salmon sat calmly, his shaved head turned so that he could see the victim, a slight smile playing across his lips.

Steckler and Chaney stopped their car some distance from the van. The searchlights had caught what appeared to be a large pool of blood on the ground near the van, and they didn't want to chance destroying or contaminating any of the evidence.

Chaney carefully approached the body and checked for signs of life. She was cold, and he couldn't find a heartbeat. So he backed off to wait for the ambulance, which arrived about thirty seconds later. The paramedics also checked for a pulse but shook their heads. They were too late. Jacine Gielinski was dead.

* * *

Back at Woldt's apartment, George was talking, too. When Salmon confessed, the police sergeant told Officer Heath to read Woldt his rights. As soon as that was done, Woldt turned to Heath and asked, "Could we talk in private?"

The police officer led him up a flight of stairs to a landing, where Woldt repeated his friend's confession about the stabbing. However, he added that after they spotted the pretty blond woman in a car next to them at a stoplight, it was Salmon who'd said, "She's the one" and insisted they follow her.

Woldt admitted that he was the first one to grab Gielinski. But the whole reason behind the abduction was that Salmon was a virgin and Woldt felt obligated "to find him a girl."

When he first started to tell his story, Woldt was emotional, his hands shaking and tears welling in his eyes. But as he got into the tale, he calmed down and he, too, gave an unemotional account of the night. The only time he got flustered again was when he asked what was going to happen to his wife.

Heath told him that she would be all right legally if she had no prior knowledge of the crime. Woldt blurted out that he "might have" told her after he came home that he'd killed someone. But he calmed down when the officer assured him that his wife was not in trouble.

After the murder, Woldt said, they drove around for a time, smoking cigarettes and discussing what had happened and its ramifications. Salmon kept accusing him, he said, of coercing him into the act "because we had talked about raping and killing a female so many times." But Woldt said he never intended to hurt anyone, "I thought it was just a joke."

# SEVEN

# "WE'RE PSYCHED!"

*April 30, 1997*
*Colorado Springs, Colorado*

Dave Young was sleeping soundly when the ringing of the telephone jarred him out of his dreams. He looked at the clock. It was 1 A.M., not a good time for a phone call to a prosecuting attorney. The news was never good.

Nor would it be this time. He recognized the voice of Sgt. Rod Walker, who headed the Homicide Unit for the Colorado Springs Police Department. The sergeant briefed him quickly. A young woman was dead, apparently raped and murdered. Two suspects had already confessed and were in custody. The sergeant paused and cleared his throat, then said, "Looks like it could be a death-penalty case."

The remark caught Young by surprise. He'd worked with Walker on a dozen or more murder cases, and the normally taciturn veteran had certainly never said anything remotely like that before. If Walker thought it was bad, it had to be really bad.

Young sighed. Thirty-two years old, clean cut, he was getting ready to leave the district attorney's office for private practice. He and his wife, Denise, were planning to start a family. It was time to make a little money, something he certainly wasn't doing as a deputy district attorney for the Fourth Judicial District Attorney's Office, usually referred to as the El Paso County District Attorney's Office.

He was already working on one murder case. It was a "Fatal Attraction" case in which a woman shot her former boyfriend, a well-liked schoolteacher, in the back of the head while he was sleeping. The case was pretty open and shut; the defendant was expected to plead to second-degree murder, and then Young thought he would leave the office.

Young had never gotten into law to be a prosecutor in the first place. He was a local boy, born and raised in Colorado Springs. He left to attend college in Texas and then got his law degree at the University of Wyoming. His first job out of law school was with the Wyoming Public Defender's Office, filing appeals for prison inmates.

In 1993, he'd been interviewed by David Vela, the head of the Colorado Public Defender's Office, for a position as a lawyer with one of the most well-funded and aggressive—especially when it came to opposing the death penalty—offices in the country. Young learned that Vela was only interviewing two applicants for the one job. When he finished, Vela asked him, "You ever think you might be better off as a prosecutor?" At that point Young figured, correctly, that he probably wasn't going to get the job.

A month later, he attended a bar association luncheon in Colorado Springs. He ended up sitting at a table with then El Paso County District Attorney John Suthers and his chief deputy district attorney, Jeanne Smith. Before lunch was over, he'd been offered a job. The pay wasn't much, abysmal in fact, but he took the job thinking it would be a good way to get to know the judges and network with the lawyers in his hometown, with the eventual goal of going into private practice.

He'd worked four years and enjoyed the work, but he and Denise had talked it over and it was time to move on. They agreed that she would quit her job and stay home with their children at least while they were young. But he would have to take up the slack in the family's finances, and the only way to do that was to go into private practice. When the call came that night, he reported to the scene figuring that he would begin the process but someone else would take over when he left the office.

On the way to the crime scene, Young thought about Walker's comment. He wasn't a big supporter of the death penalty and wasn't sure at what point he would know what side of the fence he'd be on in a particular case. Other prosecutors who'd worked death penalty cases had told him, "you'll know it when you see it." Now he saw it when he arrived at the elementary school and a patrol officer pointed to where the nude body of the young woman still lay beneath a white van bathed in searchlights that also glimmered off a red pool of blood nearby.

Young was led to a minivan where Detective Todd Drennan and Walker had set up their command post. Long years of experience had taught Walker that homicides were rarely any more complicated than they appeared at first glance. He was constantly urging his guys, especially the young ones, "don't Mickey Spillane these things." It wasn't going to take Sherlock Holmes to catch the guys who did this particular murder, but in the past supposedly slam-dunk cases had been lost due to carelessness or overconfidence. They were going to do this by the book, so a decision had been reached to wait until daylight to approach the body. There was obviously no helping the young woman now. The only thing they could do for her was to seek justice, and they could only help their cause by being careful not to damage or overlook evidence.

Young was also well aware of the pitfalls that could botch even the most airtight case. The two suspects—

whose names, he learned, were Lucas Salmon and George Woldt—had already been taken to a local hospital to have blood and hair samples taken for DNA testing. From there, they'd be taken to police headquarters to be interviewed. He'd been told that the suspects had been Mirandized and waived their rights to have a lawyer present and to remain silent.

In fact, they were talking to detectives even as Young waited in the van. During breaks in the interviews, their interrogators were relaying their information back to the command post at the elementary school. That's how Young heard the initial details about the crime—how they'd chosen her at random, then abducted, raped, and stabbed her to death.

Poor girl, Young thought. He could see her well in the glare of the lights. Even though he knew the reasons, it seemed a travesty to leave her lying naked and unprotected in the cold air, the wind stirring her blond hair and drying the dark splotches of blood on her body. Her purse had been discovered at the abduction site, so he knew her name and a little about her: Jacine Gielinski, a twenty-two-year-old college student. He could see that she was well muscled, and athletic, which made him think suddenly of his wife. She was a runner and often went out alone after dark to put in her miles. He made a mental note to stop that practice at once.

The crime scene had been taped off, but extra precautions were taken to keep the school's students and teachers from arriving and seeing the victim. The police had contacted the principal to close the school and then sealed the area as a precaution for those who might not get the word. It didn't take long for the media to hear and begin arriving with their cameras, satellite trucks, microphones, notepads, and questions. They were kept beyond the tape.

At dawn, the crime-scene unit began the process of investigating and photographing. The investigators were meticulous; for example, a crane was brought in to lift the van above the victim so that they would not have to drive the van over any evidence or move the woman.

Samples were taken from the pool of blood, now mixing with water from a nearby pile of melting snow. A tire print where the suspects' vehicle had backed through the blood was measured and photographed. Like an automotive fingerprint, it would tie the car in which the knife and sweatshirt had been found to the scene.

To the layperson, it might have seemed overdone. The police had the killers and their confessions. But no one on the scene needed to be told that confessions and physical evidence like a bloody knife had been thrown out by judges in the past. Someone willing to admit guilt in the immediate aftermath of a crime might start singing a different tune after he was teamed up with a defense lawyer.

While waiting for the sun to rise, Young had gone to the kidnap scene and the Woldts' apartment. That way, back at police headquarters he would be able to visualize the story as it had unfolded. However, he didn't need to be told that this case was worse than most. He could see that for himself back at the elementary school, where the investigators noted that the killers had apparently packed the victim's vagina with mud.

After their trip to the hospital, Salmon and Woldt had been brought to the Colorado Springs Police Department's operations center, a large redbrick building near the downtown area. There they were escorted to the second floor and seated in small, Spartan interview rooms illuminated by fluorescent lights and containing two chairs with a table between them. A box of tissues, a notepad, and a pen waited on the table for the next ruined life to come through the door and make use of them.

Set into one wall was a large "mirror" that anyone who

has ever seen a movie or television cop show knows is not really a mirror, but a one-way window. On the other side was another small room, through which the proceedings in the interview room could be watched and filmed.

There were seven detectives on the homicide unit, which was a part of the Major Crimes Division. The seven were chosen from the ranks of the 530 officers on the force who had at least four years' experience. Their job was to investigate aggravated assaults, missing-person reports, kidnappings, and murders.

They usually worked in three-person teams. One concentrated on the victim, gathering the so-called victomology. This detective became intimately familiar with the victim—likes and dislikes, hobbies, habits (both good and bad) and the names of family and friends. The second detective took charge of the crime-scene investigation.

On the third detective fell the responsibility of identifying and interviewing possible suspects. In this case, two of the unit's most experienced detectives, Terry Bjorndahl and Pat Crouch, were each assigned to one of the two suspects.

Bjorndahl drew George Woldt. Pat Crouch got Salmon. In their fifties, the two detectives were both considered the department's best at getting statements and confessions from reluctant witnesses as well as suspects. They approached their task with a similar philosophy. They treated even the most heinous murderer with decency. The detectives knew that most murderers were pretty typical people who found themselves in atypical situations, caught up in the heat of the moment, acting on impulse. Long years of experience had taught them that a gentle handshake and a soft voice would get them a lot further with a suspect than the hard-nosed, in-your-face routine television cop shows liked to portray. They generally spent ten or fifteen minutes on casual conversation, sort of like letting a car warm up on a cold day. After making sure the suspect had again waived his Miranda rights, they would begin asking the questions meant to loosen the suspect's tongue.

Sometimes it was difficult to sit and not react while listening to murderers or rapists describe their crimes. The detectives had families, people they loved, but they had to remain detached, at least while in front of the suspect, so that they could do their jobs and find justice for the victims. It would take all of their professionalism to hear Woldt and Salmon recite what they did to Jacine Gielinski.


They weren't the only ones who had to listen. Watching in the observation room and meeting with the detectives during breaks was Chief Deputy District Attorney Dan Zook. Twelve years older and more experienced than Dave Young, he would be taking the lead in the case.

Zook was another prosecutor who'd come out of law school figuring he'd be a defense attorney. He'd graduated from the University of Kansas Law School in 1979 never having had a former prosecutor as a professor. But his older brother was a prosecutor working for the district attorney in Colorado Springs, and he suggested that Zook apply. He'd been hired and worked there ever since.

He had no regrets. True, the money wasn't what he could garner in the private sector, but he'd been there long enough to make a decent enough wage to support his family and he enjoyed the work. He knew it sounded corny whenever he discussed his job, but it felt like he was doing the right thing. As a prosecutor, he had to believe that he could prove "the people's" case beyond a reasonable doubt, or he didn't file it, even if he knew in his heart of hearts that they had the right guy. His obligation was to do justice—not to any one person, but to the law.

Nothing was black and white. The prosecution also had to determine the appropriateness of the charge; for example, murder or manslaughter, which included discussing the possibilities with the victims or, in murder cases, victims' families. It also meant looking at the past records of the defendants to determine whether to pursue the tougher charge.

Zook didn't think the issues were quite so clear for defense attorneys. It was their job to make the state prove its case, but they didn't all go about it with the same integrity. Some of those who worked in that arena—the ones he respected—fought zealously but within the intent of the law without resorting to cheap tricks or theatrics, or ignoring legalties. But there were others who seemed to feel that ensuring a defendant's rights to a fair trial gave them license to bend, fold, and mutilate the law. They felt it was fair game to get away with whatever they could, knowing the judges often bent over backward so as not to be reversed by higher courts, even if it meant letting the defense get away with murder, at least figuratively. The worst of the lot treated it like a game, even if they knew that their client was guilty as sin.

What really grated on him was that what was lost in the game was the victim. And sometimes justice was a casualty as well.

The El Paso County District Attorney's Office had been stung two years earlier—losing what had appeared to be a slam-dunk murder case. In 1993, Eugene Baylis had been in a biker bar when one of the other customers threatened him. Baylis went home, armed himself to the teeth with a machine gun, four hand grenades and a handgun, then went back to the bar, where he began blasting away. He killed two men and wounded six more in the parking lot before he was apprehended by police. The man who threatened him wasn't even one of his victims.

Baylis had been charged with first-degree murder after deliberation and then District Attorney John Suthers had decided that the case warranted the death penalty. His second-in-command, Jeanne Smith, took on the case herself, doing most of the work, though joined at trial by Mary Maletesta, a death-penalty specialist with the Colorado Attorney General's Office.

The Colorado Public Defender's Office had countered with what the press called a death penalty Dream Team of experienced trial lawyers who also specialized in death-penalty cases. Although Baylis originally said he did it because he was angry, at the trial in 1995 the defense lawyers came up with the theory that he'd killed in self-defense. The attorneys also spent a great deal of time painting the victims, and intended victim, as black as possible—vicious, cruel, depraved people—while Baylis was just an ordinary Joe looking for a social drink. They also filed more than four hundred pretrial motions, which Smith admitted afterward wore her down before the trial had even started.

Legally, the premise of self-defense is that the defendant felt his life was in immediate danger. But Baylis left the bar, drove miles to his home to fetch his weapons, and then drove back to the bar. All he would have had to have done was stay away from the bar to avoid his tormentor. Even if he felt threatened by the mere existence of the other man, the law didn't make allowances for gunning down people in cold blood—much less people who had nothing to do with the initial argument—just because someone felt verbally intimidated.

The prosecutors felt that the theory was so ludicrous that no jury would accept it. Even if the jury somehow didn't believe that the crime met the requirements for premeditated murder, they would have to find Baylis guilty of second-degree murder. So they were stunned when the jury returned a verdict of not guilty and Baylis walked away a free man.

Losing cases, however, wasn't the worst thing a prosecutor had to deal with. Some cases simply left more lasting impressions, especially those involving the deaths of children and young women.

As a father, Zook had never gotten over the abduction and murder of a thirteen-year-old named Heather Dawn Church. Heather had disappeared from her home in the country east of Colorado Springs in 1991. She was babysitting a younger sister, her parents gone, when a neighbor heard a scream. When her parents arrived home later, Heather was missing.

No blood was found at the scene, and she disappeared without a trace. It was two years before her remains were found in the mountains west of Colorado Springs. Whoever had taken her had thrown her body off an overlook, where it was scavenged and scattered by wild animals. Not until her skull was discovered by a motorist on the switchback of a road below the overlook—where it had either been carried or washed down the hillside in a downpour—did anyone know what had become of her. Even then, no one knew the identity of her killer.

The case remained unsolved until the El Paso County Sheriff persuaded a near-legendary lawman named Lou Smit to come out of retirement to take on the case. Based on a single fingerprint found at the scene and tenacious detective work, Smit was eventually able to bring Heather's killer to justice. But the perpetrator's plea of guilty to second-degree murder left a number of unanswered questions that had troubled Zook ever since. How long had her killer kept her alive and in fear? What had he done to her before he left her body in the mountains so far from the people who loved her?

Sometimes he thought about how he'd been sitting on his couch with his little girls watching television when Heather was snatched from the safety of her home, murdered, and left for the animals to devour. Ever since then, he'd kept a photograph of Heather in his desk drawer—

forever smiling and happy, a soccer ball resting beneath her foot.

It was photographs like that which kept him going when sometimes he felt like throwing up his hands at the strange machinations of the system and the antics of defense attorneys. The autopsy photographs were terrible, but worse for him were the photographs that grieving mothers and fathers brought to him of their children in happier days, posing with soccer balls or blowing out birthday candles or just smiling, looking forward to a future they would never know. He would never understand how someone could bring himself to rape and kill the victims in those photographs to satisfy his perverted lusts, but he could do something about it by getting a jury to find them guilty.

Too often, the victims were all but lost in the system. The system was all about the defendants: their rights, needs, childhoods, and troubles. Meanwhile, families of the victims sat in courtrooms and listened to lawyers argue over their loved ones as if they were no more than a case file number or a legal question to be debated. Worse, they sometimes had to hear defense lawyers trash the victims and sometimes even insinuate that the victims were somehow complicit in their own murders.

Zook had prosecuted a first-degree murder case in which a nice, older gentleman with a wife and children was murdered by a man he'd befriended and given work doing odd jobs—Frank Orona, who'd recently been released from prison. The old man's thanks was to be forced at gunpoint to withdraw money from his bank and then taken to a deserted field where he was beaten and stabbed to death. The prosecution sought the death penalty.

The defense attorneys, led by Chief Deputy Public Defender Terri Brake, had come up with the theory that their client had killed his benefactor because the old man had made "homosexual advances" toward him, the idea being that a jury would understand a man being upset to the point of murder for such a thing. There was no truth to the allegation, and the man's family knew it, but that had not kept the allegations out of court or the media. Orona was convicted, but the jury sentenced him to life in prison rather than the death penalty.

It was Zook's first and only death penalty case. He walked away disgusted, not by the jury's decision as much as the defense's tactics. Not only had the old man been savagely murdered, but his reputation had been besmirched, adding to the pain his family was already suffering.

The defense attorneys had not cared about the victim. The way Zook saw it, their trial tactics weren't about justice or a defendant's rights. They were about winning at any cost. In fact, the "homosexual advances" defense became the "defense theory du jour" used by other defense attorneys in subsequent trials when trying to explain why their clients would kill another man.

Sometimes Zook wanted to quit. But then he'd win a conviction and the victim or the family would call to thank him or write a card. It made it worthwhile.


The photograph of Heather was still in his desk drawer four years after her killer was caught. Now as Zook listened to Salmon and Woldt confess their crime, he wondered what new photograph would be added.

He marveled at how Bjorndahl and Crouch could stay so calm; they'd even sent out for McDonald's breakfasts— two Egg McMuffins with sausage and two orange juices. During the breaks, they would compare notes and discuss what questions to ask to check the stories against each other. It might help them decide if they were being told the truth, but it also might give them some insight into the reasons behind the crime and how each defendant would act in the future.

For instance, Salmon wrote out in his confession, "The

roots of this incident date back to approximately a month ago. My friend, George Woldt, and I viewed a film called *Clockwork Orange.*

"This film depicted graphic scenes of violence, betrayal, and rape. It was then that we first became interested in the act of sexual assault. . . . We only joked about it at first, but as time went by we both agreed it was something we would like to do."

When Bjorndahl went back and asked Woldt about the film and its role in their crime, he'd shrugged and acknowledged that he'd watched the movie with his friend, but only found it "somewhat interesting."

The detectives and Zook knew they had to do it right the first time. Once the defendants decided to lawyer up, that would be it for questioning. When they ran out of questions, they asked the suspects to write out their statements on yellow legal pads. Both agreed and were left alone for more than an hour.

Much of what the young men said was nearly identical, even to the wording of their conversations. However, each of the suspects tended to place a greater share of the blame on the other, especially Woldt.

Salmon maintained that after watching the movie, the concept of raping and killing a woman remained a fantasy until a week before Jacine's murder. "It was then that we began formulating ideas and possibilities of performing the act," he wrote. "We took the risks into consideration and did not believe that they were high enough to keep us from doing it. . . . So we began picking places where we could accomplish our idea." They were committed after George brought out the steak knife and placed it in the glove box.

Woldt said that the reason they'd been following women was because his friend was a virgin. He complained to Bjorndahl that his friend had badgered him until he felt obligated to help him find a woman for sex. It was

Salmon, he said, who'd first placed the steak knife in the glove box, though they'd both agreed that the woman had to die so that she could not identify them.

One of the most chilling aspects was that others had come so close to becoming victims, including a child and an older woman. They learned of yet another near-victim during one of the morning breaks, though for reasons known only to themselves, the suspects had not mentioned their attempt to kidnap Amber Gonzales.

Gonzales had been watching the morning news on television when she heard about the arrest of two men who had kidnapped and murdered a young woman. A chill passed through her body; she knew they were the men who'd hit her with their car in the Garden of the Gods that previous afternoon. She told her father, and he brought her to the police to tell her story.

Gonzales was shown a photo lineup and had immediately picked out Salmon and Woldt. She told the detectives about the $170 sunglasses that had mysteriously disappeared from scene of the attack. They called out to the investigators going over the Woldt apartment looking for evidence and asked if they'd seen any sunglasses that matched the description of Gonzales's. The answer was yes, they'd been found in the dresser used by Salmon.

When Bjorndahl went back in and asked Woldt about Gonzales's allegations, the suspect said he had "totally spaced out" the incident. He then proceeded to say that although it had been his idea to go to the Garden of the Gods that day, it was Salmon's idea to "follow her."

Salmon had another story. "We regularly visited Garden of the Gods and clubs. We began to look for victims of our crime to be [but] had little luck until Tuesday—April twenty-ninth, 1997. . . .

"We left the house at 2:45 P.M. on Tuesday. We headed

for Garden of the Gods Recreation Park. We drove around for a while before coming upon a young lady about eighteen years old. She was jogging on the paths, and as we passed, we noticed she was attractive, and decided to pick her up."

They drove around again, talking about how they were going to abduct her. "This time we decided to hit her with the car," Salmon wrote. "We were in George's car and he was driving. He hit her going about 15 miles per hour. She flew forward after the initial hit. She had badly scraped her knees and her arm, but had no problem getting up immediately. She was coherent, and we asked her right away if she was all right.

"George got out of the car, walked up to her, holding her arms, and I had then gotten out of the car, and walked around the car and stopped." At this point, he saw the sunglasses and picked them up.

Salmon told Crouch that he felt bad about hitting Gonzales, but he didn't try to stop it either. "George let go of her. . . . We got back in the car, and drove in her direction. We continued to ask her if she needed a ride, and if she was all right. She continued to dodge our questions, and we drove off."

George had chastised him for not helping. Salmon said he used the excuse of the bushes getting in the way. Crouch asked him how they felt when they left the Garden of the Gods.

"We're psyched about it, excited, and it made us more determined to find someone," Salmon replied.

# EIGHT

# "AT LEAST I'M NOT A VIRGIN ANYMORE"

*April 30, 1997*
*Colorado Springs Police Headquarters*

Although Dan Zook and the detectives interviewing Salmon and Woldt knew from the investigators at the crime scene that the victim had suffered a number of what appeared to be knife wounds, they were not prepared for the horror of Jacine Gielinski's final hour, nor the matter-of-fact way it was presented to them by the two young men who sat in the interview rooms, clad in orange jail jumpsuits, calmly describing a young woman's worst nightmare.

The two young men differed on whose idea it was to follow the pretty blonde in the red sports car. "We were on Austin Bluffs, and came to a stop at a red light on Nevada," Salmon wrote. "I glanced over into the girl's direction, but could not see her because of the lighting. . . . George said he wanted to follow her, and I said okay."

Woldt claimed that it was Salmon who suggested that they follow the woman. He said, however, that he'd responded, "Yeah, we'll get you one."

After turning into the apartment complex behind the

woman, they'd come up with a fast plan to surprise her by pretending that they lived in the complex. She'd just about reached the security buzzer when Woldt pounced.

"George grabbed her from behind, putting his left arm around her stomach and his right hand over her mouth," Salmon wrote.

"He began carrying her to the car before I helped, picking up her legs. . . . We got to the car, and opened the passenger door. He began putting her into the back seat. I got the keys and went around to the driver's side and got in. I started the car and left."

Neither Salmon's version nor Woldt's mentioned the brutal assault the witnesses described for the police at the scene. And Jacine might as well have been a sack of groceries for all the resistance she put up in the killers' version.

Salmon saw the witnesses and thought, even as he was leaving the complex, that there was a good chance someone had taken down his license plate number. "We took a left on the street we were on before, and drove for about fifteen to twenty minutes through a residential area, before coming to a school parking lot," he wrote. "We entered the school's south entrance, and found a secluded spot near a white van. I parked and shut the car off."

Woldt and Salmon then talked about what to do next as Jacine cried in the backseat, lying on Salmon's Holy Bible, begging them not to hurt her. The two men decided to go ahead and rape Jacine, although in their statements they described it as "having sex" with her, as if consensual.

"I asked George if we should knock her out first," Salmon claimed. "He said, 'No.'"

Salmon claimed that when Woldt told him to go first, he'd refused. His friend then said, "Whatever," and proceeded to "have sex" with the woman. The assault lasted five minutes, Salmon said, during which the woman had cried and continued "to whimper, 'Please don't hurt me.'"

In Woldt's confession, he said Jacine was compliant, even assisting by removing her own pants. Then when he was not able to get an erection, she'd followed his directions to manually stimulate him until he was able to have sexual intercourse.

When he was finished, Woldt told Salmon it was his turn. "We then traded places," Salmon wrote. "He got into the front passenger's seat, and I got into the back seat. At this time the girl was on her knees, facing the driver's side of the car with her head down." Jacine was again told to manipulate her assailant's penis to enable him to rape her.

When at last they were through, the two men exited the car. They ordered Jacine to crawl out of the car backward. She did so leaving behind a garnet tennis bracelet and ring her parents had given her at Christmas lying on the same seat as Salmon's Bible. Her attackers made her lie facedown on the cold pavement. They placed her shirt over her head so she could not look at them but otherwise made no attempt to cover her nakedness.

As she lay there—batttered, degraded, frightened, and shivering—Salmon and Woldt began to talk about what to do with her. They spent the next ten to twenty minutes, depending on which story the investigators chose to believe, discussing the next step in their terrible fantasy. Adding to the scene, part of the time they spoke in high-school German.

During the oral part of the questioning, the investigators had asked them why they did not stop at this point. They had had time for reflection, time to make a moral choice and at least mitigate the damage already done. The girl was asking for mercy. But there was none to be had in that dark hour on that black night. They decided she had to die. She had seen their faces. She could identify them. Moreover, her death was part of the fantasy.

"At this point, George and I had a discussion on who would cut her first, and how it would be done," Salmon wrote. "I said I didn't want to do it. He got upset. He said I had to do it, that I had to make the first cut."

Woldt fetched the knife from the glove box and handed it to Salmon, who knelt in front of Jacine. "I took the knife, and prepared to cut her throat," he wrote. "I told George to lift her head up by the hair, and to cover her mouth."

Reaching down, Woldt had pulled Jacine's head up by her hair. The shirt still covered her face, but her neck was exposed.

"I then made my attack," Salmon wrote. "I placed the knife low on her throat, near her clavicle. I made a cut about 6 to 7 inches in length and pulled the knife until it was away from her. She did not scream, but made a light moaning sound."

On this point Woldt's account concurred. "Lucas told me to hold her head up so I did, and he cut her throat," he wrote. "She was still breathing so Lucas handed me the knife to do the same as he did."

The two men told their victim to roll over on her back, but to leave the shirt over her face so that she could not see them. Perhaps hoping that following orders would move her attackers to pity, she complied.

Woldt placed the knife about an inch above the wound created by Salmon. "I cut her throat as well."

Salmon noted, "Again, no scream. . . . We began to discuss again what we should do next."

The unlikely pair talked about the life and death of Jacine Gielinksi as though they were on the high-school debate team and she was the audience. The investigators and Zook were struck by how even hours later, the pair talked and wrote about their participation in Jacine's ordeal matter-of-factly and with no sign of remorse. They could have been moviegoers reviewing the last film they'd seen. In fact, they'd shown more emotion when the Egg McMuffins arrived than at any other point in their interviews.

The would-be killers were surprised by the relative lack of blood from the two gashes in the young woman's throat. Apparently, killing her wasn't going to be as easy as it looked in the movies. So they took some time to discuss how they might accomplish their task.

The further they got into their confessions, the more deviations there were in their stories. According to Salmon's written confession, "We decided to stab her in the chest. I again told George that I did not want to do this, and that I may get sick. But again, he convinced me to take the first one."

However, according to Woldt's account, after he cut the young woman's throat, "I quickly handed the knife back to Lucas, and he said that he was going to stab it into her heart. I said, 'Isn't there a bone there?' Lucas said to stab hard enough to get through the bone."

Salmon now knelt at Jacine's right side, facing her exposed chest. He then brought the knife up "about level with my mouth" above her while Woldt held the shirt down on her mouth. "When I struck her," Salmon wrote, "she screamed a faint scream."

"Now George took the knife from my right hand with his right hand. I had moved up to her head to hold the shirt over her mouth while George took my place at her side. He too brought the knife up about as high as his mouth, and brought it down. Every time the blade sunk until the hilt of the knife hit her body. This time no scream."

Woldt's version was that Salmon "stabbed her and said, 'Your turn,' and hands me the knife. I stabbed her."

After Woldt struck, the two young men traded places again. "At this time I made two consecutive strikes," Salmon recalled. "On my second she brings her hands up to where the wound is and screams. It is muffled by the shirt."

Despite her grievous injuries, Jacine did not give up. She was still alive, moaning and feebly moving her hands.

But the pair wasn't through with her. They switched once more. However, there was a slight interruption. The steak knife had hit bone and bent; Salmon straightened the blade as best he could by stepping on it before handing it back to his friend. "Again he stabs as I muffle the scream," Salmon wrote. "This time much fainter."

The murder was not going well at all. They'd cut her throat twice and stabbed her five times in the area of the chest they thought contained her heart. "By now we can see and hear blood gushing from her wounds," Salmon wrote, "and with each breath we could hear the blood gurgling in her mouth."

Blood was everywhere. Pumped out with each beat of her heart, pooled beneath her body, splattered on the sides of the car and van, and smeared into the clothes of her killers. But there was no quick end to her suffering. The men once again stopped their assault to discuss what they could do to finish her.

They came up with the idea of smothering her. Salmon began stuffing her shirt into her mouth as he pressed down. But Jacine wasn't through fighting for her life. She lifted her hands and weakly tried to remove Salmon's grip.

"At this point I was so terrified that my whole body was shaking because she was still alive," Woldt wrote. "Lucas took the clothes on her face and pressed down to suffocate her. At that time he told me to step on her hands so she wouldn't move them. I did, but it wasn't working."

Woldt, who was still holding the knife, then cut her right wrist twice: once superficially, but the next so deep it nearly amputated her hand. "She lets out a small whine," Salmon wrote.

Slicing the woman's wrist, Woldt conceded, was his idea. But when the first cut hardly bled it was Salmon who insisted that Woldt "slice her again deeper."

One more time, the men stopped their attack to consider

why she wasn't dying as expected. Despite Salmon's best attempts, she was still getting air.

The men told her to put her hands on her stomach. Even at this late stage in her torment, Jacine tried to cooperate, but she was too weak to do it on her own. So they helped her. Then as Salmon smashed the clothes into her face again, Woldt stood on her hands, pressing them into her stomach to "force the air out."

"Lucas said she wasn't breathing any more," Woldt wrote. But when he got off of her, they saw that she was still trying to draw in air.

"We think it works," Salmon noted. "But then she starts to roll around and throw her arms around. We try it again."

Woldt stepped back onto Jacine, balancing himself with his hands on Salmon's car. "This time George moves his feet up and down on her stomach to force the air out, while I press even harder," Salmon wrote. "After a minute goes by, she appears to have stopped breathing."

Finally, more than an hour after they began by raping her, Jacine Gielinski was dead. She had been kidnapped and beaten into submission; raped twice; forced to lie on cold, hard asphalt, naked and alone in the dark of night, far from anyone who cared about her as a human being; and made to listen to her captors talk about how to kill her.

The detectives who interviewed them kept their professional demeanor, but behind the façade they were stunned. They were used to shootings and stabbings—they'd seen crimes horrible to imagine. But Jacine Gielinski's torment was not only gruesome and horrific, it had been needlessly drawn out because the killers were particularly bad at their work.

Even then, they were not through with the young woman. "We then take mud from a nearby ditch, and take turns shoving it into her vagina," Salmon wrote. "First George, then me. We figure this will help avoid evidence from semen samples.

"Then I pick up her legs, and George grabs her hair, and we swing her under the nearby van, and continue to push her under until she is somewhat concealed."

The pair had then wiped the blood off their hands with her sweatshirt before putting it and the knife in the trunk of Salmon's Thunderbird. They didn't go home right away. Woldt said it was because he didn't want to face his wife and stepson "after what I had done." So they drove around and talked. About the "stupid" mistakes they'd made in committing the crime, including being seen by witnesses.

They began to talk about the ramifications of what they had done. Not just the possibility that their mistake would lead to their apprehension, but the eternal consequences. They discussed heaven and hell and their chances of making it into either and concluded they were bound for the latter.

Only now did a split in the seam of their partnership appear. Woldt said that as they drove, Salmon began blaming him for the rape and murder because he was always talking about his fantasy of raping and murdering a young woman. However, Woldt complained to the detective that Salmon had badgered him into finding him a woman with whom to lose his virginity.

At last the two decided to go back to Woldt's apartment. Salmon made one pass by the building to check for the police. The next time around, he pulled into the driveway, parked, and they went into the house. "We wash blood off our hands and shoes, sit down and watch T.V.," he wrote.

"I hear a loud conversation, camosion [sic] going on outside, and look out the peephole. I see two police officers at the door. When I tell George, he tells me to turn off the light and T.V. and to lie down."

However, the knocking and shouts woke Bonnie Woldt. She came out of her bedroom, demanding to know what was going on. George took his wife aside, Salmon said, to "to calm her down before letting her know what has happened." Then someone broke the bathroom window, and they decided to open the door.

Throughout their confessions, neither man expressed any sympathy for the victim. They didn't know her name, nor did they ask to know. If they felt sorry for anyone it was for themselves for getting caught.

Woldt told Bjorndahl, "Nothing this bad has ever happened to me before."

When Crouch asked Salmon how he felt about the murder, the young man replied, "Killing her was the worst experience of my whole life."

They apparently didn't get the irony that nothing that bad had ever happened to Jacine Gielinski before, either, or that being murdered was the worst experience of her life.

By noon, the investigators were out of questions and the killers were out of answers, except for one. They couldn't really say why they decided to hunt someone they didn't even know to rape and murder. Only that it was something they thought they might "like to do."

There was no doubt in anyone's mind who listened to them then or later that they knew what they were doing and that what they were doing was wrong. The confessions were so detailed and, except in several telling areas, so identical it was as if they'd taken notes. Particularly striking and important for the prosecution were the steps they had taken to ensure that they were equally culpable— deliberating before acting, and taking turns with the rape and then with the knife.

Yet, for all that they did tell the investigators, Salmon and Woldt left out one last telling example of their mindset that had nothing to do with philosophical discussions regarding heaven and hell or who was more to blame.

As they drove out of the parking lot, Woldt had turned to his partner, grinning, and said, "Bet you're dying for a cigarette now."

To which Salmon replied, "At least I'm not a virgin any-more." The pair then high-fived each other as though their team had scored a touchdown in a football game.

# NINE

# "... A RANDOM ACT OF VIOLENCE"

The brutal killing of Jacine Gielinski stunned the citizens of Colorado Springs, especially as it followed on the heels of another senseless killing that had also shocked the community.

While it's true that most murder victims are killed by someone they know, until the spring of 1997, random homicides in Colorado Springs were extremely rare. Of the thirty-four murders in the city during 1995 and 1996, only one had involved a victim being killed by a stranger.

Then on Valentine's Day 1997, fourteen-year-olds Andrew Westbay and Scott Hawrysiak were walking home from a party in the early evening when they were gunned down by two other teenagers, Jeron Grant and Gary Flakes, who just happened to be driving by. Several aspects of the crime made it stand out.

One thing was the racial overtone. Both victims were white and the killers were black. Another was the location: the murders took place in plain sight of witnesses on a tree-lined sidewalk near the affluent Broadmoor area, not some gang-infested neighborhood or seedy, high-crime part of town. Then there was the cold-blooded brutality of the crime. Westbay thought that Grant and Flakes were kidding as they taunted and pointed a shotgun at him and Hawrysiak—until they shot him. Hawrysiak tried to run but he was shot in the back and then executed as he lay on his stomach.

Yet, the most unnerving aspect was that the teens were killed by strangers for no apparent reason. The killers didn't know them; they'd never seen them before nor spoken to them. No angry words or gestures had been exchanged. Grant and Flakes said they just wanted to know what killing was like.

Colorado Springs wasn't immune to violence. Every month or so, the newspapers would carry the story of a new murder, but there always seemed to be some aspect to the crime that left the ordinary citizen (at least those who didn't live in the "bad" parts of town) still feeling safe in their homes and neighborhoods. There'd be a gangland shooting, or a drug deal gone awry. Two lowlifes would get drunk and argue, and somebody would pull a trigger.

In 1991, there was even a notorious love-triangle case in which Brian Hood talked his lover, Jennifer Reali, into shooting his wife in a city park, trying to make it look like a robbery. Reali was found guilty of first-degree murder and sentenced to life in prison; Hood was acquitted of murder but found guilty of conspiracy and solicitation to commit murder, for which he was sentenced to thirty-seven years. But even that wasn't the sort of threat that good, upstanding citizens worried about.

The same day Jacine was abducted the police arrested Brian Eugene Thompson, thirty-seven, for the murder of his nineteen-year-old stepdaughter, Rebecca. Her nude body had been found March 29 at a construction site. Thompson confessed that he attempted to have sex with Rebecca and then, after she rejected him, he killed her by stabbing her in the throat. He said he did it because he was afraid she would tell her mother.

Even that was easier to comprehend than what happened to Jacine. The citizens of the Springs were left to wonder what was happening to their town. Her death was the thirteenth homicide, and it was only four months into the year. But it was more than that: not only could innocent teenagers be murdered in broad daylight in a wealthy neighborhood, now according to the first statements by the police, young women driving in cars were being stalked, raped, and killed for no more reason than they were attractive and in the wrong place at the wrong time. If that was true, no one was safe.

"There's no evidence that we've been able to find to indicate any known relationship between the victim or the suspects," Lt. Steve Liebowitz, the police department spokesman, told the press. "It appears to be a random act of violence."

Poor Foothills Elementary School had suffered more than its fair share of horrors. Two weeks earlier, a fifth-grade student had committed suicide, which was hard enough to explain to his schoolmates. Now teachers, administrators, school counselors, and parents had to try to explain why a young woman had been killed by two young men in the school parking lot.

The media set about trying to find out as much as they could about the two confessed killers, only to learn that there wasn't much. Salmon had graduated from Cheyenne Mountain High School and Woldt from Harrison, where neither had been anything more than an ordinary student.

Neither had much of a criminal history. Woldt had been evicted from a previous apartment for not paying rent and had been sued for writing bad checks, according to court records. They both had traffic tickets. The press didn't immediately catch the rock-throwing incident from the summer of 1994 because the records had been expunged after Woldt and Salmon completed the terms of their probations.

The press showed up on King Street to talk to neighbors of the Woldts. Sylvia Ornelas told the *Gazette,* "They were pretty nice to me—gave me rides to the grocery store."

Most of the others, however, had a different opinion. "They were jerks," said one neighbor, who asked not to be identified.

Another, Candice Lewis, told a *Denver Post* reporter that Bonnie Woldt would visit her apartment and talk about her violent marriage. "She told me about how they would fight all the time and punch each other," Lewis said.

Tricia Martinez, who lived in the apartment directly above the Woldts, told the *Rocky Mountain News,* "We could hear them fighting. It sounded like he was hitting her. It frightened us because she was pregnant."

"That's what makes it so scary," Tricia's mother, Juanita Martinez, added. "He didn't look like he'd do something like that."

There wasn't a lot of information coming out of the police department. Liebowitz would not say if the investigators knew whether the two killers had stalked Gielinski specifically or were simply cruising the area looking for the first female they could find. "We're not into the motive part of this thing yet," he said.

The lieutenant also declined to say how she was killed "other than she sustained multiple traumas to the body." The press noted that Gielinski's family members reported that she'd been stabbed. There'd be no official word until after the autopsy.

The autopsy was performed on April 30 by Dr. David Bowerman, the El Paso County coroner, who identified four deep stab wounds and one shallow one, which had struck bone and not penetrated any farther. There was a stab wound that ran through her left hand as though she'd had it on her chest when the killer struck. He also noted the slices to her wrists and neck, as well as dozens of bruises and abrasions on her face and body.

Bowerman's main task was to ascertain the exact cause of death beyond the fact that she'd been stabbed. It wasn't the cuts to her neck. In fact, the manner in which the pair tried to kill Jacine by cutting her throat showed they were inept killers. Pulling a victim's head back actually causes the major blood vessels—the carotid artery and jugular vein—to recede and therefore, in Jacine's case, they had not been cut. Pushing her head forward when they slit her throat would have been more lethal. So while using a serrated knife had to have been painful, the two gashes Woldt and Salmon made were not fatal.

The worst of the two cuts to her right wrist had nearly severed her hand and caused a significant loss of blood. But again, it was not the cause of death. Nor was the clumsy attempt at suffocation lethal, though it would have greatly added to Jacine's agony and terror—fighting for breath as two men hacked and stabbed at her with a knife.

Bowerman opened up Jacine Gielinski's chest to examine the damage done by the stab wounds. Measurements showed that the wounds had been caused by a thin blade, only about a sixteenth of an inch at its widest. This important fact connected the murder weapon found in the trunk to the wounds of the victim.

Two of the penetrating stab wounds had not struck any major blood vessels or organs and therefore had not caused her death. However, the other two had pierced three to four inches through her breastbone and into her heart. Simply put, she'd bled to death.

The murder of Jacine Gielinski had been brutal, and her killers singularly incompetent, which had served only to prolong her torment. Almost more disturbing was the effort they made to destroy the evidence of the sexual assaults after her death. They'd packed Gielinski's vaginal vault with mud. But like everything else to do with the crime, the killers' efforts were clumsy, and Bowerman was able to find traces of semen.

The traces would help identify Jacine's assailants in case they tried to recant. Thanks to the work of a German scientist around the turn of the century, semen could be matched to blood type. Dr. Karl Landsteiner had led the research team that for the first time classified human blood into four major groups: A, B, O, and AB. In the years that followed, he and his associates had made a number of other advances in forensic (meaning applied to law) science having to do with forensic serology, or the study of blood.

One was the discovery that most people are secretors, meaning that in addition to their blood, their other body fluids (saliva, sweat, urine, and semen) could also be classified according to the four major blood groups. Landsteiner's group also discovered that a very small percentage of the population were nonsecretors.

Almost a century later, Landsteiner's work would enable Bowerman to send the semen samples, as well as the blood taken from Salmon and Woldt, to a crime lab to match the semen to the suspects. Even if one was a nonsecretor, that would be damning in itself because it would show up in the tests. Given the small number of possibilities, it would constitute at least circumstantial identification.

Given the time of night and the emotions involved, it was remarkable how well the killers' descriptions of the attack matched the physical evidence on Jacine Gielinski's body. In fact, after Crouch finished interviewing Salmon, the detective asked him if he would place a mark to indicate where wounds were inflicted on the appropriate places of a body drawn on a piece of paper. Salmon did one better by using two pens with different colors of ink, one to indicate the wounds he inflicted, and the other for Woldt's. The diagram showing the placement of the wounds was a perfect match to the autopsy.

* * *

The investigation continued at a careful pace. Even with the detailed, written confessions and the witness identifications, the crime-scene technicians collected every minute bit of evidence, including samples from stains in the defendants' underwear and hairs from the backseat of the car, for DNA testing. They identified even the tiniest drips of blood on the defendants' clothes, as well as on the Thunderbird and the van, including bloody handprints on Salmon's car where, if the confessions were accurate, Woldt had leaned to steady himself while standing on Jacine's stomach.

Every detail was important. When Detective Crouch read Salmon his rights on the morning of April 30 and asked if he wanted a lawyer present, the young man replied, "Why would I need a lawyer? I did this. I'm guilty. I'm responsible for killing her. I want to plead to it and go on." But that didn't mean that once the defendant got together with a defense lawyer, he wouldn't be persuaded to fight the charges. Confessions and other evidence had been ruled as inadmissible for legal technicalities in the past, and it could happen again now.

Everyone knew the stakes would be high. District Attorney Jeanne Smith would take her time deciding whether to file the necessary paperwork to seek the death penalty, but few doubted that she would. That would mean a bitter fight, with the defense attorneys pulling out all the stops.

The gamesmanship began early when prominent criminal defense attorney Ed Farry called the police station at 11 A.M. to inquire about the status of the murder suspects. An hour earlier, Bob Salmon, who identified himself as the father of Lucas, had called the police to ask if his son had legal representation. He was told that his son was an adult and that he had waived his right to have a lawyer present.

Farry then called. He knew he had no right to demand to see the suspects, as they had not yet been charged nor had he been retained. But he was told that they were being interviewed by Crouch and Bjorndahl. The lawyer made a snide comment about the detectives and their "McDonald's interviews" and said, "I suppose it's too late to tell them not to talk." It was, indeed.

On May 1, 1997, Salmon and Woldt appeared in court together before Fourth Judicial District Court Judge David Parrish to be advised of their rights and to hear the charges brought against them, including kidnapping, first-degree sexual assault and, of course, first-degree murder after deliberation, which carried the possibility of the death penalty.

Parrish had served on the bench since 1978, first as a county judge and then beginning in 1981, as a district court judge. In 1996, a judicial performance commission had described him as courteous and qualified. Basing its findings on interviews and surveys from attorneys, law enforcement officers and jurors, the commission had listed his retention rating as a very favorable 87 percent.

At that first appearance, the press heard some of the details about the crime as Chief Deputy District Attorney Zook submitted police affidavits necessary to justify the charges being brought against the pair. According to the affidavits, Salmon and Woldt had been planning for two weeks to abduct, rape, and kill a woman, but Jacine Gielinski had been chosen at random. The victim had been sexually assaulted in the backseat of the kidnappers' car. Then her attackers had cut her throat and stabbed her in the chest with a steak knife. The report noted that Woldt stood on her stomach while Salmon tried to smother her with her own clothes. And that they'd used mud to try to hide the evidence of their rapes.

Based upon the severity of the allegations, Parrish ordered the defendants held without bond. He also appointed lawyers to represent them.

Salmon's father had hired Farry. But having been told that death-penalty cases in Colorado could cost hundreds of thousands of dollars, he now asked Parrish to appoint Farry so that taxpayers could pick up the tab. The judge approved the request and also approved two public defenders to represent Woldt.

The public got their first look at the defendants in the evening broadcasts and on the front page of the next day's *Gazette*. They had appeared in court wearing their bright orange jail jumpsuits—bald Salmon looking dumbstruck and Woldt with every hair in place and a half smirk on his face. The photographs in the newspaper were accompanied by a story in which one of Salmon's brothers, who wasn't identified, said the family was "in shock. . . . We're very sorry for the victim's family. This should not have happened." Contacted at his home, Woldt's father declined to comment.

It was a hard day to escape death in the newspaper. On the same front page was a story with the parents of Jon-Benet Ramsey at a press conference proclaiming their innocence regarding the death of their six-year-old daughter. The child had been murdered on Christmas Day in John and Patsy Ramsey's million-dollar home in Boulder, Colorado. The story had been front-page fodder for the national mainstream and tabloid press ever since. But no one had been arrested for the latest "crime of the century," although the Boulder District Attorney's Office had intimated that the parents were prime suspects.

"I did not have anything to do with it," Patsy Ramsey told the television cameras, microphones, and assembled reporters. "I loved that child with the whole of my heart and soul."

The murder of Jacine Gielinski was a much more local affair, although the *Gazette* did the usual day-after reporting. That included a story in which another young woman, a twenty-three-year-old dental hygienist, called the paper to talk about her experience of having been raped thirty-six hours before Jacine was murdered. She, too, had been beaten into submission, but the stranger who attacked her had then cried and talked about God and the power of prayer.

"I keep thinking about her," the woman said. "This girl was living her everyday normal life. And I was living my everyday normal life. She must have known she was dying. I had that fear. We both knew that fear."

In the same story, Gail Hoagland, executive director of the Colorado Coalition Against Sexual Assault, noted that rape is not a crime about sex. "It has to do with power. It has to do with anger," Hoagland said. "So we need to begin teaching kids, starting very young, appropriate ways of handling anger."

The newspapers and electronic media had more to feed the public when they learned that Salmon and Woldt had tried to snare another victim earlier on April 29, when they struck Amber Gonzales with their car in the Garden of the Gods. The incident had been classified as a hit and run; however, now the district attorney was going to add to the charges facing the killers by tacking on first-degree assault and attempted kidnapping.

The *Gazette* also quoted a female high school friend of Salmon. She recalled a "decent student" who enjoyed drawing landscapes and animals. He was shy and polite, she said, opening doors for girls and cheering for friends during sports events. He'd told her that he was going to work after graduation to save for college. She remembered that he always carried a Bible in his car and attended church regularly.

The young woman told the newspaper that she almost didn't recognize him from the courtroom photographs and television broadcasts. In the past, she said, "He was always smiling."

\* \* \*

No one felt like smiling on Saturday, May 3, outside the Colorado Community Church in Littleton. It was a beautiful spring day, the sort Jacine would have spent outdoors in the sun and warm breezes that presaged another glorious summer in Colorado. It was a summer she would have spent camping with friends and family, stuffing S'mores into her cheeks, playing softball, visiting her girlfriends, and waiting for training camp to open for the Denver Broncos.

Instead, all that remained of Jacine were her ashes in an urn inside the church and the memories shared by her family and friends.

Nearly a thousand people showed up for her memorial service. That didn't include the gaggle of media.

As they waited for the crowd to enter the church, Bob and Peggy Luiszer stood in the sun behind the church with other members of the family and Jacine's best friends, hugging and crying and wondering why they were there. In the time it took for Jacine's heart to stop pumping, the world had changed for the Luiszers. They had gone to bed one night, a happily married couple, working two jobs, looking forward to yearly vacations and camping trips, trying to help a daughter get through college, dreaming of a future that included wedding bells and grandchildren.

Then before the sun rose, they were something different. Now they were the parents of a murder victim. That made them different than everybody else. But they were only just beginning to realize that nothing would ever be the same.

The media onslaught began the morning of April 30. Big, boxy television trucks with satellite antennae on top parked up and down the block of the Luiszers' house. Reporters walked up to the house and rang the doorbell, wanting to talk. Their voices were sad, their faces drawn, as they commiserated over the Luiszers' loss. . . . *now, if you could just answer a few questions, we'll be on our way.*

The Luiszers didn't know what to do. There was nothing in the parents' handbook about dealing with the press after one's child has been brutally murdered. At one reporter's request, Peggy handed over Jacine's high school graduation photograph, but after that she wouldn't have anything to do with them. They'd gathered around her house like vultures, a reminder of the reality she was facing even as she wandered around, commanding herself to wake up. . . . wake up. . . . wake up.

Bob Luiszer had done his best to cope with the media and take the burden off his wife's shoulders. "It was strictly random," he told the *Denver Post* when asked if he thought the killers intended to stalk and kill Jacine in particular. "The intent was what they did."

He wanted to be left alone, too, but understood that the members of the press were doing their jobs. Still, if he had to talk, he preferred to recall the vibrant young woman who called him Dad and promised that he'd give her away on her wedding day. "Everybody loved her. She was very outgoing and friendly and touched a lot of people's lives."

Bob held up pretty well until one reporter asked if they had any other children. He shook his head. "Just her," he said, as his voice broke. "She was it."

Another neighborhood friend, Tammy, took over intercepting the press on the telephone. As Peggy drifted from room to room in tears, asking unanswerable questions to the mute walls, she could hear her friend berating overly aggressive reporters: "What kind of goddamn human beings are you? These people just lost their daughter."

Lost? Lost? Lost people came home. Jacine wasn't ever coming home, she was gone, dead. Murdered!

The Luiszers knew that Jacine was well liked, but nothing had prepared them for the overwhelming response of both friends and strangers. The house was filled to bursting with flowers until the Luiszers were begging visitors to take some home with them.

Cards and letters of condolence arrived by the boxful. Although many of the messages caused Peggy to cry, some of the tears were tears of pride for the young woman she'd raised, such as the letter from the girl who had been the overweight child on Jacine's childhood soccer team. Now a young woman, she wrote that she would never forget the one teammate who reached out when no one else did and taught her to believe in herself.

Another was from the developmentally disabled girl whom Jacine had taken under her wing in high school. "She was my best friend," she wrote. "She was the only person in school that would ever say 'hi' to me."

Others had to cope with the press as well. Jacine's friends were, of course, devastated. They had been counting on Jacine to be their maid of honor, to be there when they needed a shoulder to cry on or someone to celebrate with, to raise her children with their children. Now, they were left trying to describe to reporters what made their friend so special.

Jamie Koons attempted to explain the effect of Jacine's smile on other people, then gave up except to note that it captivated all who were fortunate enough to experience it. "You could see it from miles away."

Jamie Hammers, who had known Jacine since they were both two years old, said she was closer to her than her own sister. Jacine was sincere and good; whatever happened to her killers would not be enough.

Mark Drury, the athletic director for Littleton High and Jacine's former volleyball and basketball coach, recalled how it was Jacine who brought him a cake to commemorate his one hundredth coaching victory. "She was the glue," he said, of the teams she played on. But she was more, including the much-loved baby-sitter of his children.

"My eleven-year-old son broke down crying when we heard."

Peggy avoided most of the news accounts of her daughter's murder by her own choice, as well as the efforts of her family and friends. However, by accident she was passing in front of the television in time to see one newscast. Before she realized what she was looking at and could turn away, there was the film of her daughter's body lying naked under the white van. It hurt her that Jacine had remained there for hours before she was taken away. What disturbed her the most was seeing the breeze blowing her baby's blond hair. She must have been cold, she thought, and the tears fell down her cheeks again.

One afternoon, Peggy felt she had to get out of her house where she'd been since *that night* and went over to her mother-in-law's house. Standing in the living room, she happened to glance down at the couch where a newspaper was lying, and there on the front page were drawings by a courtroom artist of Salmon and Woldt. She stared for a moment. She thought they were ugly and frightening, particularly the one with the bald head and the odd, protruding eyes. When it struck her that they were the last two faces her lovely daughter saw before she died, she felt the bile rise in her throat and thought she would throw up.

When the coroner in El Paso County called to officially notify them of the cause of death, the Luiszers had asked if they needed to drive to Colorado Springs to identify the body. He told them that it wasn't necessary. They could come if they wanted—he'd done his best to "make her presentable"—but he recommended that they stay home. He agreed with Peggy's therapist that they wouldn't want their last memory of Jacine to be of her cold and lifeless corpse.

The Luiszers had opted to have their daughter cremated. Now, as the big church filled nearly to standing room only, the only tangible things they had left were photographs and an urn with her ashes.

The two-hour service passed in a blur of friends and family talking about how much they loved Jacine, how she would be missed. Afterward, about a hundred mourners gathered at the Gielinski house.

It was also a time of reflection, as noted in the journal kept by one of Jacine's teenage cousins, Amy. She recounted how her family had been called at 4:30 in the morning on April 30 to be told that Jacine had been murdered.

"I was at a loss for words," she wrote. "I didn't know what to think or do, and I didn't even cry until at least an hour after I heard the news."

Amy had gone to school that day only to be overwhelmed when the class began discussing a rape scene in a book they were reading and some of the other boys and girls "laughed and joked" about it. "Eyes glazed over, I thought, *How cold their hearts must be.*"

Still, she had tried to go through the motions for the rest of the day. Finally, her algebra teacher asked what was wrong. "My cousin was raped and murdered last night," she replied. The teacher had been too shocked to say anything.

Amy didn't understand why this was happening. Rape and murder were something that happened to people who ended up in newspapers, not her family. Her family had driven to the Luiszers' after school. "How heavy their house felt," she wrote. "I retreated to Jacine's room and plopped myself in the middle of her bedroom floor." There, enveloped by memories of playing with Barbie dolls and surrounded by walls covered with photographs of her laughing, smiling cousin and her friends, dried corsages from school dances, stuffed animals, and high school yearbooks, she had questions she wanted answered.

"God why did you do this to us?" she wrote. "We are a perfect Christian family. We live by your Word. How could you allow this to happen?"

Amy thought back to Christmas Day 1996, the last time she saw Jacine. It troubled her that she couldn't remember if she hugged her cousin when she left. "Or if I expressed my love for her."

Peggy Luiszer was troubled by the same thoughts. After friends and family were gone, leaving just her and Bob and their memories, the house seemed empty of all joy. She wondered if that feeling would ever change. She was beginning to regret following the advice of the coroner and her therapist and wished she had gone to Colorado Springs to look at Jacine's face one last time.

*I never got to say good-bye,* she thought. *I didn't get to tell her how much I loved her.*

# TEN

## "WE GRIEVE OUR LOSS . . ."

*May 23, 1997*
*University of Colorado-Colorado Springs*

Peggy Luiszer took her place in line for the commencement exercises at the University of Colorado's campus in Colorado Springs. Only it wasn't really her place. . . . It was Jacine's, as were the cap and gown she wore as she filed into the auditorium with the students.

University officials had called earlier in the week and said they were going to award Jacine's bachelor of arts degree posthumously. They wanted to know if Peggy would accept on behalf of her daughter.

Peggy took her seat with the others and looked for her husband, Bob, in the crowd. She saw him sitting surrounded by other, happier, parents, but he looked so alone. No one else from the family had wanted to attend the ceremony, and she felt bad for him. He'd been left out in the cold throughout much of the fallout from Jacine's death. Even the press had quickly learned that he was more reserved with his emotions, but they could get her to cry easily for their cameras and stories.

They wanted her to cry. . . . It gave them something juicy to write and talk about, and made for better photographs. But so far today, she was keeping the tears pretty well in check as she talked to the soon-to-be graduates around her, and explained what she was doing there. They were kind, sympathetic. One of the young men said he knew Jacine and that she was a wonderful person. . . . But it was also as though they were uncomfortable with her presence.

The outpouring of sympathy and support had not dried up with the memorial service at the church, nor was it limited to Littleton. On May 6, another memorial service had been conducted on the University of Colorado campus in Colorado Springs, with three hundred people in attendance.

Of her own volition, campus security officer Susan Szpyrka handed out 200 white carnations. "Jacine was innocent," she explained to the *Gazette*. "Brides get to wear white at their wedding. She didn't even get to do that."

As with the previous service, most of those who spoke chose to remember how she was in life rather than the manner of her death. One of her journalism professors, Don Morley, brought smiles to the crowd when he recalled one day when Jacine was feeling poorly and told him she would have to miss class. She made him feel her head to prove she had a fever. "She made us laugh," he said. "Her loss is all of ours."

However, the service wasn't all about memories of Jacine. Sociology professor Jay Coakley spoke out against what he saw as a growing tolerance of violence against women perpetrated in music and films. Salmon and Woldt, he said, are "part of a culture where men have privilege and can talk about dominating other people without being sanctioned."

University officials announced the formation of a scholarship fund in Jacine's memory. Another scholarship fund had been established at Littleton High School to pay the $100 school athletic participation fee, as well as pay for sports equipment, for underprivileged girls.

The scholarships were all very well intentioned, and Peggy knew that people were hoping for the old adage "some good would come out of all of this." But she couldn't help but feel that such platitudes were a bunch of crap. They didn't make her feel better, and nothing good was going to come out of her daughter's murder. The scholarships were nice, but she would much rather have had Jacine.

The Luiszers had not said much to the media recently. They felt the majority were just rude and insensitive. Without so much as calling, they'd show up at the door and make demands, no matter how they tried to couch those demands. And they wanted them met right away, with the clear implication that Jacine's murder was important now, but tomorrow it might not be so important. Something new, perhaps someone else's tragedy, would knock Jacine right off the front page and the newscasts.

They'd asked if they could bring their cameras and crews into the church to record the memorial service. The Luiszers had replied, "Absolutely not." So they'd showed up outside and filmed everyone filing in, the friends hugging and in tears.

After the first memorial service, they spoke briefly to a reporter for the *Littleton Independent*, a small weekly, and the anger they felt bubbled to the surface.

"I hope that something will be addressed with the violence in the Colorado Springs area," Bob Luiszer said. "I don't know how people can do this. . . . They're sick."

"Animals don't do this to animals," Peggy said. "They are lower than . . . I don't know what." But for the most part, they stayed away from the press.

The Monday following the funeral, the Luiszers drove to Colorado Springs at the request of the district attorney.

Normally, the sixty-mile drive south along the front range of the Rocky Mountains was enjoyable. Roofed in by robin's-egg-blue skies, Interstate 25, the major north-south thoroughfare, separated the beginning of the green and grassy plains in the east and the pine- and fir-clad mountains to the west. The last of the spring snows still glimmered in the sunlight on purple Pike's Peak, hovering over their destination.

They should have been driving down to see Jacine play volleyball or take her out to lunch "just because." Instead, a feeling of dread crept up on them with every mile and landmark they passed. The town of Castle Rock, the halfway point, was named after a several-hundred-foot-tall sandstone bluff. More than a century before, pioneers in their covered wagons had thought it looked like a castle from across the prairie. Just north of the Springs was the U.S. Air Force Academy, identifiable by the triangular spires of its chapel against the mountains. Then there was the green-and-white highway sign put up to designate the exit for the Focus on the Family headquarters.

Up to this point, there had been a feeling of unreality, that sooner or later they would wake up and this would have all been a nightmare. But now they were going to go talk to people who knew the truth about Jacine's murder and who were going to put on trial the two young men accused of doing it.

They had no idea then of how many times they would make that drive and how they would come to hate it, but they knew it would never be easy as they passed the hotel where Jacine had been working on the north end of town. There would always be that reminder, and probably others.

This visit was at the invitation of the district attorney, Jeanne Smith, to meet the prosecutors and investigators assigned to the case. They arrived and were whisked to a large room with tables set up in a U-shape. Standing and sitting around the tables were a cadre of police officers, detectives, and prosecutors, as well as assorted other personnel from the district attorney's office—the combined forces arrayed against the defendants.

As the Luiszers entered, those around the tables turned and rose to meet them. They were soon feeling overwhelmed as they were escorted from grim, sympathetic face to grim, sympathetic face, and handed business cards and consoling laments "for your loss."

Although they didn't realize it at the time, one of the most important introductions was to a petite woman with short silver hair named Barbara Buchman, who they were told would be the Victim's Advocate assigned to their case. Peggy knew looking at her that she was someone at last who would understand what she was going through— maybe not firsthand—but in her heart. Buchman handed her a business card and told her to call if she ever had any questions, or just wanted someone to talk to, any time, day or night.

Deputy District Attorney Dan Zook was introduced as the attorney who would take the lead in the case. He was accompanied by a younger attorney, Dave Young, who would be something called the second chair. They were both good-looking, Peggy thought, and seemed confident, as did a third deputy district attorney, an older man named Gordon Denison. His job as an appeals specialist—an expert on the precedents and technicalities of the law—was part of the reason Smith asked them to come to the meeting.

Smith herself came off as straitlaced though she, too, softened to express her condolences. But she was all business after the introductions, when she told the Luiszers that her office was considering whether to pursue the death penalty against Salmon and Woldt. She said that she and her staff felt the punishment was warranted given the "heinous" nature of the crime, and that everything possible had been done to ensure that the prosecution would be successful.

She apologized for Jacine's body being left beneath the van for so long. But, she explained, it was all part of the extreme care the police and her office were taking to preserve all the evidence. The handwritten confessions given by Salmon and Woldt were damning, and the police had taken the extra step of having them notarized so that there would be no question as to their authenticity. She was confident that all the legal details had been followed to the letter and that they would hold up in court against the inevitable challenges by defense attorneys.

However, Smith said she wanted one more thing: the Luiszers' blessing. It would be a long, bitterly fought process that could take a year, even two years, the district attorney warned. The defense attorneys would probably try anything—from stalling to begging to intimidation—to wear the Luiszers down so that they would throw in the towel and ask the prosecutors to settle for life in prison.

"We won't pursue this if you don't want us to," she said.

Bob and Peggy looked at each other. There was no other hesitation. *These guys dying sounds good to me,* Peggy thought.

"We're behind whatever you want to do," she and her husband said.


If Smith had asked the same question of the citizens of Colorado Springs, the majority would have voted to hang the defendants from one of the ancient cottonwood trees that lined the blocks around the old courthouse, at least if the telephone calls and letters to the editor of the *Gazette,* the local radio and television stations, and the district attorney's office were any indication. And that didn't include the letters and calls to the jail from vigilantes offering to save the state the time and expense of putting Salmon and Woldt on trial.

There were a few calls for restraint, such as letters written by Father Bill Carmody, the Respect Life director of the Colorado Springs diocese. But even state legislators from the area were calling upon the district attorney to seek the death penalty.

In the climate of fear and anger immediately following the murder, there were even letters to the *Gazette* pointing fingers at the inhabitants of the apartment complex where Jacine was abducted. The writers accused the residents of standing by and "doing nothing" while the young woman pleaded for help.

Several of the residents wrote back to defend themselves. They noted that the attack occurred at the time of night when most were settled down for the night. They said that they did respond when they heard Jacine's screams, but there was little they could do except yell at the men and dial 911 before the kidnappers drove off.

People needed to place blame so that they could understand something that made so little sense. Some hurled vitriol at the parents of Salmon and Woldt. They'd raised a couple of sick perverts, which to the lay psychologists in the community meant there had to be something wrong with them as well.

Bonnie Woldt appeared in the *Gazette* complaining that she was being unfairly targeted. She'd seen the letters to the editor and heard from callers who denounced her for everything from having children by two different men, to failing to "stop the crime."

The harassment she felt took an official turn when she received a notice from the city's housing authority on May 13 saying that she was being evicted from her subsidized apartment due to a federal policy aimed at discouraging crime in public housing. The policy, informally called "One Strike and You're Out," held that if anyone in subsidized housing was accused of a serious crime any individual or family in that residence also could be evicted.

The policy was created to deal with rampant drug dealing and violence in large urban housing projects. But eight-months pregnant Bonnie said the notice gave her and her three-year-old son seven days to move out because "a guest" had been accused of murder. The newspaper article was sympathetic to the twenty-year-old, noting that her "only connection to the crime is her relationship to the men accused of committing it."

"I feel like I am being punished for something they did or are accused of," she complained.

Bonnie's dilemma brought expressions of sympathy. She was offered baby clothes and rides to the hospital when her time came to deliver. The Rev. Ted Haggard, pastor of New Life Church, urged Christian charity, though he also seemed to indicate that she had only herself to blame.

"I don't think it's appropriate to be negative towards her. I think we need to be helpful towards her," he said. "Everybody makes messes of their life to one degree or another."

The two killers certainly had done that to themselves, as well as to Jacine's life. Barring some off-the-wall decision by a judge to suppress their confessions and the rest of the evidence, the trial was not going to be about guilt or innocence.

Salmon had even begun his confession by acknowledging, "I, Lucas Salmon, am guilty of the crimes of kidnapping, sexual assault, and murder. I have been made aware of my right and have waived them." He'd then finished by noting that he "voluntarily helped the officers find the crime scene," and acknowledged that he had placed the knife in the trunk of his car and then gave the officers permission to search it. "At no time during the interview was I intoxicated, and at no time during my conversation with the police officers was I bribed, threatened or asked to make a deal."

The question at trial was going to be how guilty—as in first-degree murder after deliberation, or a lesser degree of homicide—and who, if either, was more guilty.

Salmon had claimed that after watching Woldt rape the victim, he didn't want to have sex with her. He also noted that it was Woldt who retrieved the knife from the glove box. However, he had for the most part accepted an equal share of the blame.

Woldt had been much more inclined to point the finger at his partner. Yes, he'd raped her first, but it was Salmon who took charge and told him to hold her head up so that he could slit her throat. Then it was Salmon who had initiated the back-and-forth stabbing routine, Salmon who insisted that he cut her wrist deeper, Salmon who tried to smother her.

In fact, during his interview, Woldt had insisted that all the talk of rape and murder had been just a joke to him, and he "couldn't believe" that they had actually gone through with it. And he'd felt pressured to go along because Salmon had been badgering him about finding a woman with whom to end his virginity.

Whether the two killers were conscious of it or not, the prosecutors knew when they first heard the slight differences in the confessions that the defense attorneys would latch on to the schism to make the other defendant look worse than their own. The prosecutors expected that the defense attorneys would move to have separate trials for that reason.

The police and investigators for the district attorney's office had immediately started the process of learning as much as they could about the defendants and their possible motives. Some of this would have been part of any normal investigation. However, the possibility of a death-penalty hearing made the background searches even more important and involved. If the defendants were convicted, as expected, the defense would introduce mitigators to explain why the crime occurred, such as traumatic child-hoods or a mental illness that didn't meet the legal qualifications for an insanity defense but that might save their clients from being put to death.

A personality pattern for each defendant had quickly evolved for the investigators looking into the case. According to friends and family members, Salmon was a quiet but friendly loner, socially awkward but otherwise intelligent. He had been a regular churchgoer and kept a Bible in his car. The catalyst for change had apparently been Woldt. Those same people noticed he changed when he was around his friend, especially since moving back to Colorado.

Woldt was another story. Former girlfriends and other friends talked about his general misogyny and his obsession with pornography, rape, and violence. He had shrugged off Salmon's implication that watching *A Clockwork Orange* had triggered their desire to rape and kill. But the investigator soon learned that Bonnie Woldt told friends that she was aware that after her husband and his friend watched the movie, they had talked about finding a girl for just such a purpose. She believed, according to the friends, that they had been following another woman for two weeks before the murder.

Bonnie also confided that she thought her husband would try to shift most of the blame onto Salmon and that would be a lie. But she was more worried about how she was going to support herself, her three-year-old son, and new infant, complaining that Woldt's parents were not helping.

The friends reported even odder statements. One told the police that Bonnie said she couldn't understand why her husband didn't come to her if he wanted to rape someone. She would have been more than willing to act out the fantasy. The friend said Bonnie had pouted that she thought she was prettier than Jacine and complained, "Why her and not me?"

The police found and talked to James Wilson, who described himself as Woldt's "best friend." He told them about Woldt's attempts to recruit him into abducting and raping a woman during their forays to the nightclubs.

Lisa came forward to tell the police that her former boyfriend, Derrick Ayers, used to hang out with Woldt, who would begin their evening forays with, "Let's go rape some chicks and beat up some punks." She recounted finding the rocks in her car and how Ayers eventually told her the story about Woldt wanting to kill a couple in the mountains. Her boyfriend had warned her to get her sister away from Woldt and his "strange ideas."

The police went looking for Ayers, whom they found in a jail in Seattle, where he was being held for a variety of traffic violations. The detective first reached him on the jail telephone and asked about Woldt. "He's demented," were the first words out of Ayers's mouth. He then went on to explain why.

Ayers volunteered to return to Colorado. Once there, he agreed to have his statement videotaped because the prosecution team was worried that he was a flight risk. At least if he took off before the trial, they would have him on tape. Ayers wasn't surprised that Woldt had talked someone else into helping him fulfill his fantasy. His former friend, he said, was "too chickenshit" to do it on his own.

Over and over, the investigators heard from various people about Woldt's constant teasing of Salmon about his virginity, or how Woldt manipulated Salmon by declaring they were no longer friends, just to see Salmon crawl to get back on his good side.

It was clear that Woldt was the driving force leading up to the attack. He was a sexual predator who sooner or later, prosecutors believed, would have carried out his fantasy with or without an accomplice.

Left on his own, Salmon might never have graduated from quiet loser to vicious killer. However, that did not excuse him from the full role he played in the crimes of April 29. No matter whose idea it was, by the time the pair struck Amber Gonzales, Salmon was, in his own words, "psyched." And from the moment they spotted Jacine Gielinski, he was an equal partner in the rape and murder.

In fact, the pair had gone to great lengths to make sure each was equally guilty. They'd held lengthy discussions on what to do and how to do it, traded the knife back and forth, and took turns putting mud up inside their victim.

Neither had expressed much in the way of remorse, although they noted that killing a lovely young woman was the worst thing that had ever happened to them. Yes, Salmon had declined a lawyer, acknowledging that he was guilty and wanted to go on from there. He'd also waived his bond hearing, saying it was "not appropriate" that he be released. But he never said he was sorry for what he had done.

The bizarre behavior of the two was sure to spur the defense attorneys to raise a mental defense. The definition for legally insane meant that Woldt and Salmon couldn't tell the difference between right or wrong and were incapable—because of their mental state—to form the "intent to kill." That wasn't going to wash, as the confessions, as well as their attempts to disguise the rape, proved they knew that what they were doing was wrong. They'd said they felt that they had to kill her to prevent her from identifying them to the police.

The admitted fantasy was to abduct, rape, and kill a woman because, as Salmon said, "it was something we thought we might like to do." As Bob Luiszer told the press, "Their intent was what they did."

However, even if the defense attorneys were going to

have a hard time establishing insanity, it didn't mean that they wouldn't raise other questions about their clients' mental capacities. These questions might have left Woldt and Salmon less culpable for their actions, especially if and when it came down to deciding whether to sentence them to death. That meant there would be a costly and time-consuming battle between psychological experts.

The defense attorneys might point to the clumsy murder as proof that their clients didn't really know what they were doing. But from the prosecution's point of view, just because Salmon and Woldt were particularly inept killers didn't mean they didn't try—cutting and hacking and smothering—until they eventually succeeded.

On May 22, 1997, Salmon and Woldt appeared in court to learn that District Attorney Jeanne Smith had filed the paperwork to seek the death penalty against them. If her prosecutors were successful, at some point in the future they would be strapped to a steel table and injected with drugs that would essentially put them to sleep like dogs.

The move was not unexpected. In fact, the neatly barbered Woldt and still bald Salmon showed no reaction to the announcement. The two local public defenders initially appointed for Woldt were gone. They'd been replaced by a special death-penalty team. The so-called Dream Team consisted of three attorneys handpicked from public defenders' offices and all well known to the Fourth Judicial District Attorney's Office.

The lead attorney on the case was Deputy Public Defender Terri Brake, who'd represented Frank Orona for the murder of the elderly man in the case prosecuted by Dan Zook. Brake was known for her impassioned pleas to the juries on behalf of her clients. She frequently broke down into tears when delivering her closing arguments in death-penalty cases, begging for the life of the killer. Sometimes she did this a little too conveniently so that even some of her colleagues thought that the tears were drummed up on demand.

Brake was the attorney who came up with the theory that Orona, who had several arrest convictions for male prostitution, "snapped" because the older man made "homosexual advances." It was the height of cynicism for the liberal-leaning lawyer to play on the well-known conservative nature of Colorado Springs, the home of Focus on the Family and it's antihomosexuality agenda.

Brake had most recently poured out the tears in June 1995 while pleading for the life of Robert Harlan. He had been convicted of the vicious rape and murder of a twenty-five-year-old woman, Rhonda Maloney, in February 1994. That time, the emotional appeal went nowhere and Harlan was sitting on death row awaiting execution.

Doug Wilson, the head of the public defenders' office in Pueblo, was the second chair for Woldt's defense team. Generally cordial to his colleagues across the aisle in routine cases, he was Mr. Hyde when it came time to trying to save a client from the death penalty. He believed in flooding the prosecutors with waves of motions and stalling in every way possible, partly to dismay the victim's family, hoping that they would give up and ask the prosecution to settle for life in prison.

Wilson was also very hard to beat in court. He'd never had a client sentenced to death, even though he had defended more than two dozen cases in which the prosecution had at least considered that option, including the Eugene Baylis case.

The third attorney for the Woldt defense team was Andrew Heher. He was the counterpart to Gordon Denison, a lawyer whose job it was to know precedents and nuances, and how to apply them.

Salmon was represented by Ed Farry and Lauren Cleaver, a lawyer from Boulder. Like Farry, Cleaver was in private practice. However, she belonged to the Alternate Defense Counsel—lawyers with death-penalty case experience who would represent indigent defendants if there was a conflict of interest for the public defenders' office. In this case, because the public defenders were representing Woldt, there was a conflict.

The defense teams had wasted no time filing motions and subpoenas. One subpoena demanded that the *Gazette* and three local television stations turn over any unpublished letters from the community about the case, as well as any taped interviews with citizens, including those that had not been aired.

Wilson told Judge Parrish that the defense needed the materials to demonstrate that "there appears to be a lynch-mob mentality against these two gentlemen." It was his opening salvo to get the trial moved to another city (a change of venue) because of pretrial publicity.

The public's mood also was important, he said, because he wanted to have the grand jury indictments charging the defendants to be dismissed. The grand jury, he said, had been subjected to intensive press coverage, making them "an extension of a lynch-mob mentality."

One unusual aspect of the proceedings was that the defendants had not yet entered a plea—guilty or not guilty. Nor would they, the defense teams said, until many of the motions had been settled.

The day after the hearing, the Luiszers drove back down for the graduation ceremonies. They'd had their first taste of what was to come, and they didn't like it.

They'd been told that the defense would throw everything they could against the wall and see what stuck. And they'd spare no expense doing it. While some states had a set amount that could be spent on defending death-penalty cases—such as New Mexico where the number was

$50,000—there were no restraints, beyond its multimillion-dollar, taxpayer-funded budget, on the Colorado Public Defenders' Office.

They regularly spent hundreds of thousands of dollars, and as much as a million, bringing in all sorts of experts. Their motto was that if the state was going to kill their clients, the taxpayers were going to "pay for it," literally and figuratively.

In some ways, Colorado prosecutors brought it upon themselves because compared to neighboring states, they rarely sought the death penalty. That meant the public defenders and Alternate Defense Counsel were able to concentrate their resources (manpower and finances) on a comparatively few number of cases.

Already it seemed to the Luiszers that Jacine was just something for the lawyers, especially the defense lawyers, to argue over. It was all about the defendants' rights now. Their lawyers wanted to move the trial because the citizens of Colorado Springs were angry that a young woman had been viciously raped and murdered by a couple of men acting out a fantasy. The defendants wanted the charges dismissed because their attorneys didn't like the way the grand jury did its business.

Peggy had immediately developed a strong dislike for Brake and Wilson, who had done most of the arguing. Some of her anger at them was because she believed they exhibited a lack of professionalism in court. The three prosecutors dressed like it was an important occasion. They didn't roll their eyes or scoff or whine. But she thought that Wilson looked like a rumpled bowling pin, who slept in his suit, and that Brake was a mousy, unkempt harpy. She thought they both behaved as if they thought they were acting in a play. Neither seemed to her to really care why they were there: Jacine. They seemed to her only interested in what tricks they could pull to help her daughter's killers.

At least those at the graduation ceremony cared. During her commencement address, University Chancellor Lunda Bunnell Shade spoke about Jacine. "People who knew her tell me she was a really special person dedicated to making a difference," she said. "We join her family in grieving and their loss and we grieve our loss as a university."

Peggy rose from her seat to follow the graduates onto the stage, her eyes damp but still in control. But when Shade called out, "Jacine Gielinski," the crowd began to clap. First one, then another, until nearly four thousand people were on their feet applauding.

By the time she reached out for the diploma, Peggy was weeping openly, praying that she wouldn't trip and fall, unable to see clearly in front of her because of the tears. She wished more than anything that she was sitting with Bob, watching her daughter graduate.

# ELEVEN

## LYNCHINGS TO LETHAL INJECTION

In the mid-1800s in what would become Colorado, as in much of the early West, a criminal could be hanged for crimes ranging from horse-thieving (leaving a man without his horse was as good as sentencing him to death), to rape, kidnapping, claim-jumping, and murder. At times, lynch mobs administered frontier justice without the benefit of a trial.

In 1861, territorial lawmakers decided that only murder and voluntary manslaughter were punishable by death. In 1874, two years before Colorado became a state, crimes related to mining claims were added to that list.

The Colorado Legislature abolished the death penalty in 1897, only to reinstate it four years later, although not for anyone under the age of eighteen or those convicted of murder based on circumstantial evidence. The impetus for the penalty's revival had come in 1900, when a mob in Limon broke into the local jail and burned a suspected child-killer to death. Lawmakers reasoned that the absence of the death penalty had resulted in frustrated citizens taking justice into their own hands.

Death by hanging remained the official means of execution until the early 1930s, when Eddie Ives was hanged twice for two murders. The first time, the rope broke, and Ives, who'd proclaimed his innocence right up to the last minute, was dropped on his head. The executioners strung him back up, but because Ives weighed so little, the noose didn't break his neck and it took fifteen gruesome minutes for him to strangle.

With Ives's sorry end in mind, in 1933 legislators made the gas chamber the state's preferred method of execution. One of the most infamous killers put to death in the gas chamber was John Gilbert Graham, who was executed in 1957 for placing a bomb aboard a United Airlines flight and killing all thirty-nine people aboard, including his mother, for whom he'd just taken out a $38,000 insurance policy.

The last man executed in the chamber was Luis Jose Monge, killed in 1967 for the murder of his wife and three of their children. Monge's death brought to seventy-seven the number of criminals executed by Colorado. But then a series of decisions by the U.S. Supreme Court put the death penalty on hold across the nation.

The high court had always tinkered with the particulars of the death penalty, including one decision that prohibited death sentences for rape or kidnapping. These rulings cut to the very heart of the death penalty's constitutionality, primarily on the grounds that it violated Eighth Amendment protections against "cruel and unusual punishment." The decisions culminated in *Furman v. Georgia* in 1972, when the court voted 5–4 to abolish the death penalty in the thirty-two states that then had the option, including Colorado. The majority opinion held that jurors had far too much discretion and not enough guidance, including what might set a murder that justified capital punishment apart from one that didn't, and what might differentiate one murderer from another. Therefore, the death penalty was too often handed down in an "arbitrary and capricious" manner. As a result of that decision, more than 600 prisoners across the country found their sentences commuted to life in prison.

In 1976, the Supreme Court ruled that capital punishment was constitutional as long as judges, jurors, or both were allowed some discretion on when to impose it and were given guidelines to follow. One of the ramifications of this decision was that capital cases were now divided into a guilt phase and a penalty phase, with a separate trial for each. For the penalty phase, most states created a process that included the consideration of aggravating factors that might qualify a crime for the death penalty, as well as mitigating factors that might explain why a criminal did not deserve to die, even if these factors did not excuse him of the crime.

In 1974, even before the Supreme Court paved the way for the return of the death penalty, Coloradans had voted overwhelmingly—451,401 to 286,805—to bring it back. After the high court's decision, the state legislature proceeded to pass a statute that outlined the death-penalty process in a way lawmakers hoped would satisfy the jurists.

Some changes were a matter of semantics. "Premeditated first-degree murder," for example, was switched to "first-degree murder after deliberation." The lawmakers' rationale was that premeditation invoked the image of a killing that was planned well in advance and then carried out. Legally, deliberation was defined as the time it took to consciously decide to kill someone—from a moment to months, even years.

Under the state's new statute, a district attorney would first determine whether the facts of the crime fit the criteria for a "capital case" eligible for the death penalty, either as first-degree murder after deliberation or murder committed to cover up the commission of, or in furtherance of, another felony, also known as "felony murder." Prior to trial, the DA had to file a motion with the court indicating that the prosecution team would be seeking the death penalty. Then, if the defendant was found guilty, a death-penalty hearing would follow.

That hearing would begin with opening statements from both sides. Then the prosecution would present its evidence to prove "beyond a reasonable doubt" that at least one of more than a dozen legally prescribed aggravating factors existed. The defense attorneys would present their evidence of mitigating factors, of which the Colorado statute listed five possibilities.

After the defense rested its case, both sides would present closing arguments. These were often occasions of high drama, as attorneys implored, pleaded, and demanded that the jury see the wisdom of their views. Finally, because the state had the burden of proving its case, the prosecution would get one last rebuttal before the life-or-death decision was turned over to the jury.

Under this new Colorado statute, the jurors would use a two-step process to determine their verdict. Step one would determine whether the prosecution had proved beyond a reasonable doubt that at least one aggravator existed. A murder might have occurred during the commission of another felony, such as rape or robbery, for example, or a murder might be "particularly heinous, cruel and depraved." The jury's vote had to be unanimous before an aggravator could be accepted. If the jury failed to approve at least one, there was no need to go to the next step.

Step two was to determine whether the defense had supplied enough evidence to suggest the existence of mitigators, such as if the defendant was under the age of eighteen, if he was under unusual duress, or if he was a principal with relatively minor participation—although not so minor as to constitute a defense from prosecution—in the offense committed by another. If the jury determined that there were mitigators, then the sentence was life in prison.

Following the Supreme Court's 1976 ruling, Colorado reinstated the death penalty. But in 1978, it was struck down again—this time by the Colorado Supreme Court, which determined that the mitigating factors listed in the state statute were "too restrictive." The legislature remedied this in 1979 by adding the rather nebulous concept of "any other evidence which in the court's opinion bears on the question of mitigation." And lawmakers added seven more mitigators, including the influence of drugs or alcohol and a "good faith, although mistaken, belief by the defendant that circumstances existed which constituted a moral justification for the defendant's conduct."

Lawmakers added another aggravator, too: if a defendant was a party to an agreement to kill another person. More significant, they also addressed prosecutors' concerns that aggravators were "canceled out" if the jury decided there were mitigators. The language of the statute was altered to require a death sentence if at least one aggravator had been proven, unless the jury was convinced there were "sufficient" mitigators to warrant a sentence of life in prison. This added a third step to the process, one that called for "weighing" of the aggravators against the mitigators.

The death penalty was back, although no one was particularly happy with the new rules.

Prosecutors contended that the statutes made it more difficult to get a death-penalty verdict in Colorado than it would be in other states. A major concern was that Colorado jurors had to reach a unanimous verdict, while some other states only required a "super-majority" of nine or ten of twelve. If the defense convinced just one juror to vote against the death penalty, Colorado prosecutors complained, the will of the other eleven wouldn't matter.

In 1984, the legislature amended the death-penalty

statute once again. The prosecution now had to prove the existence of at least one aggravating factor "beyond a reasonable doubt," the same standard prosecutors had to meet in a trial. The new language, however, also said that the defense did not have to prove its mitigating factors "beyond a reasonable doubt," nor did the jury decision have to be unanimous in deciding they existed. In fact, the defense had no burden of proof beyond what could be called a "burden of persuasion," which would leave it up to each juror to decide how much weight to give the defense case.

The most important change to the statute, however, was a rather innocuous-sounding addition: that based on a "consideration" of the other steps, a jury would decide "whether the defendant should be sentenced to death or life in prison"—essentially, whether he "deserved" to die. In the years that followed, this was interpreted by trial courts as adding a fourth step, making Colorado's death-penalty statute a hybrid of other states' statutes. The states were divided between "weighing states"—in which jurors compared aggravators to mitigators and determined whether the former "outweighed" the latter—and "nonweighing states." In weighing states, if aggravators outweighed mitigators, the sentence was death. In a nonweighing state, jurors heard evidence of both aggravators and mitigators. But they were required only to decide whether there was at least an aggravator before looking at the case as a whole and deciding the penalty. Only Utah, and now Colorado, combined the two versions.

Colorado's fourth step would spare many murderers who likely would have landed on death row in a "weighing" state.

Late in the afternoon of November 14, 1984, Lorraine Martelli, a fifty-four-year-old bookkeeper, left work. A devout Catholic who'd never married, she lived with her elderly mother in the old Italian neighborhood of north Denver.

As Martelli walked to her car, she was spotted by brothers Frank and Chris Rodriguez and David Martinez and his girlfriend, Patricia Thomas, who were looking for someone to rob. Too late, Martelli spotted the Rodriguez brothers approaching. The two men grabbed her and forced her into her car. Pushing her to the middle of the front seat, Frank got in on one side and Chris on the other. Martelli tried to resist, honking the horn, but the pair drove down an alley and swung around to pick up Martinez and Thomas.

After they drove to a public-housing area, Frank got out of the car and went into an apartment to buy pot with Martelli's money. While Frank was in the building, Chris raped Martelli.

Violence was nothing new for the Rodriguez brothers. In 1978, they and a cousin had abducted "Judy," a young mother who'd gone outside to warm up her car. For several hours, the trio had taken turns raping Judy vaginally and anally. They'd considered killing her, then finally let her go in a warehouse area along the Platte River. After warning her that they'd kill her and her baby if she told anyone, the threesome took off. But Judy did tell, and the cousins were arrested and convicted.

At the time of the Martelli kidnapping, the brothers had only recently been released from jail. Now they were back to their old tricks. After Frank returned with the pot, they headed to the mountains, with Frank driving, and discussed what to do with "the lady." When Martelli asked what was going to happen, younger brother Chris told her they'd probably let her go. But Frank said no, she'd seen their faces. They couldn't release her. He didn't want to go back to prison.

They ended up driving back to Denver, close to the spot where they'd let Judy go six years before. Frank got out of the driver's seat, saying it was his turn to "have my thrill" with Martelli. While the other three waited outside the car, he assaulted her. When Chris complained that he was taking too long, Frank interrupted his "thrill" long enough to get out and hit his brother, then returned to his victim, whom he raped repeatedly.

Finally, Chris got in the car and began to drive, but he only got about twenty yards when Frank started torturing Martelli with a knife. Dragged from the car, she pleaded for her life. Frank replied that she was stupid and continued stabbing her—she had a total of twenty-eight wounds—until she died. The three men then tossed Martelli's body into the trunk of the car, and they all drove to another apartment building to visit the Rodriguez brothers' girlfriends. When the killers were caught several hours later, the body was still in the trunk of the car.

Martinez pleaded guilty to second-degree kidnapping and received a twenty-year sentence. Thomas was given immunity in exchange for her testimony against the Rodriguezes, who'd been charged with first-degree murder after deliberation and first-degree felony murder as well as first-degree sexual assault and kidnapping.

Denver District Attorney Norm Early announced that his office would seek the death penalty for both brothers. Chief Deputy District Attorney Mike Little, who'd prosecuted the Rodriguez brothers for the 1978 rape, would prosecute both cases.

In 1986, Chris Rodriguez went first. The prosecution held that he was a "principal" in the felony murder. For the count of first-degree murder after deliberation, however, he was charged and convicted as a "complicitor," under the legal theory that while he didn't wield the knife that killed Martelli, his actions leading up to the murder made him equally culpable. He was convicted of all charges.

At the death-penalty hearing, the prosecution's aggravators included the claim that Martelli had been killed to eliminate the witness to a crime (her rape and kidnapping), and that the murder had been particularly "heinous, cruel and depraved." Little supplemented the facts of Martelli's torment and death with testimony from Judy, as well as from a man who'd miraculously survived after being shot four times in the head by the brothers just days before they killed Martelli.

The jurors agreed that the prosecution had proved its aggravating factors, and they felt that the aggravators outweighed the mitigators. But they balked at the fourth step. The fact that he had not stabbed Martelli saved Chris Rodriguez from a death sentence. Instead, he was sentenced to spend the rest of his life in jail.

Frank Rodriguez went on trial almost a year later; this time, Little was joined by Deputy District Attorney Craig Silverman. The jury quickly found Frank guilty of all of the charges.

At his sentencing hearing, the defense presented a fifty-page exhibit put together by one of its investigators detailing the rough childhood of Frank Rodriguez. He was the son of a convict, a child growing up in a violent neighborhood. The defense also argued that it was Chris who started the chain of events that ended with Martelli's murder.

But the defense attorneys couldn't get around the fact that it was Frank Rodriguez who'd wielded the knife. A jury sentenced him to death on January 28, 1987, and Frank Rodriguez was sent to death row.

On July 21, 1986, Virginia May, thirty-three, was living with her husband and two young children, a boy and a girl, on a ranch about twenty-five miles north of Byers. A slender, pretty woman, "Ginny" was tougher than she looked, having been raised on her parents' ranch.

Even after his daughter married, Rod MacLennan knew that if he needed a hand at his place, all he had to do was ask Ginny May. She'd stop working in her much-loved flower and vegetable gardens or turn off the computer, where she was going over cattle records, and pitch in. Like many farm people who have to rely on their neighbors in times of need, she was friendly and trusting.

That July afternoon, Ginny was home with her two toddlers when Becky Fincham, a neighbor, called to say she had some children's clothes to give her. She also wanted to know if Ginny's husband was home. When Ginny said no, he wasn't, Fincham said she'd be right over. She didn't mention that her husband, Gary Davis, would also be coming.

Fincham had met Davis, a convicted sex offender, after writing to him in prison. Once Davis got out, he'd become obsessed with acting on a violent sexual fantasy. Over the past weeks, the couple had tried to approach other women, but one thing or another—the sudden appearance of a husband or ranch hand—had scared them off.

Now, as Ginny, her daughter, and Fincham emerged from the house, Davis punched Ginny in the face. Becky told the little girl to go back inside. What occurred next was confused by the couple's changing stories, but Davis raped, or attempted to rape, Ginny in the back of the car while his wife drove to a secluded field. Stripped of her clothes, with a rope tied around her neck, Ginny was dragged from the car. Davis then raped, or attempted to rape, her again, using a knife to coerce her into submission, after which Ginny was forced to perform oral sex on Fincham.

During the ordeal, Ginny fought and pleaded for her life, even offering the couple money to let her live. Instead, Davis struck her in the head with the butt of a .22-caliber rifle, fracturing her skull. The blow didn't kill her, though, and she was able to raise her hands in futile defense when Davis or Fincham or both—their stories were contradictory—aimed the rifle and fired. Ginny was shot fourteen times in the head, chest, and pubic area. The killers covered her body with a bale of hay and went home.

For two days, Ginny's family, friends, and neighbors searched for her. Davis and Fincham were immediate suspects after Ginny's husband returned to find the children alone and his daughter told him, "Becky took her." But the couple denied knowing anything and even offered to help look for Ginny.

Late in the afternoon of the second day, the sheriff told Ginny's folks that they'd located her body. Rod MacLennan had been hoping against all reason that his daughter would be found alive. He just couldn't understand how anyone could do such a thing to a young woman who'd never harmed anybody in her life.

Davis and Fincham were arrested and charged with Ginny May's murder. Exactly one year after the killing, with Adams County Chief Deputy District Attorneys Bob Grant and John Coates prosecuting the case, Davis was convicted of kidnapping and first-degree murder after deliberation. He'd torpedoed his own defense by climbing onto the witness stand, against the advice of his attorney, Craig Truman, to confess to everything. Although he'd claimed the opposite earlier, he now insisted that his wife, who had already been convicted and sentenced to life, was not at fault. He blamed alcoholism for his conduct. The death-penalty hearing began immediately. Within three hours, the jury sentenced Davis to die.

Rod MacLennan thought the sentence was just. He'd always believed in the death penalty, but until Ginny's murder, his belief had been philosophical. Now he wanted to see for himself the execution of the man who'd killed his daughter.

He couldn't have imagined then how long he would have to wait.

* * *

The late 1980s and early nineties saw significant changes in the application of Colorado's death-penalty statute. In 1988, the state changed its method of execution from the gas chamber to lethal injection. Proponents said it was more humane, but opponents pointed out that the procedure had been botched in states already using lethal injection.

But Colorado was a long way from carrying out a death sentence by any means.

In 1988, Michael Tenneson, twenty-eight, went on trial in Denver District Court, charged with two counts of first-degree murder after deliberation for the 1987 deaths of Jeffrey Sheffield, twenty-three, and Mitchell Gonzales, twenty-two.

Before the trial had even gotten under way, Tenneson confessed to three more murders in Wisconsin. He'd broken into a home, shot and killed its owner, killed the owner's mother, and then killed the owner's girlfriend. He wasn't confessing because of a sudden attack of conscience. He hoped to be extradited back to Wisconsin, where there was no death-penalty statute.

Denver wanted him first, though. Little was again on the case. Through his attorneys, Tenneson tried to claim that Sheffield had attempted to rob him after a night of drinking and snorting cocaine. But the prosecution proved that Gonzales and Sheffield had been murdered in their sleep. Although the Denver jurors hadn't yet been told of the Wisconsin murders, they easily convicted Tenneson of two counts of first-degree murder after deliberation.

At Tenneson's death-penalty hearing, his Wisconsin confession came into play, as did a previous conviction for raping an elderly woman.

The defense attorneys brought in a psychologist who testified that Tenneson suffered from fetal alcohol syndrome. The result was a "serious personality defect" that impaired the defendant's ability to tell right from wrong.

The syndrome wasn't enough to save him from prosecution, his lawyers argued, but it was enough that Tenneson should be sentenced to life in prison, not death. The prosecution brought in its own psychologist, however, who testified that even if Tenneson were a victim of fetal alcohol syndrome, which he doubted, it wouldn't have caused him to murder people.

And at closing, Little had his own description of Tenneson's personality defect: "He kills people." As the jury went off to deliberate, Little was confident that the defendant would soon be on death row.

In fact, the jurors accepted the prosecution's aggravators and determined that they outweighed any mitigating factors. But they were tripped up by the fourth step.

Eleven of the jurors quickly agreed with Little's assertion that Tenneson deserved to die. The last juror, however, refused to even participate in the deliberations. She had a "gut feeling" it wouldn't be right to vote for the death penalty. The rest of the jurors decided to go home and return the next day, when they might be able to convince the holdout to at least take part in the discussions, as she'd been sworn to do when she was put on the jury. But the next day, she sat in a corner with her back to the others.

In any other criminal case, a vote of eleven to one either for or against the defendant would have resulted in a mistrial, and the whole process would begin again with a new trial and jury. But in a death-penalty case, a jury had to be unanimous if voting for the ultimate punishment. Otherwise, the sentence was life in prison. Angry, the eleven jurors were forced to surrender, and Tenneson went to jail for life.

When the Colorado Supreme Court reviewed the Tenneson case, the justices reaffirmed the validity of the fourth step. In 1988, the Colorado Legislature revised the death-penalty statute to do away with the fourth step, or so lawmakers thought.

One night in June 1989, Dan Smith and Steve Curtis returned home from a double date and were accosted by two men who'd broken into their house in southeast Denver. The intruders were Joe Young and Kevin Fears, who were there to murder another roommate, Frank Magnusson.

Several months earlier, Magnusson had witnessed an armed robbery. He was able to identify Joe Young's older brother, Roger (also known as Roy) Young as one of the gunmen. With his trial for that robbery coming up, Roger Young, who'd been sent back to prison on a parole violation, was worried that one more conviction would land him behind bars for life as a habitual offender. He decided that Magnusson needed to be silenced, and he arranged for it over the phone.

The plan was to make the murder look like a burglary gone bad. Joe Young and Fears broke in and waited in the basement for Magnusson, while Roger Young's common-law wife, Christa, sat in the getaway car. The problem was that neither of the hit men knew what their target looked like. So they grabbed Smith and Curtis and knocked them around, demanding to know which one of them was Magnusson.

When they finally figured out the man they wanted wasn't home yet, they made Smith and Curtis lie on the living room floor and called Christa to figure out what to do. While their victims listened, they decided they were going to have to kill them. The burglary-gone-awry plan wasn't going to work if they left witnesses alive.

Fears had the gun and shot Smith in the back of the head, killing him. He then shot Curtis, but the wound wasn't fatal, and Curtis was able to fool his assailant by playing dead. Magnusson arrived home just as Young and Fears were leaving through the back door. They chased him across the backyard, and Fears shot him to death.

Once again, Mike Little was on the prosecution team seeking the death penalty, this time for Fears and the

Young brothers. But there was a legal hitch. The defendants' lawyers, including David Vela, the director of the Colorado Public Defenders' Office, and David Kaplan, a former public defender, went to the Colorado Supreme Court, arguing that the death-penalty statute that lawmakers had just revised was unconstitutional. The third step now specified that the mitigators had to outweigh the aggravators or a defendant would receive the death penalty. That meant that even if the mitigators were judged equal to the aggravators, the defendant would be sentenced to die, and that was unfair, the defense attorneys argued. The court agreed, ruling that the new statute was unconstitutional since it could subject clients to "cruel and unusual punishment."

In other states where the three-step process had been reviewed and judged constitutional, the wording was reversed. That is the aggravators had to outweigh the mitigators in order for a death sentence to be imposed. If they were equal, the defendant would not face execution. But rather than correct the statute's language, state lawmakers quickly endorsed the previous four-step process, and Colorado again had a death penalty. The next time the legislature decided to change the death-penalty statute, lawmakers were careful not to tinker with the four-step process.

Almost a year after the trial had first been scheduled, prosecutors Little and Al LaCabe finally opened their case against Kevin Fears. With an eyewitness, Curtis, testifying to the murder of another eyewitness, the jury easily found Fears guilty of first-degree murder after deliberation, felony first-degree murder, attempted first-degree murder, and burglary.

Little believed they had a strong death-penalty case. Fears had shot three people, not in the heat of the moment, but in cold-blooded executions. Two of his victims had died. The third lived to testify against him. But the fourth step would again trip up the prosecution.

The Fears trial and death-penalty hearing took twelve weeks and involved more than a hundred witnesses. The case also set a number of legal precedents. Prosecutors were used to dealing with testimony about tough childhoods and abusive parents, but the defense went to new extremes to present "any other evidence which in the court's opinion bears on the question of mitigation." They delved into the background of Fears's parents, into his other relationships, and into his school record. His attorneys took advantage of the fact that Fears was a handsome young man who didn't look like a cold-blooded killer. On the stand, he begged for his life, saying he'd found religion—he'd converted to Islam—and even moving some jurors to tears.

After two hours of deliberations, the jurors returned with a verdict. They'd split over the fourth step, and therefore Fears would not be sentenced to die. In light of the Fears outcome, the death-penalty filings against the Youngs were dropped, and they pleaded to lesser charges.

Denver Chief Deputy District Attorney Bill Ritter hadn't been part of the prosecution team, but he talked to several jurors after the Fears verdict. He came away with several observations that would affect his strategy when the Colorado Legislature again began talking about changing the death-penalty statute. One was the jurors' resentment over how long their lives had been disrupted. Another was that many of the younger jurors seemed swayed by the defense's emotional arguments rather than by the law.

Years later, Mike Little would look back at the Fears death-penalty hearing and see it as the moment when defense strategies began to swamp jurors and, later, judges, with what prosecutors would deride as the "abuse excuse."

\* \* \*

The next man to be sentenced to death was already behind bars when he confessed to the murder that landed him on death row. In April 1988, Ronald White had been sentenced to life in prison after he pleaded guilty to the murders of a Pueblo hotel clerk and a bicycle salesman. Then twenty-eight years old, White would have been eligible for parole in 2046.

In prison, however, White complained that he was regularly assaulted by Cañon City guards. So he came up with a plan to get away from his tormentors. He confessed that in 1987, he'd shot his roommate, Paul Vosika, in the head, decapitated him, and then chopped off his hands to prevent identification.

A self-professed serial killer, White—who'd later claim he "couldn't begin to count" the number of people he'd murdered—hoped that by pleading guilty, he'd be allowed to transfer to a Wyoming prison. Instead, in May 1991, he was sentenced to join Gary Davis and Frank Rodriguez on Colorado's death row.

In November 1993, an opinion poll showed that 80 percent of Colorado's voters endorsed capital punishment. In the almost twenty years since Colorado had voted to reinstate the death penalty, there had been more than 3,500 murders in the state. Although fifteen killers had been sentenced to death, one had died while waiting on death row, nine had had their convictions or sentences overturned on appeal, one had had his sentence commuted to life in prison, and one had been executed for a murder in Texas. Of the thirty-eight states in which the death penalty was legal, only four—New Hampshire, New Mexico, Wyoming and South Dakota, all states with much smaller populations—had fewer killers on death row.

But those same Coloradans who favored the death penalty philosophically often balked when they were sitting in the jury deliberation room. It took a particularly heinous crime to move all twelve jurors through that fourth step.

* * *

On December 14, 1993, the employees of Aurora's Chuck E Cheese restaurant had locked the doors for the night when nineteen-year-old Nathan Dunlap emerged from the rest room where he'd been hiding. Fired a few months before, he wanted revenge.

First he shot nineteen-year-old Sylvia Crowell, a student at Metro State College. Next he walked up to seventeen-year-old Ben Grant, a junior at Smoky Hill High School, and shot him in the face. Colleen O'Connor, a seventeen-year-old senior at Eaglecrest High School, saw her killer coming and got down on her knees to plead for her life; Dunlap shot her through the top of her head.

He then went into the kitchen, where he shot nineteen-year-old Bobby Stephens in the face. The bullet knocked Stephens to the floor but didn't kill him. After Dunlap walked on, Stephens got up and went for help.

Proceeding to the office, Dunlap ordered assistant manager Marge Kohlberg to open the safe. Kohlberg, the mother of two daughters, had just moved into her dream house with her husband. She'd been working at the restaurant for only two weeks and had had nothing to do with Dunlap's firing. But after she did as ordered, Dunlap shot her in the ear. When she fell to the floor, he shot her through the other ear. He then emptied her purse, filled it with about $1,500 from the safe, and left the restaurant.

Dunlap wound up at the apartment of a friend, who helped him count the money. "I did it," Dunlap told his friend. "Chuck E Cheese." Next, Dunlap went to his girlfriend's home, where he called his mother. She said the police were there looking for him. He was arrested the next morning.

Denver was still reeling from the Chuck E Cheese murders when another killing shook the community.

Early on February 12, 1994, twenty-five-year-old

Rhonda Maloney was driving home from her job as a Central City cocktail waitress. Although the job paid well, Rhonda had plans that went beyond slinging drinks. She and her husband managed the apartment complex where they lived, and she hoped to go to school to learn to be a hairdresser. At some point, she wanted kids.

It had snowed that night, and Rhonda's car got stuck at the intersection of Interstates 76 and 25. A man pulled over—Robert Harlan.

Driving home from work, Jaquie Creazzo had just exited eastbound I-76 for northbound I-25 when she noticed two cars parked on the highway. As she slowed to see if there was a problem, a woman emerged from the passenger side of one of the cars and frantically gestured for help. Creazzo stopped, and the woman, Rhonda Maloney, jumped in, saying she'd just been raped and that a man in the car had a gun and was going to kill her.

The pair took off with Harlan in pursuit. Pulling alongside, he fired several shots, striking Creazzo in the face, knee, and spine. She lost control of the car on the lawn of a police station. As the car came to a stop, Harlan ran up with his gun, warned Creazzo that he'd kill her if she told anyone, then dragged Rhonda out and put her in his car.

Creazzo, who was left paralyzed from the waist down, was able to give police a description of her assailant. But it was Harlan's own family that found bloody evidence of his crime and turned him in three days later.

Rhonda Maloney's body was discovered four days after Harlan's arrest, near the intersection of Colfax Avenue and I-70. She'd been raped, beaten (there were more than sixty injuries on her body, including a fractured skull and facial bones), and then shot in the head.

In the wake of Dunlap's rampage, Coloradans grew more vocal in their support of the death penalty, and the

Jacine Gielinski, pictured here at about age five, loved being active in the Littleton, Colorado, neighborhood where she was raised.
*(Courtesy of Peggy Luiszer)*

Jacine joined the Brownies, and anything else where she could be around friends.
*(Courtesy of Peggy Luiszer)*

Bob Luiszer (on left) helped raise Jacine since she was two years old with her mother Peggy Luiszer (right) and dreamed of the day he would walk down the aisle with her at her wedding. *(Courtesy of Peggy Luiszer)*

Jacine and her mother, Peggy, were best friends. *(Courtesy of Peggy Luiszer)*

Jake Gielinski was Jacine's biological father, but the two did not become close until he was diagnosed with terminal cancer and she cared for him in his last days. *(Courtesy of Peggy Luiszer)*

Lucas Salmon (as he appeared at his arrest for the rape and murder of Jacine Gielinski) was a former Christian missionary in Mexico.
*(Courtesy of the Colorado Springs Police Department)*

George Woldt (as he appeared at his arrest for the rape and murder of Jacine Gielinski) was a smooth-talking ladies' man and pornography addict.
*(Courtesy of the Colorado Springs Police Department)*

Salmon and Woldt planned to make Amber Gonzales their first victim on April 29, 1997, when they knocked her down in the Garden of the Gods park in Colorado Springs, Colorado.

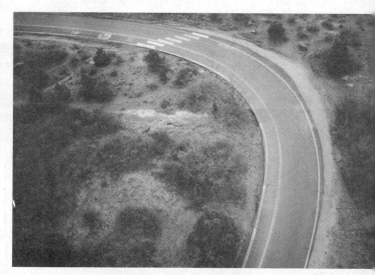

Amber Gonzales was jogging around this corner when Woldt and Salmon drove up behind her and struck her with their car.
*(Courtesy of the Colorado Springs Police Department)*

Jacine was on her way to visit her boyfriend at this apartment complex in north Colorado Springs when she was followed by Salmon and Woldt.
*(Courtesy of the Colorado Springs Police Department)*

Jacine had just reached the security door for the apartment complex when Woldt grabbed her from behind. He and Salmon dragged her to their car.
*(Courtesy of the Colorado Springs Police Department)*

George Woldt at his home at the time of his arrest. Note the missing index finger on his left hand; it was severed in a bread-making machine when he was five years old.
(Courtesy of the Colorado Springs Police Department)

Lucas Salmon at the hospital where he was taken after his arrest, holding up his hands to determine whether he had wounds on them from Jacine's struggle.
(Courtesy of the Colorado Springs Police Department)

Lucas Salmon gave police investigators permission to search his Ford Thunderbird, which he and Woldt used to abduct Jacine Gielinski.
*(Courtesy of the Colorado Springs Police Department)*

Police investigators discovered Jacine's bloody sweatshirt and the murder weapon, a common kitchen knife, in the trunk of Salmon's car.
*(Courtesy of the Colorado Springs Police Department)*

After the discovery of Jacine Gielinski's body beneath a van
in a school parking lot, the police asked neighbors
to turn on their lights while they searched for evidence.
*(Courtesy of the Colorado Springs Police Department)*

To avoid disturbing evidence during the night,
the police left Jacine's body beneath the van near
a pool of her blood until morning.
*(Courtesy of the Colorado Springs Police Department)*

Lucas Salmon has his blood taken at a Colorado Springs hospital after his arrest.
*(Courtesy of the Colorado Springs Police Department)*

George Woldt smirks as blood is drawn for DNA testing purposes.
*(Courtesy of the Colorado Springs Police Department)*

Jacine's bra was soaked through with her blood
that had poured out onto the concrete of the parking lot.
*(Courtesy of the Colorado Springs Police Department)*

Leaving the scene of the crime, Woldt drove the Thunderbird
through Jacine's blood, leaving behind tire imprints
that would help identify the vehicle.
*(Courtesy of the Colorado Springs Police Department)*

The murder weapon, still smeared with blood, was a kitchen knife.
*(Courtesy of the Colorado Springs Police Department)*

The passenger side of Salmon's vehicle was splattered with droplets of Jacine's blood, identified and circled by crime scene technicians.
*(Courtesy of the Colorado Springs Police Department)*

Salmon and Woldt used Jacine's sweatshirt to wipe the blood and mud from their hands and then threw it in the trunk of Salmon's car.
*(Courtesy of the Colorado Springs Police Department)*

The prosecution team of Dan Zook, Dave Young, and Gordon Denison devoted nearly four years of their lives to bringing Salmon and Woldt to justice.
(Author's photo)

Victims' advocate Barbara Buchman was the "angel" who guided the Luiszers through four years of court hearings and trials.
(Courtesy of the El Paso District Attorney's Office)

George Woldt
smiles during
a court
appearance.
*(Courtesy of the
Colorado Springs
Gazette)*

Lucas Salmon
scratches
nervously during
one of his
hearings.
*(Courtesy of the
Colorado Springs
Gazette)*

APRIL 29, 1997
IN COLORADO SPRINGS...

JUNE 24, 1999
IN COLORADO SPRINGS

NEWS ITEM: LUCAS SALMON TESTIFIED ON TAPE HE AND GEORGE WOLDT EXCHANGED HIGH-FIVES WHEN THEY FINALLY SUCCEEDED IN KILLING JACINE GIELINSKI!

SALMON DEFENSE ATTORNEYS

DEATH PENALTY

ASAY @ GAZETTE.COM

The tactics of Salmon's defense team were the subject of this cartoon by Chuck Asay that ran in the *Gazette*. *(Reprinted with permission of Chuck Asay and Creators Syndicate, Inc.)*

RATS!

DEATH PENALTY DEFENSE TEAM

WOLDT

DELAYS

APPEALS

TAX

JURY

JACINE GIELINSKI

JUSTICE

ASAY @ GAZETTE.COM

The jury's guilty verdict was applauded by the citizens of Colorado Springs, including cartoonist Chuck Asay. *(Reprinted with permission of Chuck Asay and Creators Syndicate, Inc.)*

This tabletop in the Luiszer foyer became a shrine of sorts to Jacine, with mementos left by friends and family.
*(Author's photo)*

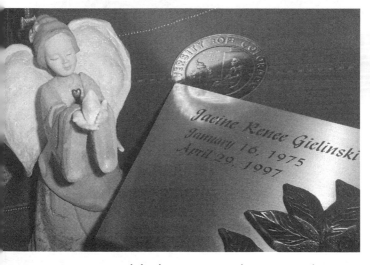

Peggy Luiszer carried the bronze urn with Jacine's ashes to the witness stand when testifying during Salmon's and Woldt's death penalty hearings. *(Author's photo)*

A memorial with lyrics from a song recorded by Celine Dion
was placed at Highland Elementary, where Jacine
had attended school, three blocks from her home.
*(Courtesy of Peggy Luiszer)*

legislature added multiple murders to the list of aggravating factors that prosecutors could use when arguing for the death penalty.

The debate intensified after Maloney's killing. Some arguments were emotional, focusing on society's right for retribution versus the moral admonition that killing does not stop killing.

Other arguments were economic. Proponents of the death penalty pointed out that keeping a prisoner alive for twenty, thirty, forty, or fifty years of a life sentence would cost taxpayers more than $30,000 a year. Opponents of capital punishment countered with the high cost of prosecuting and defending such cases, including the inevitable appeals. But the proponents fired right back, accusing the state public defenders' office, which defended the vast majority of death-penalty cases, with having ulterior motives for keeping costs high. Not only was the office trying to expand its budget, and thus its clout, but it was also using economic coercion to convince the public to abandon the death penalty altogether. The public defenders' office countered again, noting that prosecutors had the investigative and forensic services of law-enforcement agencies, including the Colorado Bureau of Investigation, on their side, as well as legal assistance from the Attorney General's Office.

Some law-enforcement officials complained that prosecutors weren't aggressive enough in pursuing the death penalty, claiming that the threat of capital punishment was being used as a chip to gain plea bargains. But if death sentences weren't carried out, they argued, the threat of capital punishment would not work as a deterrent to crime.

Two members of the Colorado Supreme Court, Justices Howard Kirshbaum and George Lohr, came under fire for saying that the death penalty was unconstitutional, and for voting to overturn the sentences of Frank Rodriguez, Gary Davis, and Ronald White. Because theirs was the minority opinion, the sentences were upheld. But that didn't prevent former governor Dick Lamm, who'd appointed both Kirshbaum and Lohr to the court, from vowing to vote them out when they came up for retention in 1996 and 1998, respectively. "We ostensibly have the death penalty, but it's a cruel hoax," Lamm said. "It's a legislative illusion. . . . Both of these judges disregard the vote of the people and are writing their own social policies."

State Senator Bill Owens accused the Colorado Supreme Court of setting up a roadblock to executions. "The will of the people has been thwarted by the Colorado Supreme Court," he said.

By early 1995, the legislature was willing to let a judge decide the will of the people. State Senator Ray Powers, a Republican from El Paso County, introduced a bill that would take the death-penalty decision away from jurors and instead give it to the judge who presided over the trial.

The Colorado Criminal Defense Bar and the Colorado Public Defenders' Office, as well as traditional opponents of the death penalty, fought hard against the proposal. Prosecutors would find it easier to win death sentences from hard-hearted judges, they complained. If the death penalty was to be used at all, it should be because a jury of the defendant's peers had made the decision.

Powers had the backing of both police associations and the Council of District Attorneys, although not everyone favored a single judge making the decision. Many DAs, including Adams County's Bob Grant, who'd been elected to his post in November 1992, Jefferson County's Dave Thomas, and Bill Ritter, who'd taken over when Early had stepped down and had then been elected to continue as Denver DA in 1994, supported the idea of a panel of judges. They thought the system should still have a deliberative process and opportunity for debate, if for no other reason than that there was less chance of a sentence being overturned if several judges, rather than a single judge, kept an eye on the legal issues.

Even Governor Roy Romer preferred a three-judge panel, the system used in Nebraska, and said he'd refuse to sign legislation creating a single-judge system. Ultimately, the measure's proponents settled for the compromise, although some, including Powers, weren't too pleased by it.

District attorneys came to legislative hearings armed with assorted travesties of justice under the jury system. Grant, for example, used the case of Allen Thomas, Jr., who'd broken into the home of a seventy-one-year-old woman to get money for drugs, but wound up raping and beating the woman, then slashing her throat. Because an Adams County DA's employee was peripherally involved as a witness, the case had been moved to Arapahoe County, where it was tried by prosecutor Eva Wilson.

Thomas was convicted of first-degree murder after deliberation. But when it came time for the jurors to deliberate the evidence presented at his death-penalty hearing, one juror refused to participate. No amount of reasoning by the other jurors could budge her. The other eleven jurors went through the four-step process anyway. They agreed that the prosecution had proved its aggravators, which outweighed any mitigators. Once again, it was the fourth step that tripped up the prosecutors. Once again, all it took was a single juror.

Prosecutors told legislators that a panel of judges—who would rule based on the law, not emotions—would bring "consistency" to death-penalty decisions. They said they were also thinking of future jurors, who would have the time-consuming, stressful death decision lifted from their shoulders. Instead, it would be borne by judges, who were better equipped to handle it.

Ritter said he didn't know if the ultimate outcome in the Fears or Tenneson cases would have been different if judges had made the decision, but he testified that placing such an emotional burden on private citizens was asking too much.

"Death is different" is a common saying in the judicial system. In one sense, the comment reflects the huge workload engendered by death-penalty cases, including a mountain of legal paperwork created before, during, and after the trial and subsequent hearing. And if the defendant is sentenced to die, several more mountains are created during appeals at the district, state, and federal levels. But there's also an emotional load, not just for friends and families of the victims, but also for prosecutors and defense attorneys who try the cases, as well as the judges who preside over them.

The emotional load was particularly heavy for jury members. To hear a case carrying a potential death sentence, jurors had to be "death qualified," which meant that regardless of their personal feelings about the death penalty, they had agreed that they could, and would, participate in the step-by-step process that might lead to a death sentence. Defense lawyers had long complained that such qualifying tilted the playing field toward the prosecution. But without it, a juror might be seated who was adamantly opposed to the death penalty, making the entire penalty phase an exercise in futility before it even began. For prospective jurors to say they didn't approve of capital punishment did not always get them excused from duty, however; unless they demonstrated to the judge's satisfaction that they would never impose the death penalty no matter what the law said, they were still eligible.

While for non-capital cases, jury selection rarely lasts longer than a couple of days, and usually closer to a few hours, the process was much more complicated when the crime was murder and carried the possibility of a death-penalty sentence. Simply selecting twelve jurors and four alternates could take weeks. Knowing that lawyer challenges and a general reluctance to serve on death-penalty cases cut into the pool, court administrators often called in hundreds of prospective jurors to ensure that there would be enough to choose from. Because the trial would likely run long and then might move into a second phase, judges often were inclined to let people off on hardship excuses—the housewife with young children at home, for example, or the small-business owner who couldn't afford such a loss of time. But once solid citizens with jobs and inescapable responsibilities were dismissed, the jury pool was not just smaller, it was narrower and less representative of the community.

Lawyers took particular care when choosing juries for death-penalty cases. They phrased their questions carefully during voir dire, when they could quiz prospective jurors. Lawyers from both sides had a limited number of peremptory challenges with which they could dismiss someone without giving a reason. But they could also challenge the seating of a juror for cause—if, for example, a juror had already formed an unalterable opinion about the case based on media reports. The judge had to agree to any for-cause dismissals, and the other side had the option of arguing against them.

Attorneys for both sides wanted to determine which potential jurors might say they were willing to take the steps to determine if a convicted criminal should be put to death, but would balk at actually doing so. They needed to know who would be willing to carefully weigh the evidence and do the right thing, no matter how many weeks, even months, they'd been sitting in a courtroom.

But while serving on a death-penalty case could be a lengthy ordeal for a juror, judges were paid to make difficult legal decisions every day. In fact, a death-penalty case was the only one in which the judge did not sentence the defendant—and that included first-degree murder cases for which the death penalty wasn't sought. Making those tough calls was the judge's job.

A poll showed that 62 percent of the Colorado population approved of taking the death-penalty decision away from juries and giving it to judges. Although the defense bar fought it bitterly, lawmakers approved the proposal to replace juries with three-judge panels. Under the bill, each panel would consist of the trial judge and two judges selected by a computer at random from that judicial district and neighboring districts. The measure didn't outline how the judges were to arrive at their conclusion, nor did it take note of the fact that the judges were not required to be "death qualified," as jurors assigned to such cases had been.

Passed in the 1995 legislative session, the new system was to go into effect for murders committed after July 1, 1996.

Public defender Terri Brake already had tears in her eyes when she began her opening statement at Robert Harlan's death penalty hearing. "This is the hardest thing I've ever done, to stand here with Robert's life," she said, her voice cracking. "I feel like it's in my hands, and it's tough.

"You have assured with your verdict that he will perish in prison. You have assured with your verdict that he will die a captive man, as punishment for what he has done. . . . Robert Harlan will die in prison."

It was June 22, 1995. Unless the new death-penalty statute was thrown out by a higher court, this would be the last time that Brake would try to convince a jury to spare the life of a killer. At the start of the trial, she and her co-counsel, Kathleen Lord, had admitted that their client had murdered Rhonda Maloney. But they'd also maintained that the murder was a crime of opportunity rather than a premeditated act. Harlan had been driving along and stopped to render assistance, and then everything had turned sour. Drugs had caused him to do what he did to Maloney, they'd contended.

But the jury hadn't bought it and found Harlan guilty of first-degree murder after deliberation, first-degree sexual assault, and kidnapping. Then it was on to the death-penalty hearing.

Opening for the prosecution, District Attorney Bob Grant argued that Harlan killed Maloney to avoid being arrested for her rape and kidnapping. The state was seeking four other aggravating factors that made Harlan eligible for the death penalty, he said, including the fact that the murder was committed in a "heinous, cruel and depraved manner."

Brake was fighting to save her client's life. "You deserve to hear more than just a very small piece of a person," she told the jury. "We as citizens don't condemn people for only the bad things that they do. We listen to it all. We will show you the value that exists in Robert Harlan that you deserve to know about."

The crimes for which Harlan had been convicted "were evil acts," she admitted. "Nobody's denying that. But the soul of the man is not evil. You cannot kill only a small part of another life. . . . If you decide he must die, then the good dies with him."

Brake had to pause several times during her one-hour opening, and she got several jurors crying along with her. At one point, the judge halted the proceedings so that the jurors could compose themselves.

The hearing was generating a great deal of interest outside of Adams County. Jefferson County District Attorney Dave Thomas and two of his prosecutors were there; the preliminary hearing of Albert Petrosky was less than a week away. Two months earlier, on April 28, Petrosky had driven to the grocery store where his estranged wife, Terry, worked. He'd shot her to death, then turned the gun on Dan Suazo, the thirty-six-year-old store manager, and killed the father of two. In the parking lot, Petrosky had set up a sniper position with a high-caliber rifle. He then shot and killed the first police officer to arrive on the scene, Jefferson County Sheriff's Deputy Terry Mossbrucker, a father of six. One of Petrosky's public defenders, Jim Aber, sat on the defense side of the aisle at Harlan's hearing. And Arapahoe County Chief Deputy District Attorney Jim Peters was also watching this first day of arguments to prepare for Nathan Dunlap's upcoming death-penalty hearing.

The prosecutors presented evidence that Rhonda was not Harlan's only female victim. One woman testified that she'd been sexually assaulted by Harlan in the bathroom of his house; another claimed he'd tied her up and raped her for two hours at his grandmother's. Female coworkers reported that he'd sexually harassed and frightened them. His ex-wife, Colleen Harlan, testified that he'd told her he drove around at night, looking for women walking alone so that he could think of ways to rape and kill them, then get away with it.

In her opening, Brake had promised that she'd call many witnesses, including Harlan's parents, siblings, former teachers, and friends, to testify about his good side as a loving father, son, brother, and friend. Belt Harlan, a Denver police detective, had done his duty when he'd turned in his son after another son showed him Robert's bloody clothes and a gun. But it was as a father that Belt Harlan addressed the jury.

Killing his son wouldn't help "bring that lady back," he pleaded. "If you ask me if I'm begging for my son's life, yes. If you ask me if you should kill him, no. If this comes about, I'll accept it as God's will. But I'm begging you not to kill him."

On July 1, the jury returned with its verdict: Robert Harlan would be the first man in four years to be sent to death row.

Harlan showed no reaction other than to pour himself a glass of water. "I think the only thing he has remorse for is that he was caught," Donna Sutherby, Rhonda Maloney's mother, told a reporter. "The only thing I'm sorry for is that he will not die the same way my daughter did."

Although it had been almost thirty years since Colorado had executed a killer, DA Grant told the press that he was confident Harlan's death sentence would be carried out. And he contended that the death penalty deterred a certain type of killer.

"I believe that folks commit murder for a number of reasons, and some of them commit them in a calculated, planned fashion," the DA said. "And for those people, the operation of the death-penalty statute can and will be a deterrent. And if it stops one person—just one person—from being killed in the state of Colorado, it's absolutely appropriate."

"If not now, when? If not this, what? If not him, who?"

Arapahoe County Prosecutor Eva Wilson strolled near the defense table where Nathan Dunlap sat, staring. She was trying to convince a jury of El Paso County citizens that Dunlap should die.

Dunlap's attorney, Forrest "Boogie" Lewis, had persuaded Arapahoe County District Judge John Leopold that extensive pretrial publicity could prevent his client from receiving a fair trial. Lewis himself had been on the receiving end of death threats. But the change of venue didn't make a difference for Dunlap. On February 26, 1996, after a five-week trial, the jury had returned with four guilty verdicts for first-degree murder after deliberation, a verdict for each of his victims.

During the penalty phase, the prosecution presented twenty-eight possible aggravating factors. The murders had been committed because Dunlap wanted revenge for being fired, wanted to rob his former employer, and had a desire for fame. And they were also committed, the prosecution argued, because Dunlap, who was black, was motivated by racial hatred for his white victims.

The defense attorneys countered that their client had grown up in a dysfunctional family. Dunlap, Lewis said, was a "human wreck" whose upbringing had left him unable to distinguish between right and wrong.

Lewis told the jury he understood the community's outrage. "If you choose to kill my client on the facts of this case, I will respect that," he said. "Nathan Dunlap chose to kill. He should be held accountable. He has been held accountable. But you have a choice now, too. Choose life. Not violence. Not killing. But life."

During her rebuttal, Wilson noted that "there's one person who isn't grieving for the victims." She turned to face Dunlap, who didn't look up. "There's one person who hasn't shed a tear or shown remorse. We ask you to come up with a verdict that remembers the victims. Remember the bloom of life. Remember the youth. Remember the promise. Remember the innocence.

"Remember how no mercy was shown."

The jurors remembered, and they unanimously agreed that the prosecution had proved every one of its twenty-eight aggravating factors. After only five hours of deliberations, the jurors returned with four death sentences, which Leopold read as Dunlap sat with his chin in his hand, showing no reaction.

A month after Dunlap received his death sentences, the statute calling for a three-judge panel took effect. There were now five men on death row.

Three of them were there for raping, torturing, and killing women, although only one had specifically targeted his victim. Another prisoner was there because he'd made a habit of killing men, two of whom had died quickly. The fifth was on death row because he'd methodically killed four people in cold blood, motivated by nothing more than a desire for revenge and notoriety.

They lived in five seven-foot-by-twelve-foot cells, each of which contained a steel sink, steel table, steel shelf, and, anchored to the floor, a steel stool and bed. The bed held a thin mattress, sheets, a pillow, and blankets. Each cell also had a black-and-white television that received only local channels and educational programs. The door to the cell was solid steel, except for a one-foot-square window and a slot for passing plates in and out.

Each resident of death row had very little human contact other than meetings with his lawyer and one hour per week with one visitor. They remained in their cells twenty-three hours a day, with an hour out for exercise or showering.

By now, Frank Rodriguez, whose execution date had come and gone a number of times, symbolized a death-penalty system so mired in paperwork and legal maneuvering that it could not serve its original purpose. And in November 1996, U.S. District Judge Wiley Daniel postponed Rodriguez's execution date yet again so that his lawyer, David Lane, could work on another appeal.

Denver Deputy District Attorney Craig Silverman told the *Rocky Mountain News* that the paperwork for Rodriguez's appeal would create a stack several feet tall. That pile included hundreds of reasons why the defense counsel thought that the verdict should be overturned, and each one required prosecutorial replies to the contrary. Silverman estimated that Rodriguez's appeals would keep him alive until at least 1998.

It was "unconscionable" that Rodriguez hadn't been executed, he said.

That same month, however, a federal appeals court upheld Gary Davis's sentence. By the fall of 1997, Davis was out of options.

On October 13, 1997, the morning of Davis's execution, Rod MacLennan drove to Cañon City. More than eleven years had passed since his daughter's murder, and he knew that anyone who said time heals all wounds had never had a child raped and killed.

He thought of Ginny often, especially on holidays or her birthday. Or when he saw her kids playing basketball for their high school and thought, *Gosh, she would have been so proud.*

But he was tired of thinking about Gary Davis. Tired of the appeals, tired of being reminded that Davis was alive while Ginny was dead.

At the prison, MacLennan and the other official execution witnesses were led into a room and seated. A curtain was pulled back, and there, on the other side of the window, was the fifty-three-year-old object of MacLennan's hatred. A minister was with Davis, holding his hand, whispering in his ear. Davis looked drugged, sleepy.

MacLennan couldn't help but think about the difference between this death and the one his daughter had suffered. This wasn't justice. Maybe if Davis had been stripped of his clothes, raped, then dragged into the execution chamber by a rope around his neck and forced to beg for his life before being riddled with bullets—maybe that would be justice.

Davis turned his head and looked at the witnesses. Then he shut his eyes as though he were going to sleep. *How lucky you are,* MacLennan thought. *I don't feel sorry for you—not one little bit.*

Even as Davis closed his eyes a final time and his victim's father looked on dispassionately, four other men were awaiting trial to determine if they would faced the same fate. Two of them were George Woldt and Lucas Salmon.

# PART III

## TRIALS AND RESOLUTION

*"What gets into you all? We study the problem. We've been studying it for damn well near a century, yes, but we get no further with our studies. You've got a good home here, good loving parents; you've got not too bad of a brain. Is it some devil that crawls inside of you?"*

—*A Clockwork Orange*

# TWELVE

# "THIS IS A CASE ABOUT DARKNESS"

*February 8, 1999*
*Colorado Springs, Colorado*

"I, Lucas Salmon, am guilty of the crimes of kidnapping, sexual assault and murder."

Nearly two years after the murder of Jacine Gielinski, Deputy District Attorney Dave Young finally opened the prosecution case against Lucas Salmon in front of a jury by reading the now-twenty-three-year-old's confession. The courtroom was packed, mostly with Jacine's family and friends, although Salmon's family sat in the pews behind the defense team's table.

A jury of seven men and five women had been picked from a pool of more than five hundred prospects, an unusually high number to call but necessary because of the intense publicity the case had received. If they found Salmon guilty of first-degree murder after deliberation, he would face a death-penalty hearing; but because of the new law empaneling three judges to make the decision, they would not have to vote whether he lived or died.

"The roots of this incident date back to approximately

one month ago. My friend, George Woldt, and I viewed a film called 'Clockwork Orange.' The film depicted graphic scenes of violence, betrayal and rape. It was then that we first became interested in the act of sexual assault. We had only joked about it first, but as time went by, we both agreed that it was something we would like to do."

When Young first heard about the reference to *A Clockwork Orange*, he went out and rented the film. He vaguely recalled having seen it when he was in high school, but didn't remember much about it. While he was at the video store, he also rented some of the other films that Woldt was supposed to have liked, such as *Faces of Death*.

Young wanted to watch the movies in case the prosecution team had to counter any defense assertions that the film had caused Salmon to act out. He had not spent much time thinking about the issue that jumped into the public arena whenever a violent crime was linked to some type of media—films, video games, music—whether media caused impressionable young people to become violent. But after reading Salmon's confession, Young, too, had wondered if there might be some correlation.

However, after watching the movies, Young was convinced that it made no sense to blame a film, or a video game, or even violent rap music for criminal acts. Millions of people had seen *A Clockwork Orange*, including himself, without being induced to rape and murder anyone.

At most, he thought, the movie had added another log on the fire already ignited in Salmon's mind by Woldt's constant diet of violent pornography, teasing about his virginity, and his own twisted desires. But that didn't take away from the fact that the two killers knew that what they were doing was wrong and also knew the difference between the fantasy of a movie and the reality of what they were doing to Jacine Gielinski.

It was just another excuse, like the one the prosecutors

expected Salmon's lawyers to use, claiming that their client was defenseless against the manipulations of George Woldt. Yet, the film was important to the prosecution case because it demonstrated how long the pair had planned—deliberated—their crimes, and the length of time they had to reflect and stop themselves.

Young had stayed on with the district attorney's office rather than follow his plan to go into private practice to make more money. He felt he owed it to the Luiszers, to Jacine, and in a way to his hometown.

Colorado Springs was just not the same since the murder of Jacine Gielinski. It wasn't so much the brutality of the murder, although the virulent calls for retribution against the killers had surprised even the prosecutors. Woldt's lawyer, Doug Wilson, who in July 1997 complained to the *Rocky Mountain News* in Denver that "I have not been involved in many cases where the atmosphere against the defendants is as bad as it is," and was still contending that a change of venue was necessary for his client to get a fair trial.

However, it was more the randomness of the crime that affected people so much—that someone, especially a young woman, could be driving in her car or jogging in a park, and that would be enough to be singled out for a violent death. The crime changed how citizens in Colorado Springs lived and thought. Women said they were afraid to drive anywhere at night alone. Without Young even asking, his wife, Denise, had stopped running by herself, and her fears were echoed by many others.

Over the past two years, Young had spoken several times to Amber Gonzales, who said she had avoided getting involved with any men—a problem with trust—and could not even get herself to go past the place where she was struck by the killers' car. She still was troubled by survivor's guilt, looking for answers to the question "Why her and not me?" and finding none.

Salmon and Woldt had both been charged with first-degree murder after deliberation, felony murder (in which the murder was committed to cover up another crime; in their case, sexual assault), first-degree sexual assault, and kidnapping. They'd also been indicted on charges of attempted second-degree kidnapping and second-degree assault for trying to kidnap Amber Gonzales. While the charges for the Gonzales assault might have seemed like overkill, if Salmon was convicted of murder, the additional charges would show that the attack on Jacine was not some spur-of-the-moment decision.

In the days before the trial, Young had contemplated how to make his opening statements, which are generally used to give a jury an overview of the evidence that they can expect to be presented by the prosecution at trial. While they are not supposed to be argumentative, they can also set the emotional tone for the rest of the trial.

Young knew that the defense was going to say that the rape and murder of Jacine Gielinski was Woldt's fault—that Salmon had been either an unwilling participant or unable to resist his partner's more powerful personality. As a prosecutor, he was going to have to show that Lucas Salmon was a full partner and that he had deliberated and formed the intent to kill her. Recalling how Salmon's confession read as if he were writing a school paper on a movie he'd seen, Young decided that there was nothing he could say that would be any better than the defendant's own handwritten words.

"George and I then got out of the car and told her to crawl out backwards, keeping her face to the ground. . . . At this point, George and I had a discussion on who would cut her first and how it would be done."

As he read, the jury leaned forward in their seats, listening with horror as Salmon described how he "took the knife and prepared to cut her throat. . . . I told George to lift her head up by her hair and to cover her mouth. I then made my attack." One of the female jurors swiped at her eyes with a tissue, while others stole furtive glances at Salmon or bowed their heads as if praying. "Again, no scream. . . . We began to discuss again what we should do next."

At the defense table, Salmon sat between his defense attorneys looking like an out-of-place store clerk or nerdy college student. He wore civilian clothes including a sweater-vest and button-down shirt, rather than the jail jumpsuit he'd appeared in during the interminable hearings leading to the trial. What hair he possessed had been allowed to grow back, softening his features from the harsh, shaved look he'd sported when he went hunting for a victim. He kept his head down as the prosecutor read his statement, doodling on a yellow legal pad, as if the proceedings had nothing to do with him.

"By now we can see and hear blood gushing from her wounds. . . . with every breath we could hear the blood gurgling in her mouth."

In the first row behind the prosecution table, Peggy and Bob Luiszer had stuffed red plugs into their ears when Young began his opening remarks. They had never read the confession nor asked to hear the details of how their daughter had suffered and died. They did not want to hear it now.

"This time George moves his feet up and down on her stomach to force the air out, while I press even harder. . . . After a minute goes by, she appears to have stopped breathing."

On her lap, Peggy clutched a framed photograph of Jace, the one taken the Christmas before her murder. Now, as the actors in the courtroom moved through their scenes in silence, she reached for her husband's hand and allowed the tears to roll down her cheeks.

Standing in front of the jury, Dave Young briefly held up a photograph of Jacine. In it, she was smiling, happy.

"They knew what they were doing," he said. "Their plan was not only to rape someone, but to kill them."

Two years. Two long, miserable years, the Luiszers had waited for this day. When District Attorney Jeanne Smith first asked whether they wanted her office to pursue the death penalty, she told them that it would be a long process. It might take a year or two before the trials and penalty phases were over.

Yet here it was, two years, and they were only starting the first trial. If Salmon was convicted there'd be a period of time—at least sixty days, and likely more—before the death-penalty hearing. Then the whole process would start over with George Woldt, and the way the defense attorneys had managed to delay the proceedings so far, God only knew how much more time would pass.

The prosecutors had warned them that the defense attorneys would do more than simply attempt to win their battles in the courtroom. They would try to wear the Luiszers down—hoping that by dragging things out, the victim's family would ask the prosecution to stop pursuing the death penalty.

The pressure started nearly from the beginning. On June 20, 1997, the defense attorneys representing Salmon and Woldt asked that their clients be tried separately. They'd been seated at different tables, as though they had nothing to do with one another.

The district attorney's office had anticipated the request. It was obvious that the defense strategy for each side would be to point the finger at the other defendant as the instigator of the crimes and hope that the jury would buy that their client was less guilty. The prosecutors did not object to the motion; they knew they would most likely lose, and it would make it easier for the prosecutors to use the conflicts in the confessions against the other defendant if Salmon and Woldt were tried separately.

Judge Parrish had granted the motion. However, to expedite the proceedings, he decided that the two would attend the same pretrial hearings because the motions, as well as the arguments for and against each, would be similar.

As they had a month earlier, the defense attorneys again demanded that all communications—written and oral—about the case between the public and any agencies, including the district attorney's office, the judge, all law enforcement, and even the city's newspaper, the *Gazette*, be turned over to them.

The defense had a right to such documents, defense attorney Heher said, because "it acts as a barometer of public sentiment." Their concern was that the district attorney was seeking the death penalty due to pressure from the citizens of Colorado Springs. Citizens, he noted, had sent threatening letters to Salmon and Woldt in jail, which had also been published in the newspaper.

Parrish said he would take the matter under consideration. But, he added, any threats made against the defendants should be relayed to the defense. He also promised not to read any letters about the case sent to him by the public.

The defense attorneys said that their clients were still not prepared for the arraignment in which they would have to enter pleas. The lawyers said they needed more time to view the evidence and read the grand-jury transcripts. Until the pleas were entered, the defendants' constitutional right to a speedy trial would not begin, so Parrish asked the two killers if that was agreeable with them.

Salmon nodded and quietly said, "Yes." Woldt, who acted as if he was enjoying the fuss, grinned and said, "No problem."

The defense lawyers managed to postpone the arraignments until December 1997 when Salmon and Woldt both entered pleas of "not guilty." However, one of the attorneys for Woldt, Doug Wilson, said he reserved the right to change that plea to "not guilty by reason of insanity" depending on the outcome of testing by a battery of psychologists and psychiatrists. Parrish scheduled the trials for June 1998.

It was clear early on that the trials were going to be a battle of the expert witnesses—in these cases, psychologists. Eventually, both defense teams had decided against trying for an insanity finding. The legal definition of insanity is whether the defendants knew the difference between right and wrong at the time of the offense, and whether they intended to kill the victim. It was clear from their confessions—they both said Jacine had to die to keep her from identifying them—as well as their attempts to destroy evidence of the rapes with mud that they knew what they were doing was wrong. Their confessions made it clear that they had also intended to kill Jacine, and indeed had spent quite a bit of time discussing how to do it.

However, that didn't mean the attorneys wouldn't attempt to present a mental defense at the trials that would argue their client was under the influence of the other, or had some other mental deficiency that would somehow mitigate the degree of guilt. That meant shopping around for psychologists who could come up with some sort of explanation for why the defendants were not responsible for their actions the night they murdered Jacine. Indeed, the defense attorneys sought out a variety of experts to overwhelm the jury, even though these experts would all say essentially the same thing but in different ways. Of course, that meant that the prosecution had to find experts of its own, from either the state mental institutions or private practice, to counter the defense theorists.

Another time-consuming practice was for the defense attorneys to overwhelm the prosecution team with paperwork. The attorneys for both defendants filed more than three hundred motions each, many times the number in non-death-penalty murder cases, and many of them repetitive. All of them had to be answered by the district attorney's office, mostly by Gordon Denison. The prosecution filed one hundred of its own, mostly to counter the defense attacks. Then time had to be scheduled for a hearing on the motions, and even those were often delayed when the defense lawyers would come to court and say they had not had enough time to prepare.

Some of the defense motions were fairly standard, such as demanding that the defendants be allowed to wear civilian clothes at their trials so as not to influence the jury by appearing in jail jumpsuits. Some were just silly, such as squabbling about what side of the courtroom the prosecution and defense would sit on, or demanding that the deputies who would provide security in the courtroom wear civilian clothes—otherwise their armed, uniformed presence would give the impression that the defendants were dangerous. On occasion, the defense motions were aimed at the other defendant, such as when Cleaver asked for confidential records about Woldt and his wife, Bonnie, that might contain information about his having sexually molested a neighbor.

Others motions seemed to the Luiszers designed only to batter them into submission. For instance, the defense attorneys insisted, and Judge Parrish had gone along, that the prosecution not refer to Jacine by her first name during the trials. It was too personal, they said, and might cause the jury to react emotionally. Instead, she was to be referred to as "Ms. Gielinski."

The defense attorneys also won a motion requiring that the prosecutors only be allowed to show the jury a single photograph of Jacine before she was murdered, and even that was to be limited to less than a minute during opening and closing statements.

Peggy was horrified by the decision. She thought that a

photograph of her daughter, happy and smiling, should have been set on the prosecution table to remind everyone—the jury, the lawyers, the judge, and the spectators—what the trials were really about: the senseless murder of a twenty-two-year-old woman. But it wasn't. Again, it was all about the defendants, about their rights, and about what they were going through.

Actually, the defense would have preferred to keep all of the photographs of Jacine, living or dead, out of the courtroom. In August 1998, the defense attorneys had tried to prevent the "gruesome" photographs from being shown to the jury. Cleaver's new co-counsel, Mike Enwall, had argued that autopsy photographs (which are normally shown during murder trials) were a "ploy" to make the jurors react emotionally. How Jacine Gielinski died was not in question, he said; nor did the photographs prove who inflicted which wounds.

"The photographs are upsetting and outrageous," prosecutor Zook had agreed. "That's what this crime is. . . . upsetting and outrageous. These photographs depict the injuries this defendant inflicted on the victim." The judge had agreed that the photographs were relevant to the prosecution's case.

Defense attorney Lauren Cleaver even asked Parrish to move Salmon, her client, to a jail in Boulder County, which is where she lived. Cleaver was now the lead counsel for Salmon because his first attorney, Ed Farry, had asked to be removed from the case in December 1997. He'd filed a motion stating that he and his client had agreed that he should step down "in the interest of justice."

Cleaver told the judge that Salmon, who was segregated from the rest of the prison population, was being "harassed mercilessly" by other inmates in the El Paso County Jail. They would walk by and bang on his cell door, and let him know what was going to happen to him if he ever got into the prison population. Rapists were only a step above child molesters in the hierarchy of inmates. Salmon was "going crazy" as a result, his lawyer complained.

Of course, that would have meant moving him back and forth for hearings and eventually his trial, more than two hundred miles round-trip. The judge denied her request after the El Paso County Sheriff complained about the additional costs and problems with security. But to Peggy and Bob Luiszer, it was just one more example of the whole affair was geared toward poor little Lucas Salmon: his rights, his comfort, and his sanity. Meanwhile, it seemed to them that Jacine had been reduced from a beautiful young woman to a case number, a legal theory for the lawyers to debate, citing statutes and Supreme Court decisions.

Such machinations did nothing to endear Cleaver to Peggy Luiszer, who was surprised in April 1998 to receive a letter from the defense attorney. "I have tossed and turned for some time trying to write you this letter," the lawyer began. "I am profoundly saddened by the loss of your wonderful daughter and extend my heartfelt sympathy to you and your family and friends.

"Lucas Salmon's family is devastated as well and would do anything in this world to bring your daughter back to life. While you may doubt these words or be so full of feelings, be they anger, disgust, sadness, or some other feelings, that my message cannot be heard, it is said with complete honesty and sincerity."

Cleaver went on to say that she had a small practice with her husband and a family of her own. "I have never lost someone as you have, and thus do not presume to 'know how you feel.' I can imagine such feelings, but I believe that the depth of such feelings are incomprehensible to those who have not experienced them," she wrote. "Thus I hope that my message does not further increase the pain or in some other way make things worse for you."

The lawyer said she would be willing to share whatever

information she might have that would be "useful," except of course what was considered confidential between herself and her client. She also offered to set up a meeting with Salmon's parents so that they could "convey their deepest sympathies and apologies."

"I can tell you that his mother, father, brothers, sister, grandparents, and family friends cannot fathom why this terrible thing has occurred. I believe there is an explanation and am more than willing to sit down with you and talk to you about that."

Peggy wondered why the lawyer would be writing to her. She had received dozens of letters from Bob Salmon and had answered him once, but had no desire to speak to him further or to his son's lawyer. But then Cleaver got around to the real reason for her letter.

If the death penalty would be dropped, Lucas Salmon was willing to plead guilty to first-degree murder, "which would automatically guarantee that he would never be released from prison," Cleaver wrote.

"Lucas would die in prison. I have conveyed this information to the district attorney, and I presumed they had conveyed it to you. However, after the other day in court, I was less sure of that fact."

Cleaver tried to persuade her that Salmon's death would not serve society's interest. She wanted to assure her that any perceptions that prison inmates "play tennis and have a great time" was wrong. "There have been many times when the question of whether this existence is not harsher than death itself is asked, and I think that is a question each of us must decide for ourselves."

Peggy ignored the letter; in fact, she couldn't believe that the woman had the gall to write it. She and Bob had indeed been told by the district attorney's office that Salmon would plead guilty in exchange for life in prison.

If asked before Jacine's murder how they felt about the death penalty, both would have said that in certain cases they were for it, but otherwise had no real strong feelings. When Peggy Luiszer learned more about the murder of Virginia May by Gary Davis, she thought that his death by lethal injection in October 1997 was appropriate.

As they'd been warned, the defense had stopped at nothing to wear them down. But if anything, the defense's insensitivity and the way it toyed with the system had only hardened the Luiszers' resolve to see Salmon and Woldt receive the ultimate punishment.

The first time Peggy saw them she was surprised at how small they were: less than six foot and slim; she had been expecting large, hulking monsters. Still, she thought that they were ugly and grieved that they were the last two faces her daughter had seen. It hurt her to think that Jacine may have wondered where her father, whose ghost had been haunting her, was as she suffered with those two hideous men doing such terrible things to her.

Peggy hated them and would have gladly killed them herself. When the hearings for the pair had first started, the Luiszers were shocked at how close they were allowed to sit to the defendants—no more than ten feet and separated only by a low, wooden barrier. They'd even discussed jokingly but with an element of truth how they might accomplish killing them. They knew they'd never get through the metal detectors with a gun or a knife, but they considered how they might smuggle in a blowgun with poison darts.

Of course, they had no idea where they would get such a murder weapon. More practically, they'd been approached by several people who said that for as little as $5,000, Salmon and Woldt could be killed in jail. If she'd thought it might actually work, Peggy would have paid any amount. She even joked that if she was caught, she could probably get off with a few months in a mental institution

by hiring a good defense lawyer to argue that she was insane at the time.

There were certainly times that she felt that she might
lose her mind to anger and bitterness. Salmon and Woldt
had taken more than Jacine's life. "You have all these
hopes for your kid and then they're gone," Bob Luiszer
told a reporter from the *Rocky Mountain News* in July
1997. "It changes your whole life."

Peggy added, "Everything we had was going to go to
Jacine when she got older. Not anymore. It rips a hole in
my heart."

Worried about the graphic nature of the crime, the
*Gazette* had run a disclaimer Editor's Note with its coverage, stating: "The 1997 slaying of Jacine Gielinski was
one of the most brutal in the city's history. Readers may
find some of the details in this story unsettling." Even
then, some readers had complained that they didn't need
so many details in their family newspaper.

Yet no newspaper article could adequately express what
the Luiszers had gone through in the two years since, or
how much their lives had changed. They couldn't go anywhere with friends without Jacine's murder hanging like a
dark cloud over them, even if everyone politely avoided
the subject. They didn't celebrate holidays like Christmas;
Bob stopped baking his thousands of cookies to send to
friends and relatives. Jacine's birthday was just another day
spent in tears.

The grief wasn't necessarily constant after two years of
mind-numbing court appearances and dozens of trips to
the courthouse in Colorado Springs. But it would sneak up
on them unexpectedly when they least suspected, like
when they'd see a red car like Jacine's or a song would
come on the radio that she'd liked. Then all the memories
would come flooding back, and so would the anguish.

In some ways, they kept the memory fresh themselves.
They didn't touch her room except to add a large portrait

of her. Peggy had a purple ribbon tattooed on her ankle; then Bob, who was normally rather conservative, surprised her by coming home one day with one tattooed on his arm. There were photographs of Jacine scattered all over the house; many of them were on the refrigerator, surrounded by two years of newspaper clippings about her case and other murders and trials.

Constantly they were reminded of time passing and what they were missing. Jacine's friends were going on with their lives, getting married, and having babies. Meanwhile, the Luiszers looked at each other and wondered if their marriage would survive, not because they fought or thought poorly of each other. It was just that all happiness seemed to have been sucked out of whatever future there would be when the trials and death-penalty hearings had come and gone. They were polite and friendly, but in many ways they were just two people who shared a house, a house full of memories that only increased the sadness. Neither had any interest in intimacy—the very thought of sex to Peggy reminded her of what Jacine had gone through and made her sick to her stomach. Bob would go to work sometimes and be fine, or he might just sit there, staring at nothing, and then begin to cry.

They were no longer just a nice, middle-class couple. They were the parents of a murder victim and that made them different. Some of their friends and relatives had reached the point of suggesting that they "get over it." Or they offered platitudes like "time heals all wounds," which Peggy thought was bullshit; there were some wounds that time had no effect on whatsover.

Some friends acted as though having a child murdered was like a disease they or their children might catch, and made up reasons not to see them. Others were simply insensitive. Peggy told the woman who ran the child-care center where she worked that she needed to take a break because the sound of happy children was too much. The woman asked, "Well, when do you think you might come back to work?"

Fortunately, Barbara Buchman, the victim's advocate in the district attorney's office, was there to answer their questions about the legal proceedings and be a shoulder to cry on when the going was especially rough. As she'd said when they met, she made herself available any time of the day or night, and Peggy in particular had leaned on her.

As the proceedings dragged on, the Luiszers grew close to the prosecution team as well. The prosecuting lawyers genuinely cared about them and invited them over for dinner or to watch their children play soccer. When the deputy district attorneys came to court, they dressed professionally and lent a certain dignity to the proceedings; the defense lawyers seemed to the Luiszers to go out of their way to show up looking like they had slept in their clothes and could hardly be bothered to arrive at all.

The Luiszers thought the defense lawyers seemed to have no shame. A few months before the trial, Cleaver followed up on her letter by calling Peggy, who had no idea why this woman who had done her best—along with Doug Wilson and Terri Brake, whom the Luiszers despised—to make the proceedings more traumatic would call.

Cleaver was always asking for more time to prepare. She would complain about the amount of work (though she filed hundreds of motions) and to the Luiszers, she seemed to either act like a little girl or flirt with the judge when making her requests or explaining why she wasn't ready. The judge would invariably grant her requests for more time, but the next hearing day would arrive and she still wouldn't be prepared. Instead, she'd repeat her routine with the judge.

Peggy found the act offensive and was angry that the judge never reprimanded the lawyer, though he had no such compunctions if the prosecutors had not met some deadline. Curious why Cleaver thought she could call like an old friend, Peggy talked to her. In fact, they spent forty-five minutes chatting, learning that they'd both had hysterectomies in the same year and that the attorney had a daughter and two sons. But with the small talk out of the way, Cleaver again got around to the reason for her call. She wanted Peggy to ask the district attorney to drop pursuing the death penalty.

"If Salmon and Woldt had done that to your daughter, what would your answer be?" Peggy asked.

Cleaver paused. "Probably the same as yours," she admitted. There was nothing more to say, and they hung up.

However, any chance of Peggy at least now viewing Cleaver as someone just doing her job, or even someone who was morally opposed to the death penalty, soon disappeared. After the telephone call, the lawyer picked up where she left off with her delaying tactics and efforts that seemed designed to cause the Luiszers more pain.

Both trials had originally been set for June 1998, but when the date approached the defense attorneys had asked for a delays to better prepare. One issue was what order the defendants would be tried. This time, the defense attorneys fought with each other rather than the prosecution. Whichever team went second would have the advantage of seeing the prosecution's case beforehand.

Parrish decided, with the prosecution in agreement, that Woldt would go first, in August 1998. But a week before the trial was to begin, Woldt's attorneys announced that they would be presenting expert testimony that a small growth in his brain affected his thought process the night Jacine was murdered. The prosecutors had to ask for more time so that they could find an expert to look into the defense assertions. The judge granted the continuance and instead set Salmon's trial for January 1999.

"Let us put our lives on hold for another four months,"

a tearful Peggy Luiszer told the press outside the courtroom that afternoon. "This is ridiculous."

Meanwhile, Cleaver complained that making her go first violated an agreement she had with the district attorney's office. Because of the broken promise, she said, the charges against Salmon should be dismissed. Of course, she didn't mention that in the beginning, her client wanted to plead guilty to first-degree murder and accept the death penalty as his just deserts. However, she and her co-counsels had refused to "let him die," though she had gone to the district attorney to offer his guilty plea in exchange for life without parole.

The Luiszers couldn't believe that the lawyer believed that a killer should escape justice because of an argument over which defendant should go first, and it only increased their contempt for her.

The contempt turned to hatred the morning of the trial. Back in June 1997, more than five hundred people got together at a fund-raiser for the scholarship in Jacine's name at the University of Colorado-Colorado Springs. For the event, her friends had made hundreds of small purple ribbons. Purple was Jacine's favorite color and her high school's color. The family had then found a vendor to make metal replicas of the ribbons, which were about an inch wide.

The Luiszers had given several of the metal ribbons to the prosecution team, which wore them on their lapels for the trial. But Cleaver noticed and complained to the judge that the ribbons might unduly influence the jury, even though the jurors wouldn't have known what they were. The judge then told the prosecutors to remove the ribbons, but allowed the family to wear theirs. Peggy seethed with anger, perceiving the look on Cleaver's face as simply smug that she had won.

\* \* \*

After Young finished his opening statement, Cleaver got her chance. She knew better than to try to persuade the jury that her client was innocent of the charges and conceded as much. Her only hope—his only hope—was that she could convince at least one person on the jury that he was so far under the spell of George Woldt that he was unable to stop himself. "No matter how crazy that sounds as you sit here this morning," she told the jurors.

Having only that morning argued vehemently against the prosecutors being allowed to exhibit even a small photograph of Jacine when she was alive, Cleaver now set up a four-foot-by-five-foot poster of Salmon and Woldt at a party. The poster depicted a smirking, confident Woldt in front of a shyly smiling Salmon in the background, the obvious implication being that Woldt was the leader and Salmon his shadow. Where the prosecutors were allowed to show the photograph of Jacine for a minute, the more than life-sized faces of her killers remained in front of the jury for the entire length of the trial.

Cleaver said she would be calling to the stand five expert witnesses who would testify that Salmon "suffers from dependent personality disorder." Such people, she said, have "pervasive and excessive need to be taken care of, have difficulty expressing disagreement with others, rarely initiate any projects, go to excessive lengths to get nurturing, and often feel helpless and alone."

Another of the defense's mental health experts, she said, would testify that Salmon suffered a type of autism—a state of mind characterized in his case by daydreaming, hallucinations, and disregard of reality—that prevented him from thinking objectively.

Salmon had the maturity of a "five-year-old," Cleaver said, and "clings to reality by a thread. She pointed to where her client was doodling like the village idiot on a legal pad at the defense table, his head down. He liked to draw hot rods and old cars, she said.

Going on, she said her witnesses would testify that Woldt manipulated Salmon into "fulfilling his sick fantasies," which he initiated by having his friend watch *A Clockwork Orange*. Salmon "lacked the free will" to resist Woldt's desire to act out the violence and rapes depicted in the film.

"He could not use his own reflection," she said. "He could not use his own judgment. Lucas couldn't and didn't think for himself." Her client was a "very vulnerable . . . outcast with no friends," she said. "One of the best days of his life was when Woldt told him the two were best friends.

"Lucas Salmon was the perfect killing companion for a sexual sadist."

Cleaver contended that Salmon would have never been involved in Gielinski's murder if not for Woldt. They would hear from Woldt's wife, Bonnie, that Salmon was "a sweet young man" when she first met him, but that he changed to a darker personality after he spent much time with her husband.

Bonnie Woldt had also told friends that she and George had a kinky, sometimes violent sex life, Cleaver said. The wife's testimony in addition to that of the experts would show that George Woldt was a "crazed sexual sadist . . . a psychopath, who became sexually aroused by another person's suffering and was fascinated by pornography, bondage and role playing."

Woldt hated his mother and took it out on other women, she said, noting that he had talked to two other men about his desire to rape a woman. But he was unable to fulfill his fantasy until he met Salmon.

"This is a case about darkness, a case about loneliness," Cleaver said. "It's about a young man so lost that no one knew he was missing."

Peggy Luiszer snipped open the clear plastic bag and removed the contents. She knew exactly what she was looking at on the witness stand, even through the tears that flooded her blue eyes behind their wire-rimmed glasses.

"This is her garnet tennis bracelet we gave her for Christmas." She'd promised herself to hold it together, but her voice quavered and drops rolled down her cheeks.

Following opening remarks, the prosecution team had begun its "case in chief" with Salmon's confession fresh in the jurors' minds and entered into evidence so that the jury could reread it in the deliberations room after the trial. The prosecution intended to keep their presentation short and simple. The facts of the case would speak, in large part through Salmon's words, for themselves. The more difficult task would be later, after the defense presented its case. Then the prosecutors would have to counter the defense team's expert witnesses.

In quick succession, the prosecutors had called their first witnesses: the police officers who had responded to the crime scenes and had gone to the Woldts' apartment. The police testified about conducting interviews with eyewitnesses, finding the knife and bloody sweatshirt, hearing the initial confessions of the killers, and finding Jacine Gielinski's body beneath the van.

"We were hoping and praying that we might be about to save somebody," Officer Olav Chaney said, remembering how he and Sergeant Steckler ran from their patrol car to the van. "I got down on my knees and looked and knew at that time, there was not a chance."

The women who'd seen the abduction and taken down the license plate number made their way to the stand and recalled for the jury a night that they'd never been able to forget. Margaret Zarate wept as she described standing twenty feet from where Woldt was straddling Jacine in the backseat of the Thunderbird, punching her repeatedly in the face. He'd looked at Margaret Zarate three times, she said, the first "as if he was curious why I was there"; the second time he looked scared; and the third "he smiled."

Peggy Luiszer had been called to identify her daughter's personal effects found in the backseat of Salmon's car, next to where crime-scene technicians had found his Bible, embossed "Lucas Salmon." Each piece of jewelry had been sealed for two years, requiring her to cut the bag open to release the contents and the memories each brought with it.

"This is her garnet ring," she said. She paused to recover for a moment and then carried on. "This was her gold chain."

As the mother of his victim testified, Salmon sat with his head down, no expression on his face, drawing on the legal pad. Mercifully, his attorneys had no questions for Peggy and she was allowed to step down and flee the courtroom with her husband.

The Luiszers left the courtroom again the next day when Dan Zook rose to show the jury photographs taken at the crime scene on a four-foot-by-eight-foot screen. He gave them a signal to let them know what was about to occur, then turned to his task as they walked quickly out.

The photographs were shown at the end of a day in which Pat Crouch, who had since retired as a detective from the Colorado Springs Police Department, testified about his interviews with Salmon. Crouch's testimony was going to be key when added to Salmon's own words to proving that the defendant was more than just a toy to be wound up by Woldt—that he'd participated in the planning and execution of the rape and murder of Gielinski as an equal partner. As the former detective noted, Salmon took pains to point out that they'd taken turns cutting and stabbing Gielinski.

On the morning of September 30, 1997, Salmon didn't try to blame the killing on Woldt or claim that he was coerced. The defendant spoke in a monotone voice and showed no emotion or remorse except to say, "Killing her was the worst experience of my life."

Crouch noted that Salmon ate his breakfast from McDonald's while calmly going over the details of the rape and killing. "I would have thought it would be real difficult to continue eating while describing what happened," he said. "But he had no problems with it."

On cross-examination by Enwall, the detective agreed with the lawyer's statement that he thought Salmon's behavior, given the circumstances, was "extraordinary."

Enwall asked Crouch if he thought that the pair intended to "torture" Jacine Gielinski. No. The detective shook his head. "There's no doubt she felt a great deal of pain. They just didn't know how to kill her."

With Crouch's testimony at an end, Zook turned slightly to the Gielinskis and looked at them. It was time for them to leave—he was going to show the photographs.

The jurors, of course, had no such option. Instead, they had to endure the scene of Jacine Gielinski's nude body lying facedown in a large pool of blood. Other close-ups showed the slashes to her throat, the puncture wounds in her chest, and the wounds to her hand and wrist.

As two jurors began to cry openly, the defense attorneys jumped to their feet and angrily demanded that the judge declare a mistrial. The photographs were "prejudicial," they said. But the attorneys had been over this territory before. The photos were going to be admitted into evidence; the jury would just have to deal with them the best they could.

For the first time in two days, Salmon stopped drawing and put his pen aside. However, he did not look up at the screen where the photographs were being displayed, but instead dropped his chin farther yet and stared at the floor beneath the defense table. *They just didn't know how to kill her.*

\* \* \*

On the third day of the trial, it was a lawyer who cried first. The defense was again objecting to showing the jury more of the murder scene, this time a videotape made by the police.

Excusing the jury, Judge Parrish decided to view the film first before ruling. Watching the camera pan slowly along the length of Jacine's body, pausing to show the knife wounds and the mud between her legs, Cleaver broke down. "I am moved to tears," she said. "Her hair is blowing, and it reminded me how alive she was and how cold and empty she is now. . . . I'm sorry about that, but I can't bring her back to life."

She pleaded tearfully with the judge to keep the videotape from the jurors. "I don't know how much of this they can take."

As she cried, her co-counsel Mike Enwall, a former judge and also a member of the Alternate Defense Counsel, sat quietly in his seat. He and Cleaver had worked before on a first-degree murder trial, defending Thomas Luther, who had been charged with killing twenty-one-year-old Cher Elder in 1993 and burying her body in a clandestine grave in the mountains. Through tenacious work, a detective named Scott Richardson found Elder's body in 1995 and arrested Luther in West Virginia, where he was serving time for sexual assault.

In her mid-forties with long brown hair pulled back, Cleaver had angered Elder's family the way she had fawned over Luther during the trial, touching him, leaning against him, tilting her head so that they could talk in conspiratorial whispers, and laughing at their private jokes. The victim's family saw it as cheap theatrics meant to demonstrate to the jury that Luther was a nice guy, harmless to women. Of course, the jurors didn't know (because it wasn't allowed into the testimony) that Luther had already been convicted of the violent rapes of two women and was a suspect in the murder of several others. Elder's family didn't understand why Cleaver, who did know Luther's past, felt it necessary to act as if he were some sort of wrongfully accused Boy Scout. It was one thing to represent him as a professional, as they felt Enwall had done in his role, but this game of pretend was sickening.

It didn't work either: eleven jurors voted to convict him of first-degree murder, which would have subjected him to a death-penalty hearing, except for one holdout juror who insisted on a lesser, second-degree charge. In the end, the rest of the jury had to go along with her or risk a mistrial. As a result, Luther received a forty-eight-year sentence for second-degree murder and didn't have to face a death-penalty hearing.

Cleaver behaved the same way around Salmon. The Luiszers had early on been taken aback by the way she touched and joked with him, as if he were a kid brother who had gotten himself into a little bit of trouble, rather than a man who had raped, then hacked, stabbed, and smothered a young woman to death. She wasn't the only female at the defense table who carried on the sham, either. One of the defense's investigators was an attractive blonde who also sat as close as she could to the defendant, placing a hand on his shoulder, giggling at things he said, and taking an extraordinary interest in his drawings.

The defense attorney's comment angered Zook, who rose quickly and said, "Attorneys are supposed to keep their emotions in control. She's been on this case for two years and she's never cried. . . . Just because jurors get upset doesn't mean it's unfair."

Parrish agreed that the videotape had a stronger "emotional tenor" than the still photographs. So he compromised. The prosecutors could show only a portion of the video, including one pan of Jacine's body. Even at that, the jurors, when they returned and the videotape was played, were visibly shaken as they left the courthouse for the day.

The horror show didn't get any better when the trial resumed the following morning. This time the Luiszers didn't bother even going into the courtroom, but sat in the hallways as the coroner, Bowerman, discussed the autopsy, and the jury once again had to view disturbing photographs. That past August, Zook had agreed with Cleaver's assessment that the photographs were "upsetting and outrageous," just as the crime against Jacine had been. Now, as the jurors looked at the photographs, several of them had to turn away quickly and avert their eyes.

Finally, there was relief from the barrage of photographs. But Amber Gonzales's testimony sent a whole new chill through the courtroom as she described being struck by a car while jogging. "I felt like it was intentional for some reason," she said. "I was very scared. I just had an instinct . . . everything just didn't seem right."

The prosecution wrapped its case on the fourth day of the trial by calling forensic experts to testify about the blood and hair samples found at the scene or in the car, and about the stains found in Salmon's underwear that matched Jacine's DNA.

The prosecutors had expected their case to go on for several more weeks. But the defense attorneys did not challenge the DNA evidence or the police investigation. Nor did they engage in much cross-examination of their witnesses.

The public's interest seemed to have dropped off as well. While the courtroom had been packed for the first day, most of the rest of the time spectator seating was only about a third full.

The final prosecution witness was Laura Shugart, the waitress who served Salmon his beer at the Corner Pocket pool hall the night of the murder, who remembered the way the defendant kept watching her. "It was a spooky stare," said Shugart, who'd recognized Salmon and his friend on a television newscast a couple of days after the murder. "His head followed me. He made me uncomfortable."

As he raped Jacine Gielinski, Lucas Salmon imagined that he was on a date and that the sex was consensual. The "extraordinary distortion" came out in one of three interviews California psychologist J. Reid Meloy testified he conducted with the defendant.

Tanned, gold chains hanging around his neck, his long silver hair swept back and held in place by plenty of hair oil, Meloy looked something like old-time movie star Fernando Lamas. But he was a past president of the American Academy of Forensic Psychology and would be the main defense witness to assert that Salmon was a mere pawn for Woldt's sexual depravity and incapable of making decisions for himself the night of Jacine's murder.

After the prosecution rested its case the day before, the jury was excused. When they had left the courtroom, Cleaver announced that she planned to call as many as sixty witnesses, most of them to testify that Salmon was a good person, raised in a devoutly Christian home, but had become a different person under the influence of Woldt.

The prosecutors objected that the defense was trying to sway the jury by sheer numbers when most of those the defense intended to call would be "character witnesses," whose testimony would have little bearing on the actual charges against Salmon. Their testimony—and even that should be limited to avoid repetition—would be more appropriate at a sentencing hearing.

Judge Parrish agreed with the prosecutors, saying the defense could not call witnesses simply to testify about Salmon's character. Cleaver shrugged and said she would then call her five expert witnesses first and determine how to proceed from there.

She opened her case the next day by calling Meloy. He'd

been a defense consultant at such trials as that of Susan Smith, the mother accused of murdering her two sons by rolling her car and them into a pond, and Oklahoma City bombers Timothy McVeigh and Terry Nichols.

Meloy said he was basing his opinion on seventeen hours of interviews with Salmon, his family, and acquaintances; as well as reviewing 6,000 pages of documents and three psychological exams. He'd been paid handsomely for his work, having billed taxpayers $60,000, at $300 an hour.

Back in December 1997, he'd written a report largely placing the blame for the rape and murder of Jacine Gielinski on George Woldt, whom he described as a "budding sexual sadist," and a "psychopath."

Some aspects of his report were not brought up by the defense attorneys at the trial. That included his discussions with Salmon family members about Bob Salmon's alleged affairs with baby-sitters.

Lucas's father told him, "His rationale for his actions was that Gail was 'too good' and too perfect, not interested in sex, not loving and affectionate enough, and too involved with the children." Bob Salmon felt his first wife suffered from "low self-esteem" but that was "not my fault."

Lucas Salmon acknowledged that he'd been told by his siblings about his father's indiscretions. "It happened." He shrugged. "I didn't judge it."

However, he was not so kindly disposed toward his former best friend anymore. Meloy noted in his report that when Salmon's brother, Micah, had visited him at the jail in July 1997, Lucas told him that at the time of the murder he'd felt that his bond of friendship with Woldt was stronger than the difference between right and wrong. But two months after the crime, he was angry with Woldt for trying to place the blame on him.

Salmon told his brother that he'd heard that his "friend" had told the police and his lawyers that the crime occurred because Lucas kept whining about needing a sexual partner, that it was Lucas's idea to follow the blonde in the car, and Lucas who had insisted on killing her.

Salmon told the psychologist that he didn't want to have sex with Jacine when he realized that she was "unwilling," and only did so when George insisted. Then he'd fantasized that he was on a date with Jacine and the sex was consensual. "I was trying to fool myself," he told the psychologist, even though Woldt was telling the girl to shut up and not look at them.

Then Woldt, who had fetched the knife from the glove box, said that because he was the first to rape the victim, Salmon had to be the first to cut her.

Meloy's testimony at the trial would last two days, in which he described the defendant as "a seriously disturbed young man." His diagnosis was that Salmon suffered from "dependent personality disorder," one of ten personality disorders formally recognized by mental health experts. Salmon met seven of the eight criteria for the disorder, including: has difficulty making everyday decisions; needs others to assume responsibility for major areas of his life; has difficult expressing disagreement with others because he fears loss of support or approval; and goes to excessive lengths to obtain nurturance and support to the point of volunteering to do things that are unpleasant.

It was difficult to say how the personality disorder developed, Meloy said. It was probably a mix of inherited traits and early behavior used to get attention.

Salmon's mother told him that it was apparent that Lucas was different than siblings, and she felt that he had been depressed all his life. As Lucas aged, the disorder became more apparent until he was a "shadow figure" following the rest of his family members from one state to another.

Meloy said he asked Salmon how it felt when Woldt called him his best friend in May 1993. Salmon replied, "I finally have a friend. It felt good." The defendant saw Woldt as more worldly and was concerned that Woldt would abandon him.

By the time he moved in with the Woldts, Salmon was a "cipher" willing to do whatever his friend wanted, Meloy said. He was "willing to suffer any humiliation just to keep his friendship," including constant taunts about his virginity, his sexuality, and the size of his penis.

Meloy noted that Woldt's defense team had not allowed him to interview their client. But, he sniffed, he'd seen enough evidence to know that the events of the night of April 29, 1997, were Woldt's fantasy, not Salmon's. He pointed out that two other acquaintances of Woldt reported that he tried to "recruit them as partners" to rape and kill women.

Unable to persuade those two to help him fulfill his fantasy, Woldt targeted Salmon. Meloy said the first attempt to lure Salmon into his web was at Woldt's wedding in Delaware, where he suggested that they "go in and rape" the neighbor having car troubles. Although Salmon resisted the suggestion that time, he said, he wouldn't remain strong in the face of constant suggestions by his friend.

Salmon told him that he knew Woldt could be dangerous. Asked why then he moved back to Colorado Springs in Februay 1997, Meloy said the defendant replied, "George was here. He asked me to be the godfather of their baby."

Watching *A Clockwork Orange* was the spark that ignited the fire, Meloy said. From that point on, the pair talked constantly about how to go about abducting, raping, and killing a woman. Although it started as a fantasy, Salmon gradually began to believe that he actually should participate in such a heinous act.

Salmon started drinking heavily to silence the voice of his conscience. Meloy quoted him as saying, "I knew God was not pleased. I didn't care what God wanted—it was me me me. I didn't want George Woldt to think I was a wuss. I started considering sex outside of marriage."

At first, Salmon didn't think they'd go through with the rape and murder; then when he realized that they might, he didn't believe that they would get caught. It wouldn't have mattered; what mattered was Woldt's opinion. "I wanted him to stop teasing me. If I went along with this, he'd accept me."

Regarding the assault on Amber Gonzales in Garden of the Gods, Salmon told him, "I saw it was wrong, but part of me was convinced by George to do it." Besides, he was angry with his father for firing him for sexual harassment at work, but not firing the women he felt had led him on.

After hitting Gonzales, "I felt pretty bad," Salmon told him. But he didn't say anything because he didn't want to "make George a liar in front of her." He took her sunglasses, he said, simply because he wanted them.

Woldt had berated him after the incident. "Why did you just stand there? We almost had her." Salmon gave his excuse of the bushes getting in the way, but admitted that he was excited to his friend, who then replied, "Now we have to go do the old in and out."

Later, as Salmon, who would only refer to the sexual assault as "having sex," watched Woldt raping Jacine, he said he felt "uncomfortable," like he had when he could hear the Woldts having sex in the apartment. He thought, "We're going to have sex. It became real. I knew what would come next."

Salmon said he asked Woldt if they should knock her out, but his friend said no. "George was going to get what he wanted again," Salmon said and admitted, "I wanted sex, too."

After the rapes, Salmon said he argued with Woldt about killing her, but finally agreed that she had to die to keep them from being arrested. Woldt said that because he'd had sex first, Salmon had to be the first to stab her. "All right, whatever," Salmon said he replied. When he cut her throat, "I felt sick," then as he watched Woldt repeat the act, "I felt contempt for him."

Salmon admitted that it was his idea to suffocate Jacine when nothing else seemed to be working. However, the act "disgusted me . . . but it didn't seem to bother George. He was into it."

In fact after Jacine died, Woldt had asked him if he wanted to have sex with her again. When Salmon declined, he said, Woldt then said something even more shocking, "Do you want to cut her pussy out?" The idea was to hide the evidence of the rape, but Salmon came up with the idea of using the mud instead.

As they drove away that night, Woldt had said, "Bet you're dying for a cigarette now." That's when Salmon said, "At least I'm not a virgin anymore." They'd then gone home to wait for whatever came next and "tried not to think about it." He wanted George to protect him. "I was also afraid of him."

Salmon seemed to have reached some sort of religious understanding about the rape and murder of Jacine and its impact on his soul. While God was against crime, Salmon believed he would still be forgiven for what he'd done. He said he was praying for both George and Jacine and hoped that "some good can come of this."

The death of Jacine was "predestined," he said. While he believed that he should not have committed the acts against her, he also believed that there was nothing he could have done to change it from happening.

"It was God's will for Jacine to die as bad as that sounds," he told the psychologist. "It happened regardless of what I wanted. Everybody dies . . . it's not right to question God."

Still, Salmon also acknowledged that he had the "free will" to choose between God and the devil. Woldt, he said, "pulled me away from God and what I knew was right."

Now, his future was up to God. "I learned Jacine was born again," he said, "and she is with God." And if he was put to death for killing her, he too would be with God and judged again "when Jesus returns."

Meloy said that Bob Salmon had told him that he thought it would be best if Lucas accepted the death penalty, then repented so that he could be forgiven and go to heaven.

There was something that troubled Salmon. He sometimes thought about his experience of "having sex" with Jacine. "I feel guilty about any pleasure I have at the memory of sex with her." He admitted that he frequently masturbated while in jail, fantasizing about having sex with one of his former girlfriends. However, he denied having any rape fantasies. "I don't think about sex with Jacine as rape. I fantasized that it wasn't."

Salmon also admitted that he had a shoe fetish, particularly red shoes, and had once fantasized about having sex with little girls.

Meloy noted that while each defendant tended to blame the other, Woldt had done so to a much greater degree. Both had minimized "the horror the victim must have felt," but it was Woldt who in his confession indicated that he thought the victim had "some complicity" in what occurred.

The psychologist described Woldt as a "budding sexual sadist" who wanted an accomplice but needed to find someone who was dependent and had strong feelings of inadequacy. Meloy felt that Woldt might be a "lust killer," someone who killed as part of sex and "got off" on killing. He hated his mother and took it out on other women.

Meloy noted that Woldt told Rayna Rogers, another forensic psychologist who worked for Woldt's defense team, that it was Salmon who liked pornography that involved rape and sexual abuse. Meloy could scarcely conceal his contempt for his colleague's opinion that

Salmon was the instigator. He said it was obvious that
Rogers was "basing her data entirely on what Woldt told
her. . . . I find that to be remarkably naïve."

Salmon's personality disorder prevented Salmon from
exercising deliberation in Gielinski's murder, Meloy said.
He also suffered a "thinking disorder" that affected his
ability to differentiate between fantasy and reality. "Lucas
Salmon told his attorney and then told me that he thought
when he was arrested for this crime that he could be given
a ticket and allowed to go home.

"I find that extraordinary," Meloy said.

Even after two days on the witness stand, Meloy stuck
to his story that, contrary to evidence that seemed to imply
otherwise, Salmon was incapable of making decisions for
himself on the night of the murder. Young kept him there,
asking question after question as he cited Salmon's confession, but couldn't shake the psychiatrist.

At the end, Young noted that Meloy had written a book
in which he said many people have had homicidal fantasies without acting on them. "Do you?" Young asked.

"I have had homicidal fantasies, yes," Meloy conceded.

Noting the length of time he'd cross-examined the psychiatrist, Young smiled and said, "Hopefully you're not
having one now."

Meloy smiled back and for one of the few times since
the trial began, laughter was heard in the courtroom as he
replied, "Am I under oath?"

*March 4, 1999*

The courtroom was packed for the first time since early
in the trial. A hush fell over those assembled, who rose at
the command of the bailiff as Judge Parrish entered and
took his seat.

Peggy looked at the clock—a few minutes after 10:30

A.M. News that the verdict was in had come unexpectedly. The jury had only heard closing arguments and received its instructions from the judge late the previous afternoon, deliberated for perhaps a half hour, and then went home for the night.

After two days spent with Meloy, on both direct and cross-examination, the defense had trotted up its remaining experts, essentially to say the same thing as the first psychologist—that Salmon was brainwashed into committing the crime by Woldt, and that his personality and thinking defects rendered him incapable of any other choice.

The defense attorneys had shown a videotape of Salmon talking to one of the experts, hoping the tape would demonstrate his odd behavior. In it he spoke in the same unemotional, explicit detail that had struck Detective Crouch, such as his statement about stabbing Jacine: "It was surreal to me, an amazing disembodying feeling. I could feel the knife going into her."

The Luiszers thought that the videotape simply showed a killer who had no remorse and had found the whole experience interesting. But otherwise he was articulate and calculating, not the childlike "sweet little bunny," as Cleaver had referred to him during her closing arguments, sitting at the defense table, drawing on his pad as if the proceedings had nothing to do with him.

The prosecutors had countered the defense's mental health experts with their own. One of them, Kenneth Kassover, a Colorado Springs neuropsychologst, testified that the defense team learned but ignored that Robert Salmon was "disturbed sexually," which perhaps influenced his son's actions. He said the defense team interviewed one of the former baby-sitters who said that Robert Salmon, at about the same time he was being named an elder in his church in California, fondled her and engaged in oral sex when she was fourteen.

The same baby-sitter, Kassover said, told the defense

team that she was aware of other sexual liaisons Salmon had with other underage sitters, including her sister. The incidents, according to the psychologist, led to the breakup of Robert and Gail Salmon's marriage when Lucas was a boy.

Kassover conceded that he had not spoken to the babysitter himself, nor was Salmon arrested for sex with the underaged girls. (He declined to comment to the *Gazette* after Kassover's testimony as well).

Kassover said his revelation was "the most important aspect of this case," as it pointed to a background for Lucas Salmon to develop his own "perverse yearnings" rather than the defense claim that the idea to rape and murder was all George Woldt's.

Kassover said Lucas learned at a young age of his father's indiscretions and had a hard time reconciling the behavior with the strict, religious discipline of the household. "I think Lucas learned a lot from his dad," Kassover said. "For Lucas, even thinking about sex is a bad thing. . . . I think Lucas has been a very angry person, and he learned to stuff it."

The defense claims that Woldt's influence combined with Salmon's alleged brain disorders and diagnosis of a dependent personality disorder were "medical gymnastics that don't come close to explaining Lucas," Kassover said. "Lucas wanted what he was getting from George. He knew George was the way he was when he met him—and he liked it and wanted more of it.

"He made choices and they were choices he wanted. He was not just a pawn."

Peggy and Bob thought the prosecution experts came off as not so obviously in someone's hip pocket, like the defense experts. Essentially, their testimony pointed out that Salmon had on a number of occasions taken the lead in the crimes, and that even if he had a dependent personality disorder, it was not considered one likely to lead to criminal behavior, such as an antisocial personality disorder. Lucas Salmon helped rape and kill Jacine Gielinski because he wanted to, they said.

The Luiszers had not listened to much of the defense witness testimony. They either wore their earplugs, or even took a day or afternoon off from the trial when it got to be too much. One of the experts had testified that Salmon was so heavily influenced that he was "a victim, too," and that had pretty much done it for them.

On the day of the closings, Peggy was reading a magazine when she turned to a page with an advertisement that stopped her short. The ad contained a photograph of row after row of red shoes—dress shoes, running shoes—with a caption that read, WAS IT A FETISH? For one of the few times in the days since the trial began, Peggy laughed out loud. She cut out the ad and showed it to the media who gathered around her every morning before the court reconvened.

During the closings, Deputy District Attorney Young again went over Salmon's confession, pointing out the places where the defendant was obviously an equal partner or occasionally, the leader in the crimes against Jacine Gielinski and Amber Gonzales: "I took the knife, and prepared to cut her throat. I told George to lift her head up by the hair, and to cover her mouth. I then made my attack."

When it was over, Young said, Salmon had noted that at least he wasn't a virgin anymore. And to celebrate their accomplishment, they'd high-fived each other.

One more time, for a brief minute, Young was allowed to show the jurors the photograph of Jacine alive and remind them that the trial was about her, not the sullen, balding man doodling at the defense table. The rule about the photograph was silly, since the jury would have it in the deliberations room.

Cleaver, in the meantime, got to point to the poster of

the two defendants and note sadly how it clearly showed Salmon's position in the relationship. A shadow of the evil, sociopathic, "sexual sadist," George Woldt. She asked the jury to remember the defense experts' testimony that showed he was a "profoundly immature" young man and pawn. Yes, she conceded, he deserved to be punished. But he wasn't able to use the judgment and reflection necessary to be convicted of first-degree murder after deliberation and thus be subjected to the possibility of the death penalty.

Cleaver reminded the jury of her opening remarks, "That this is a long journey. Easy answers are not always the right answers." She pointed to posters created by the defense and hung in front of the jury to illustrate Salmon's thinking disorder—for example, that he thought he would be given a "ticket" for killing Jacine and allowed to go home; that he thought he would be allowed to learn woodworking in jail; and that he'd participated in the crime so that Woldt would not kick him out of the apartment.

"You've got to wonder about Lucas Salmon when you hear he placed George Woldt over God," she said. "No matter how much you hate him, you have to stop and say, 'What's going on?' Thank God this is something wrong with Lucas Salmon."

Zook came back on rebuttal and agreed "there's something wrong with Salmon, but so what? "Of course he has a personality disorder," he said. "So what? That's not a defense to anything."

He compared the defense theory to the story of Alice in Wonderland "depicting a world where absurdity reigns and no one cares. . . . There's where they want you to go. They want to pull you down a hole where nothing makes sense."

The prosecutor also ripped into the defense experts, noting they'd been paid more than $150,000 to testify to anything the defense wanted. "Money is a powerful motivator," he said. "That's what these people do . . . they fly around the country and testify."

Zook noted that Salmon led an active social life even when not around Woldt—he'd been in a band, had friends, girlfriends. "He wasn't a puppet on a string for George Woldt.

"Why did he do it? The shocking answer is he did it for fun." Zook paused and then repeated himself. "He did it for fun."

When the jury left the courtroom to begin deliberations, Peggy was asked by the media how she felt toward Bob Salmon, who'd told them about sending her letters and cards trying to apologize for his son. She said she'd called him once. "I know he's sorry, this is tragic for his whole family."

However, she added, her sympathy did not extend to his son or George Woldt. "I don't want these guys to see another sunrise and sunset another day. They don't deserve it."

After reaching the courthouse the next morning, Peggy and Bob split up. She wanted to get a cup of coffee, while he wanted to head to the victim's advocate office to see if there was any news. Then the courthouse loudspeaker crackled and a voice announced, "The verdict in the Salmon case is in."

The Luiszers met outside the courtroom and hurried in to the first pew behind the prosecution table. The Salmon family took their places behind the defense table, except for his mother, who wasn't yet in the building.

Peggy's heart soared. She believed that the quickness of the verdict could mean only one thing: Guilty.

The courtroom had quickly filled with the media, friends, and onlookers fortunate enough to find a seat before the guards stopped the rest. "No more room."

As the jurors filed in and took their seats, Parrish cautioned the spectators that he would not tolerate any outbursts. Accepting the papers from the jury, he cleared his throat and at 10:40 A.M., read the verdict.

In her seat, Peggy sobbed. Lucas Salmon had been found guilty on all counts. A minute later, Salmon's mother, Gail, rushed into the courtroom and up to where his family sat stone-faced. They whispered the outcome as she sank into her seat.

At the defense table, Salmon wasn't doodling for once. He sat in his chair next to Cleaver, wearing a sweater and button-down shirt, his face blank.

A few minutes later outside the courtroom, the attorneys addressed the assembled scribbling reporters with their microphones and cameras.

"A couple of our experts thought he was legally insane because he's so weird," Cleaver said after the verdict. "But we thought credibility was a real issue—and asking for insanity might have been asking too much."

The verdict was not unexpected. "I think there are some cases that are clear-cut, but we knew this case wouldn't be like that. This whole case is very subtle." On reflection, she said she thought showing the videotape of Salmon talking to the psychologists had backfired. "It showed him more normal than you would expect."

Now the defense would gear up for the death-penalty hearing. Cleaver noted that Salmon had been willing "from the beginning" to plead guilty if he could be sentenced to life in prison.

Asked about that comment by Cleaver, District Attorney Jeanne Smith said, "This case has never been about just first-degree murder. It's been about the death penalty. What Lucas Salmon did to Jacine Gielinski deserves the death penalty."

With Bob Luiszer standing behind her, Peggy also talked to the reporters. "Last night, I kept telling her to be with the jury—*Help them out, help them out,*" she said. "I imagine she's up there, and I bet she's having a Zima or something."

"It doesn't take the pain away," she said. "The pain is always going to be there because Jace isn't here."

The trial, she said, had not accomplished something she dearly wanted: an explanation. "That's what's always bothered us—there's never been a reason for what they did."

She said she'd kept trying to get Salmon to look her in the eye. "I think it would be big of him to say he's sorry," she said. "But it's not going to mean anything to him."

Asked what she would have said to him if he had looked her in the eye, Peggy said, "The Golden Rule applies."

Did she prefer life imprisonment or the death penalty? "Death," she said without hesitation.

Now, however, all eyes turned north, where another man's life would hang in the balance under the new legislation placing the burden of the death-penalty decision in Colorado on a panel of judges.

# THIRTEEN

# THE DEATH-
# PENALTY BAR

*April 14, 1999*
*Jefferson County, Colorado*

Robert Lee Riggan, Jr., a petty criminal for most of his life, sat at the defense table, staring at the panel of judges before him. "You're a motherfucking egomaniac," he snarled at Jefferson County District Court Judge Frank Plaut, who was presiding.

Pale, his face scarred and his hair shorn to an uneven stubble, Riggan was demanding to be allowed to return to his jail cell rather than attend his own death-penalty hearing. R. Brooke Jackson, another Jefferson County District Court judge, asked the defendant why he wouldn't want to be present for such an important life-or-death matter.

"I've got fifty pounds of shit on my back, and I don't want no part of this garbage," Riggan yelled. "Go ahead, kill me and get it over with. . . . I did not kill that girl, but there's nothin' I can do about it."

The "girl" was twenty-one-year-old Anita Paley, the mother of two young daughters and a crack addict who'd turned to prostitution to feed her habit. On May 16, 1997,

Riggan had been spotted dragging Paley up a mountain trail. Suffering from a severely fractured skull and brain damage, she'd died the next day. An emergency-room surgeon had also found a deep, three-inch-long cut inside Paley's vagina that had severed a major blood vessel; the physician had testified at Riggan's October 1998 trial that the cut had been made deliberately with a sharp instrument.

At that trial, Riggan had claimed that Paley had jumped from his van, fracturing her skull in the process. Although he had no explanation for the vaginal wound, his lawyers, Bob Hartley and Nathan Chambers, offered the theory that Paley must have been carrying a small glass container for drugs or money inside her vagina that broke when she struck the ground. The jurors didn't buy that, and they'd convicted Riggan. Still, the defense had won an important point when the jurors hung 8–3 (a twelfth juror had been released because of illness) on the charge of first-degree murder after deliberation, and instead found him guilty of first-degree felony murder.

The verdict came almost four years after the Colorado Legislature had changed the death-penalty statute, taking the decision of whether a convicted murderer should be put to death away from jurors and giving it to a panel of three judges. Now Riggan was about to find out if those judges would do what Colorado juries in the past had consistently refused to do: sentence a man to die for felony murder.

The new system had generated a firestorm of debate within the legal community. It played out in the media and would heat up even more due to the circumstances surrounding another death-penalty hearing some seventy miles to the south in Colorado Springs, that of Lucas Salmon.

In the days before Riggan's death-penalty hearing, the legal community had debated the new system in the media. Defense lawyers, who'd fought the switch back in 1995, predicted a population explosion on death row, currently occupied by Frank Rodriguez, Robert Harlan, and Nathan Dunlap. Gary Davis had been executed in October 1997. Ronald Lee White, forty-three, a self-professed serial killer, had been moved off death row because the Pueblo County District Attorney had recently received a box of investigative files related to White's case from the sheriff's office that had never been turned over to the DA, much less White's attorneys. Although the documents appeared to be duplicates of materials already presented, the DA had decided to go ahead and stipulate that White should get a new sentencing hearing. The date for that was still pending results of tests done on White for hepatitis C, a potentially fatal disease.

But while Colorado's death row had few residents in April 1999, six death-penalty hearings in addition to Riggan's, including Salmon's, were coming up. Colorado district attorneys also had announced that they'd seek the death penalty in four as-yet-untried murder cases, including George Woldt's. With judges now deciding whether defendants should die, defense attorneys were bracing for the worst.

"In Colorado, there have usually been one or two death-penalty cases pending anywhere in the state," David Lane, an outspoken critic of the death penalty who'd represented White in civil suits filed against prison guards, told a reporter. "Now there are a dozen. This never happened before. Murders here haven't all of a sudden gotten worse. Prosecutors know they're going to start filling up death row and are champing at the bit trying to do it. Judges are far quicker on the trigger."

The Riggan case had "serious issues of guilt or innocence," Lane added. And compared to other murders, Paley's death didn't rank "among the 1 or 2 percent of heinous murders the death penalty is designed for."

David Kaplan, the former public defender who five years earlier had represented killer Kevin Fears, declared that "the floodgates have opened up." He'd testified before the legislature against giving death sentence decisions to judges. In another month, he'd be standing before another death-penalty panel, trying to save the life of convicted killer Francisco "Pancho" Martinez.

"I call it the 'Texasification' of Colorado's death penalty," Kaplan told the press, referring to the Lone Star State's execution of 173 inmates since the U.S. Supreme Court reinstated the death penalty there in 1976. (Colorado had executed just one man—Davis—during that same stretch of time.) "Are we going to be a better community because we have twenty-five people on death row? I don't think that makes Texas a better community."

Kaplan mocked prosecutors' assertions that the three-judge panels would bring "consistency" to death-penalty hearings. "DAs wanted more calloused people to make the decision because they didn't trust the public," he said. "Jurors were taking their obligation seriously and not putting everyone on death row that prosecutors thought should be there."

Now district attorneys were trying to lower "the capital-punishment bar," he said. "Usually the death penalty is reserved for a certain group of defendants who are unique," Kaplan warned, "even among the group of individuals who have committed a homicide."

Riggan's own defense team added to the furor. Experienced, well-respected attorneys, they had been appointed from the Alternate Defense Counsel, the same group of which Salmon's lawyers, Cleaver and Enwall, were members.

Hartley, a former marine who'd tried several dozen murder cases, pointed out that while polls indicated that Coloradans overwhelmingly favored the death penalty, juries had been reluctant to impose it. "There's a difference between favoring the death penalty and imposing the death penalty in only the most extremely aggravated crimes," he said. "It doesn't mean you're in favor of killing every single person charged with first-degree murder."

Riggan had been convicted of first-degree felony murder, which meant a murder connected to the commission of another felony, in this case sexual assault. No Colorado jury had sent a man to death row for felony murder; historically, they'd balked unless the verdict was first-degree murder after deliberation with its requirement that the jury find that the murder was "intentional" and "premeditated."

"Do you think there's any possibility that a jury would impose a death penalty in my case?" Chambers, a former prosecutor, asked the press rhetorically. "There is none, and the prosecutors know it. The only reason they are seeking it is because it's in front of judges instead of citizens."

The defense bar had complained long and hard when, after the first-degree-felony-murder verdict came in, Jefferson County District Attorney Dave Thomas announced that his prosecutors, Chief Deputy District Attorney Dennis Hall and Deputy District Attorney Mandy Easter, would continue to seek the death penalty for Riggan.

The Riggan trial had not been a clear-cut case in which Riggan's guilt was never in doubt. But defense lawyers also knew that sooner rather than later, a felony-murder case would be brought before a panel of judges to test the new law.

The law was already being tested in other ways. On April 22, the day before the Riggan death-penalty hearing was to start, El Paso District Judge Michael Heydt resigned from the bench rather than sit on a death-penalty panel that would be considering the fate of Lucas Salmon.

The death-penalty panels comprised the trial judge, Plaut in Riggan's case and Parrish in Salmon's. As was previously mentioned, the other two members on a panel were selected by a computer from the pool of judges in the county in which the crime occurred, as well as surrounding counties. The computer had picked Heydt and Pueblo District Judge James Frasher and the hearing was scheduled for June 1999.

The new system was "unworkable," Heydt said in his letter of resignation to the Colorado Supreme Court. "I do not believe that a fair and just decision can be made by a panel of judges from a paper record. I do not wish to participate in a death-penalty process unless I believe that it is one that I can live with, not only as a judge but also as a human being."

Although in the past, judges had allowed jurors to be excused from death-penalty trials because they were adamantly opposed to the death penalty or believed that all killers should be put to death, as stated previously, judges did not have to be "death qualified" in order to sit on panels. They were sworn to uphold the law, but their oath of office did not specifically address whether they could participate in sentencing someone to death.

Heydt's objections to the new statute weren't all philosophical, however. He was concerned that, unlike the judge who'd presided over the trial, the two appointed members of the panel would have to rely on reading transcripts of the courtroom proceedings. What the judges would know of the witnesses and the crime would come from those transcripts; the rest they'd learn at the hearing.

Heydt's resignation had, of course, stoked the debate, even among other judges. "I guess if you were to extend his logic one step further, you would probably say that unless an appellate judge sat in a trial court, there could never be a fair and just decision," former Denver District Judge Federico Alvarez told a reporter. Appellate courts made their decision by reading the transcripts of a case and allowed lawyers only to argue the technical aspects of an appeal, such as improper decisions by the trial judge.

Defense attorneys applauded Heydt's moral choice, but they also worried about what it portended. Kaplan lamented that the resignation of "people of conscience" from the bench could actually mean more death sentences. The judges who remained, he said, would be those more favorably inclined toward the death penalty. Fighting the proposed statute in 1995, the former public defender had argued that judges would already be under political pressure to appease the voting public by handing down death sentences.

Even Judge Plaut entered the media fray. "I know judges well enough," he countered, "to know that they will not compromise their integrity by doing something just because it's popular. I don't know any judge that takes an issue like this lightly."

Plaut certainly did not. Until his appointment to the Jefferson County bench in September 1996, the sixty-seven-year-old jurist had spent most of his legal career as a civil lawyer. Before the Riggan trial, he had never presided over a first-degree murder case.

Although he had personal reservations about the death penalty in all but the most extreme cases, such as that of a convicted killer who killed again in prison or escaped from prison by killing a guard and then murdered again once in the community, he also believed that when he'd accepted his appointment to the bench, it became his duty to carry out the will of the people as expressed through the Colorado Legislature. And the will of the people was to have a death-penalty statute with an established set of guidelines to determine who qualified for the ultimate punishment and who did not. If a judge could not participate in the application of the death-penalty statute for philosophical or moral reasons, Plaut felt that the judge should remove himself from the case.

When the Riggan trial ended, the computer had selected Judge Jack F. Smith of Arapahoe County and Jackson of Jefferson County to sit with him on the panel. The sixty-one-year-old Smith had been a judge since 1987 and had presided over murder trials, but never a death-penalty case. Jackson, fifty-one, who'd also spent most of his career in civil law, had been on the bench only four months.

Plaut's chief concern with the Riggan case was how the three-judge panel should go about reaching its decision. The legislation that created the death-penalty panels did not address the process judges were to use. But about a month before Riggan's hearing began, the Colorado Supreme Court, in reviewing Nathan Dunlap's death sentence, had reaffirmed the four-step procedure that juries had been using to make that decision. Riggan and his colleagues agreed that they would follow the same steps at the Riggan hearing.

Riggan—foul-mouthed and virulent, spitting on his own lawyers—had refused to participate in the hearing and was allowed to spend it in his cell. Instead, he listened to the proceedings as they were transmitted over a speaker there.

Other than a panel of three judges instead of twelve jurors, the death penalty proceedings were still a minitrial. Following opening statements by both sides, the prosecution had presented its case of aggravating factors, statutorily defined reasons for imposing the death penalty. Then the defense had presented its mitigating factors, reasons the defendant might deserve a life sentence. In Riggan's case, the defense focused on his abysmal childhood. The lawyers had then given their closing statements, after which Judge Plaut announced that the panel would render its decision on April 23, 1999.

The courtroom was full that morning as members of the legal community and the media waited to hear the judges' decision. However, the courtroom was curiously subdued. The debate over the death penalty had suddenly taken a backseat to an act of violence so overwhelming that such wars of words seemed trivial. Three days earlier, on April 20, 1999, the worst high school massacre in American history occurred when Columbine High seniors Eric Harris and Dylan Klebold slaughtered thirteen people, injured two dozen more, and then turned their guns on themselves.

The life and death of a career criminal who'd murdered a prostitute hardly seemed to matter except to Riggan, those who'd argued whether he deserved to live or die, and those who would make the decision. The defendant, looking both frightened and angry, sat at the defense table for the first time since demanding to skip the hearing. On the dais above a silent Jefferson County courtroom, Plaut cleared his throat. He was well aware that he was about to make Colorado history by handing down the first sentence from a three-judge panel in a death-penalty case. The other judges sat on either side, gazing solemnly at the packed spectator gallery.

Plaut announced that the panel did accept the aggravating factor that "the offense" was "especially heinous, cruel or depraved." However, the judges agreed that Riggan did not have a significant criminal history, one of the mitigators, and had been "raised in what can only be described as a horribly dysfunctional family. Regrettably, this was a family plagued by incest, sexual abuse, squalor, poverty and emotional neglect of Mr. Riggan and his siblings."

The third step of the process required that the aggravators be weighed against the mitigators, and the judges unanimously concluded that the aggravator outweighed the mitigators. In other weighing states, this finding would have meant a death sentence for Riggan. But Colorado had the fourth step: The decision had to be made whether, all things considered, the defendant "deserved" to die.

In Colorado's history, jurors had refused to take that fourth step in felony-murder cases. And now, so did a panel of judges. "We unanimously conclude, beyond a reasonable doubt, that a sentence of death is not appropriate in this case," Plaut announced, reading from the decision, which had been written by Jackson. "It is, in our view, entirely appropriate that Riggan be removed from society and pay a price that, at least in the view of some, may even be more severe than death itself. But a civilized society should not and cannot take the life of a human being, even one who commits an especially heinous, cruel and depraved offense, if a jury could not conclude beyond a reasonable doubt that the individual in fact administered the fatal injury.

"As much as we are all pained by the loss of Ms. Paley and the unspeakable affront to her body that was performed by Mr. Riggan, our values must be different than that."

When it was over, even defense attorneys had to concede that the Riggan panel had not "lowered the bar" for the imposition of the death penalty as they had feared. Now Hartley told the press that he'd never believed that judges would impose more death sentences.

"This decision means the same thing juries have been telling us for years," he said. "They don't like to sentence to death on felony murder without more. The death penalty should be reserved for only the most aggravated and extreme cases."

With Riggan out of the way, the Colorado legal community's attention now turned to two death-penalty cases that would be heard simultaneously beginning April 27: Jacques Richardson's in Denver, and that of Daniel Martinez, Jr., again in Jefferson County. Each would test the new system in different ways.

Jacques Richardson had accosted Janey Benedict, a thirty-four-year-old tour guide, in her Capitol Hill apartment in June 1997. He'd put a noose around her neck and then hog-tied her. A neighbor heard the commotion and called the police, who arrested Richardson after he jumped from Benedict's second-story window. By the time the police reached Benedict, the young woman had strangled and was unconscious; she would die soon after.

The twenty-eight-year-old Richardson was not just a burglar, he was a serial rapist. After his arrest, he was charged with three unrelated rapes and convicted of two, for which he was sentenced to 216 years in prison. Denver District Attorney Bill Ritter charged Richardson with first-degree murder after deliberation and first-degree felony murder for the Benedict murder; he said his prosecutors, Bonnie Benedetti and Martin Egelhoff, would be seeking the death penalty.

Richardson's was the first death-penalty case in Denver since the 1997 trial of Jon Morris, who'd kidnapped, raped, and strangled five-year-old Ashley Gray. At the trial, Morris's public defenders argued that he was mentally ill and therefore didn't know the difference between right and wrong, even though he'd tried to conceal the girl's body in a dumpster. The jury had acquitted Morris of first-degree murder after deliberation and agreed instead on a verdict of first-degree felony murder, as well as charges of kidnapping, sexual assault, and sexual assault on a child. Given the historic reluctance of juries to sentence a defendant to death for felony murder, Ritter decided not to seek the death penalty and settled for life in prison without parole for Morris.

In Richardson's case, any hope of a death-penalty verdict ended before the trial even started, although that wasn't immediately apparent. The prosecutors had hoped to introduce Richardson's "prior similar criminal acts"— the rapes he'd committed—to show that his motive in binding Benedict was not simple robbery and that the sexual assaults were escalating in violence with each victim.

Usually, defense lawyers are able to keep a defendant's

prior criminal history out of evidence, on the grounds that the defendant is to be tried for the crime for which he is on trial, not his past. However, the legislature had passed a "prior similars" statute, designed to deal with serial rapists in particular, which allowed prosecutors to present testimony of previous acts if they could demonstrate to the trial judge that the current charge fit into a pattern. The statute was rarely used because defense attorneys fought such motions tooth and nail, and judges tended to view the law very narrowly and in favor of the defendant.

In the Richardson case, public defenders Terri Brake, who'd represented death-row inmate Robert Harlan a year earlier and would be representing George Woldt, and her co-counsel Charles Garcia won a major victory after the prosecutors asked Denver District Judge Stephen Phillips to allow Richardson's rapes into evidence. Phillips determined that the prosecutors would be allowed to use the evidence only if they agreed to two trials for Richardson: one for first-degree murder after deliberation, the other for first-degree felony murder. And, the judge said, he would only let them use the "prior similar acts" at the felony-murder trial if the argument was that Richardson had killed Benedict while committing the felony of rape.

Although he was accustomed to judges rejecting motions to present prior similars, Ritter had never heard of a judge separating a single murder into two trials. The Denver District Attorney tried to protest Phillips's decision to the Colorado Supreme Court, but the state's top judges said they wouldn't even listen to Ritter's arguments until long after Richardson's case was scheduled for trial.

Ritter was stuck. He was sure that with the evidence of the earlier rapes, a jury would understand that Benedict's murder was no accident by a frightened cat burglar and would convict him of first-degree murder after deliberation. Without the rapes in evidence, it wasn't going to be easy.

On the other hand, there was no question, as there had been in the Riggan trial, that Richardson had killed Benedict or that she had suffered a long, torturous death. Ritter thought that there was still a good chance that the state's case, even without the rapes, would be enough to have Richardson sentenced to death. He also didn't want to put Benedict's family through two trials and then a death-penalty hearing, so he rejected Phillips's compromise. Richardson would be tried once without the rapes becoming part of the evidence that the jury would hear.

At Richardson's trial, prosecutors argued that Benedict was bound so tightly that the slightest movement caused the noose around her neck to strangle her just a little more. But the defense countered that Richardson only wanted to subdue Benedict so that he could rob her. The jury ended up split on the charge of first-degree murder after deliberation. Instead, as in the Riggan case, Richardson was convicted of first-degree felony murder—killing Benedict during the felony of robbery.

Defense attorney Brake believed that by keeping the prior similars out of the testimony, and by gaining the lesser murder conviction she'd saved Richardson from a death sentence. The jury couldn't agree that her client had deliberated before killing Benedict, which, as in the Riggan case, would be a "very significant factor" for a panel of judges to consider, she told the media.

When the felony-murder verdict had come down in the Morris case, Ritter had decided against pursuing the death penalty. But he thought the Richardson case stood a better chance. He was well aware that the panel of judges had refused to condemn Riggan to death for felony murder, but there were dramatic differences between the Morris, Riggan, and Richardson cases that he thought judges might find compelling.

Morris, for instance, did not have Richardson's history of violent sexual assault, and although the prosecution had been prevented from presenting Richardson's history at trial, it would be fair game at a death-penalty hearing. And while Riggan's guilt had been hotly contested by the defense and also by several jurors, there was never any question that Richardson had killed Benedict. Richardson's criminal history would also be a slam-dunk aggravator, whereas Riggan's comparative lack of a criminal history had served as a mitigator in his case. Ritter decided to go for the death penalty.

Richardson's panel would include three judges from Denver: trial judge Phillips, as well as Paul Markson and Joseph Meyer III. Phillips decided to take a different approach to the hearing than Plaut had in Jefferson County. His panel would listen to the evidence for each of the four steps and make a decision in each before moving on.

Since the first step was to determine if the prosecution could prove beyond a reasonable doubt the existence of at least one aggravator, the panel listened to the prosecution's case, then heard arguments for and against the aggravators. Phillips then announced that the panel had determined that Benedict's murder was not "especially heinous, cruel and depraved," because it did not fit in "those murders which are 'conscienceless, pitiless and unnecessarily torturous to the victims,'" a definition handed down by the Colorado Supreme Court in an appeal of the Gary Davis case. But the judges did grant the aggravator that Richardson had committed the murder in the course of another felony, robbery.

And so they moved on to the second step, determining whether any mitigating circumstances would cause them to hesitate in imposing the death sentence. Nothing in Richardson's past or present mitigated his accountability, the judges concluded, moving on through the third step and determining easily that the prosecution had met the necessary standard for Richardson to be considered eligible for the death penalty. Then, one last time, the lawyers from both sides again squared off to argue, this time over the fourth step, whether Richardson deserved to die.

On May 8, 1999, the panel announced its verdict: Richardson would be spared. Echoing the Riggan panel, the Denver jurists noted that neither a Colorado jury nor a panel of judges had ever sent a defendant to death row for anything less than first-degree murder after deliberation.

"We all see Richardson as a morally culpable, despicable and dangerous human being who, prior to being a felony assailant, burglar and murderer, was a manipulator, freeloader and abuser," the judges determined. "But the statutory scheme is one designed to distinguish the most horrendous first-degree murders from the rest. That statutory scheme has, to date, produced no death penalty except for premeditated, intentional murder."

Outside the courtroom, Mary Sue Hoaglin, Benedict's mother, said she was satisfied with the verdict. Richardson would spend the rest of his life in prison, where he couldn't harm anybody else. "I thank the state of Colorado for what they've done for us," she added.

"I think it was a correct decision, a legally correct decision," said defense attorney Garcia. "My goal in doing this was to save Mr. Richardson's life, and this is what we did. I don't believe in the taking of human life by the state, particularly in this case."

Ritter told the press that he didn't think the decision necessarily indicated that judges' decisions would mirror those of juries past. Nor did he think the switch to death-penalty panels had been a mistake. "It's too early," he said.

As Ritter spoke, he was aware that that same afternoon, a third murderer had escaped a death-penalty verdict, this time back in Jefferson County. Despite the fears of defense attorneys, the bar had again remained firmly in place, even for a man accused of one of the state's most horrific crimes: the murder of Brandaline Rose DuVall.

On May 30, 1997, Brandy was a petite fourteen-year-old who loved her mother, got good grades, and looked forward to graduating from middle school in a couple of days. She was growing up; just a few weeks earlier, she'd brought home her first rose from a boy.

Brandy took a bus to a friend's house that evening. They smoked pot and persuaded a man to buy them a six-pack of beer. A little before midnight, she said good night to her friend and walked to a bus stop on Federal Boulevard to catch a ride home. Brandy was waiting there, wearing a bright red Chicago Bulls jersey bearing the number of her favorite player, Michael Jordan, when a carload of young men pulled up. The shirt, a favorite of those in the Bloods gang, had attracted their attention.

No one knows why Brandy got in the car that night or whether she was forced to do so. But the young men took her to a house in Adams County, where older core members of the Deuce Seven subset of the Crenshaw Mafia Gangster Bloods had spent the day getting drunk and smoking pot. The house was rented by Jose "Uncle Joe" Martinez, Jr., the uncle of Daniel Martinez, Jr., known on the streets as "Bang" and one of the Deuce Seven founders.

Another original Deuce Seven member, Francisco "Pancho" Martinez, Jr., was also there. He and Danny had been inseparable since elementary school, and as young teens they had been "beat in" to the CMG Bloods at the same time. The last two members of the core group present were Sammy "Zig Zag" Quintana, Jr., a first cousin of Danny's, and sixteen-year-old Frank Vigil Jr., a protégé of Danny's nicknamed "Little Bang."

Over the next several hours, Brandy was stripped, raped, sodomized, and cut with a knife; Francisco Martinez shoved a broom up her rectum. When they were through raping her, the gang members handcuffed and hooded her and began talking about how she had to be killed so that she couldn't go to the police.

Brandy was placed in the backseat of Quintana's car, between Danny Martinez and Vigil. Quintana drove, with Francisco Martinez in the front passenger seat. As they headed into the mountains, Brandy pleaded for her life, promising she wouldn't tell what had happened to her. Instead of showing mercy, Francisco turned around and began stabbing her in the chest and stomach with a knife. When Quintana complained that he was getting blood on the seats, Francisco stopped stabbing Brandy and instead started strangling her.

Several miles up Highway 6, Quintana pulled over next to a steep embankment above Clear Creek. Brandy was pulled from the car and knocked to the ground. As Quintana held her head and Danny and Frank looked on, Francisco stabbed her repeatedly in the neck, cutting the carotid artery and jugular vein. Quintana and Francisco then picked up the girl and threw her down the embankment.

The gang was back in the car when Francisco announced that he'd misplaced the murder weapon. Danny got out and retrieved it. Then, on their way back to the city, Danny Martinez remarked, "I guess this makes us serial killers now."

Although she'd been stabbed twenty-eight times, at least twice fatally, Brandy didn't die immediately. She tried to struggle up the embankment, hands still cuffed behind her back, then fell back down. Finally, she bled to death next to the stream, where her body was spotted later that morning, May 31, by a tourist.

Angela Metzger, who'd been desperately searching for her daughter, didn't know what had happened to Brandy until the next day. She hurried to the morgue and identified first her daughter's jewelry, then her daughter's body.

"Wake up, baby," she cried, pounding on the glass partition that separated her from her child. "Wake up!"

Eventually, Jose Martinez told a friend what had happened at his home; his friend contacted the police. Confronted, Martinez told police that his nephew and other members of the Bloods gang had acted like they were "possessed by the fuckin' devil" when they tormented the girl. "Uncle Joe" was soon joined on the prosecution's star witness list by Quintana, who'd been charged with two counts of first-degree murder after deliberation. Like the others, he'd been arraigned for Brandy's murder, but he was also charged with the shooting death of nineteen-year-old Venus Montoya a year earlier. Faced with two possible death-penalty hearings, Quintana had an attack of conscience, found religion, and quickly agreed to testify against the others in exchange for being allowed to plead guilty to two counts of second-degree murder.

Frank Vigil, charged with first-degree murder after deliberation, was the first of the gang members to go on trial for Brandy's murder, in January 1998. Since he was still under eighteen, he was not eligible for the death penalty.

Vigil was represented by Randy Canney, a former public defender now in private practice. Canney had never tried a first-degree-murder case, and there wasn't much he could do with this one other than try to get the jury to go for something less than first-degree murder and life in prison without parole.

Canney's strategy was to convince the jurors that his client, the smallest and youngest gang member, was the least involved. But the prosecution team pointed out that Vigil had plenty of involvement that didn't suggest he was afraid of anything other than getting caught. It took the jury only six hours to convict Vigil of first-degree murder after deliberation, and he was sentenced to life in prison.

Francisco "Pancho" Martinez went on trial in August

1998, before Jefferson County Judge Michael Villano. He was defended by David Kaplan and Patrick Ridley. On September 3, after only two hours of deliberation, the jury came back with its verdict: guilty of first-degree murder after deliberation, sexual assault, sexual assault on a child using force, and kidnapping.

Danny Martinez went on trial in February 1999, represented by Dave Lindsey and Forrest "Boogie" Lewis, whose last death-penalty client had been Nathan Dunlap. Jefferson County Judge Leland Anderson presided. This jury took a little longer than Francisco's had to reach a verdict, but the result was the same: guilty of first-degree murder after deliberation.

Danny Martinez was in front of Judge Anderson again on April 27, 1999, just four days after the conclusion of Riggan's death-penalty hearing in the same courtroom, and a week after the Columbine shootings. Anderson was flanked by Judges Timothy Fasing of Arapahoe County and John Coughlin of Denver, the panel that would decide whether he would be sentenced to death.

"The presumption of innocence is gone," Deputy District Attorney Ingrid Bakke said, delivering the Jefferson County prosecution's opening statement for the fourth time in the DuVall case. "Mr. Martinez sits before you, a convicted murderer." Bakke was normally assigned to the unit that deals with sex crimes against children; this had been her first homicide case. And this was the first time she would ask for another human being's execution. To do so had taken a lot of soul-searching for the prosecutor, who wasn't sure where she stood on the death penalty when she was assigned to the case. But as she'd assembled the aggravators with her two colleagues on the case, Deputy District Attorneys Hal Sargent and Mark Randall, she'd come to believe that the punishment fit the crime.

That decision had its price. Defense attorneys with whom she'd once been on friendly terms went out of their way to avoid her, wouldn't even speak to her, because she was helping prosecute a death-penalty case. She'd crossed the line. Now she was more than just a courtroom adversary; she was the enemy.

Bakke didn't waste a lot of time making an emotional pitch. The three judges wouldn't be swayed by courtroom theatrics, or so prosecutors had argued when pushing for the statute that gave judges, rather than a jury, the responsibility of issuing a death sentence. Instead, she laid the groundwork for the four-step process that the judges would follow to reach their decision. The prosecution, she said, would prove beyond a reasonable doubt five of the seventeen possible aggravators allowed by law, several of which—such as killing a kidnap victim—had been added after Gary Davis murdered Ginny May.

For the second time in a month, Jeffco prosecutors were testing whether judges would do what juries had not. Danny Martinez had been convicted of first-degree murder after deliberation. The prosecution theory presented to the jury was that while Danny had participated in the rape and torment of Brandy DuVall and had called the shots as the gang's leader, Francisco Martinez had stabbed the girl to death. So the wording in Danny's first-degree murder count included the "complicity instruction," which meant the jury didn't have to find that Danny had done the actual stabbing, just that he was a "principal in the offense."

It was essentially the same instruction that a Denver jury had been given in the death-penalty case against Chris Rodriguez, who'd raped Lorraine Martelli back in 1984 and stood by as his brother, Frank, raped and then stabbed her to death. The jury had found Chris guilty of first-degree murder after deliberation, too, but then wouldn't go for the death penalty because he had not done the actual killing. He got life in prison; Frank was sentenced to death.

Danny Martinez's case would be another test of what separated killers who got life in prison from killers who got a lethal injection. This time, though, Jeffco prosecutors thought they had a better chance than they had with Robert Riggan. The Danny Martinez case was as good as they were going to get for a complicitor case. He'd done everything except stab the girl, and in some ways—the amount of sexual contact, for example, and his role in deciding her fate—he'd gone beyond even that of Francisco Martinez. It was hard to imagine a more heinous case or what more a complicitor would have to do in order to qualify for the death penalty.

Bakke was almost at the end of her opening. Before the hearing, she'd told friends that it had given her a strange, unpleasant feeling when she wrote down the last line: "The People respectfully request that you sentence Danny Martinez, Jr., to death." Now she felt comfortable saying it out loud, but she took no joy in it.

In Lewis's opening statement, the defense attorney outlined Martinez's rough childhood and said his client had many good qualities. But it was clear what the crux of the defense would be: blaming Danny's childhood friend. "Danny is guilty of complicity," Lewis conceded. "But the blood of Brandy . . . is on the hands of Francisco Martinez."

The judges had an alternative to sentencing Danny to death. "He'll never get out of prison," Lewis pointed out. "He'll never see his children except through bars. He should be in prison for the rest of his life, and he will be. But the death penalty . . . is excessive."

As Lewis spoke, Jim Aber, the chief deputy for the state public defender's office, sat listening on the defense side of the spectator gallery. The Golden-based Aber was a frequent critic of the Jefferson County DA's Office for its death-penalty decision. But he was also the lawyer who'd represented Sammy Quintana in his dealings with the prosecution; he'd even spoken up at Quintana's sentencing following Danny's trial, praising his client's "truthfulness" on the witness stand. "Mr. Quintana has really brought down the Deuce Seven gang and the CMG Bloods gang," he told Judge Villano. In Quintana, he'd seen "more remorse and rehabilitation than I think in any other client I've ever seen."

The irony of Aber sitting on the defense side now was not lost on court observers. He might have saved his client from the death penalty, but Quintana was one of the main reasons that two others, his cousin and his friend, were facing the possibility of a death sentence.

It took the prosecutors only that one day to lay out their case for the aggravators. The defense attorneys would use the next three to present their side. Over the objections of the prosecution, they were allowed to bring in witnesses who testified regarding the "evil" Francisco Martinez, to contrast him to Danny.

And again over the prosecution's objections, the defense was allowed to call one of its own investigators to the stand, where she discussed death-penalty statistics she'd obtained from the NAACP Legal Defense Fund. According to those statistics, of the 6,331 people sentenced to die since the Supreme Court had reinstated the death penalty in 1976, only seventy-six were "non-triggermen," or complicitors. Defense attorney Lindsey told the panel that those statistics provided a "moral sense" of the record regarding complicitor sentencing around the country.

At the end of the defense case, Danny Martinez shuffled to the podium for the traditional show of remorse. "Your Honors, I just want to apologize to both families—my family, Brandy's family—for what has taken place. Also to your Honors about putting them in a position like this," he said.

"I know it's not easy for nobody, and there's really not no words . . . you know, there ain't no words that could really just explain anything about this. So, you know, there's no—any hard feelings against anybody, no matter what happens, and I'll just make the best out of whatever happens. And thank you for being respectful to my lawyers. Thank you."

The prosecution's closing arguments fell to Randall. He started right in on what he knew would be the heart of the defense's closing argument: that Danny was not the man who'd actually stabbed Brandy. "He intended her death after her torture," Randall said. "The only thing that he does not do is physically place the knife into her body. He has Francisco for that."

Randall reviewed the prosecution's five aggravators and pointed out that no mitigator came close to balancing them. And when the prosecutor arrived at his case for the fourth step, he didn't even try to argue that the death penalty served as a deterrent. Instead, he asked for retribution: "Some crimes are simply so shocking that society insists on the adequate appropriate punishment. He should die because of every horrible, torturous act that he did to that girl."

There was no need to compare Danny Martinez to his friend, Randall continued. "The standard of the death penalty is not Francisco Martinez. The bar is not Francisco Martinez. Francisco Martinez may be a hundred miles above the bar. There's other people that go over that bar, too, and he's one of them," he said, pointing at Danny. "Sentence him to the only appropriate sentence there is: death."

As soon as Randall finished, Lewis rose to deliver his closing. "I'm so tired of seeing the carnage in these cases, and there is much in this one," he said. But although what his client had done was bad, it was not as bad as what others had done. "He's not a killer," Lewis said of Danny. "This man was not on the road to killing anybody. He's no Francisco. He's not an evil person.

"Do we kill a person who did not himself kill this little girl? Or should the death penalty be reserved for those worse cases, for the worse people, for those by whose hand the death of sweet, innocent people was caused?"

Although the prosecution had argued against their inclusion, during the rebuttal that followed Lewis's closing, Randall used the NAACP statistics to his advantage, noting that some complicitors had been sentenced to death. "We don't know the facts of all those cases," the prosecutor said. "But what those statistics do tell us is that there are some cases in which it is absolutely appropriate for even a non-triggerman to be sentenced to die, and Colorado is now facing one, right here and right now."

Randall pointed out that many people, including some of Danny's own family members, had grown up in the same bad neighborhood and yet had not become killers or gang members. "He comes out of that neighborhood as the evil murderer that he is, and other people do not. Why? Because he's different. Because he's capable of what he did to Brandy, and the others are not," Randall said. "There is only one punishment appropriate for the horror of this crime. It must stop. It must stop. He's been given enough chances. No more.

"Brandy's now dead. Danny Martinez must be sentenced to death."

On the morning of May 7, the courtroom filled quickly as everyone waited for the judges to deliver their verdict.

Angela Metzger sat behind the prosecution table, numb. Although she didn't believe that Danny would get the death penalty, the thought didn't disappoint her; she knew that he would spend his life behind bars. And her heart went out to Theresa Swinton, Danny's mother, who was losing her child, too. She'd been upset when the defense attorneys had attacked Swinton, as if what had happened to Brandy had been her fault. Danny Martinez was a grown man who had made his choices.

Behind the defense table, Swinton fought to control her fear. When called by the defense to testify, she'd taken the opportunity to apologize to Angela Metzger and the rest of Brandy's family. Now all her thoughts were on her first-born. *Please don't let them kill my son,* she prayed.

The judges came into the courtroom, and Anderson warned the standing-room-only crowd that anyone who felt that he might not be able to control himself should leave. "Those people of courage, respect and civility," he said, "are welcome to sit with me at this time."

Then Anderson quickly announced, "We cannot reach a unanimous verdict." The words took a moment to sink in: Danny Martinez would not be sentenced to die.

Only later would those in the courtroom learn how close Martinez had come to death. Anderson and Fasing agreed that the prosecution had proved three of the five aggravators and that those aggravators outweighed the mitigators. In particular, they rejected the idea that Danny's participation in a murder "committed by another" was "relatively minor." Nor did they allow him to blame drugs and alcohol for his behavior. They did, however, sympathize with his "difficult and even tragic childhood" and allowed that as a mitigator.

Still, at the fourth step, Anderson and Fasing noted that Danny's history and background included a long series of decisions to engage in criminal conduct and that he evinced an attitude of reckless indifference to the possibilities of violence and confrontation between gangs. "The fact that the defendant did not administer the lethal wounds is a circumstance which pales when measured against the series of brutal acts leading up to the killing of Brandy DuVall," they determined. And they agreed that it was constitutionally permissible for a complicitor, "under appropriate circumstances, to be executed in a capital case." And the circumstances in this case were appropriate because Martinez's "participation was substantial and his intent murderous." For this reason, they would have imposed a sentence of death.

But Judge Coughlin had disagreed. In fact, he didn't even get as far as the fourth step. He accepted only one of the aggravators: that Danny Martinez had conspired with others to kill Brandy. In rejecting the aggravator that he'd "committed the offense in an especially heinous, cruel or depraved manner," Coughlin said he interpreted "offense" to mean only the act of stabbing Brandy to death.

Coughlin was also much more generous in accepting mitigators. Again interpreting "the offense" to mean only the stabbing, he agreed that Martinez was not the "principal in the offense" and that his participation was "relatively minor." He accepted the mitigators that Danny was drunk and had had a difficult childhood that influenced his actions. Those mitigators, he said, outweighed the single aggravator, and so there was no reason to proceed to the fourth step.

Although Coughlin had already eliminated any possibility that Martinez would be put to death, he went on to contradict Anderson and Fasing, asserting that the Colorado Supreme Court "clearly holds that the death penalty may not constitutionally be imposed on a defendant convicted on a complicity theory."

For the third time in as many attempts, a killer had avoided the death sentence. And even though judges were now in charge of the decision, once again the will of the majority had been overruled by a single vote.

Going into the trial, the prosecution team had concerns about Coughlin, a staunch Catholic who went to Mass daily. But they'd gone on the assumption that if Coughlin was philosophically opposed to the death penalty, he would have removed himself from the process.

Coughlin's holdout raised concerns among the pro-death penalty faction that judges did not have to be death qualified, as jurors had been. But Jefferson County District Attorney Thomas, echoing the words Denver DA Ritter uttered that same afternoon, said it was too early to dump the new statute. "We've just started the process," he said.

The district attorneys recognized that all three of these cases had issues that would have troubled juries, too. But in just a few days, Thomas's prosecution team would take a fourth case before a panel of judges, a case with no such issues.

If black came in different shades, as Randall had remarked, it didn't get any darker than Francisco "Pancho" Martinez, Jr.

Deputy District Attorney Hal Sargent of Jefferson County took a last glance at his notes before looking up at the judges. It was May 19, 1999, just two weeks shy of the day two years before when Brandy DuVall's savaged body was found alongside Clear Creek. Two years of prosecuting members of the Deuce Seven Bloods gang for Brandy's rape and murder were nearly at an end.

The task had been monumental. Endless meetings with defense attorneys to make deals and get co-defendants to roll over and testify against the others. Innumerable hearings to quibble over legal technicalities. Three murder trials. Two death-penalty hearings, including this one, for Francisco Martinez, Jr.

Francisco's defense team alone had filed more than three hundred motions between his trial and the hearing. Most of the motions contested the constitutionality of the three-judge death-penalty panels, attacking the statute from every conceivable angle. Others seemed designed merely to take up time and resources, such as the motion that demanded to be informed of any "known side effects" of the drugs used for lethal injection and whether those drugs had been approved by the Food and Drug Administration. The defense had won perhaps half a dozen of its motions, although none that challenged the panel's authority or greatly affected the prosecution's strategy. Yet each issue had to be researched and answered.

The prosecution team was physically and emotionally spent. The prosecutors' workdays began at six in the morning and continued until ten at night. There was never any downtime; another hearing or trial or sentencing always loomed a week or two away. None of the members had taken a real vacation in nearly two years. Even weekends were spent working.

The emotional demands were just as wearing. They all had dreams about the case: the crime, the people, the testimony. And it never got any easier. Every glance at the photographs of Brandy's mangled body brought back all the horrors.

Things had gotten even rougher after Danny Martinez's death-penalty hearing had ended in a life sentence. Sargent worried that his material was growing old, flat. He didn't want Brandy DuVall to be remembered as a two-dimensional footnote in the law books, but rather as a young girl who'd died horribly at the hands of these young men.

Francisco's lawyers looked worn out, too. The saying "death is different" applies to defense attorneys as well as prosecutors. They weren't immune to the tears shed by the victim's family; they had to look at the same photographs and listen to the testimony describing their client's monstrous act. But it was their job to try to save the lives of killers.

David Kaplan and Patrick Ridley had fought hard and bitterly, filing ten times the number of motions that Danny Martinez's team had filed. The prosecution called them obstructionist, but Judge Coughlin's position on Danny's case was proof that it took just one argument, heard by just one judge, to prevent a death-penalty verdict. The defense attorneys weren't counting on that, though. And in every motion that was turned down, every objection that was overruled, they saw the possibility of an appeal. Even if the three judges sentenced Francisco to death, the fight would not be over.

Francisco Martinez sat at the end of the defense table. His hair had been shaved to a dark bristle that matched his goatee. He wore a long-sleeved white dress shirt that hid the gang tattoos on his arms and covered the electric-shock belt that bulged from his lower back.

Like Riggan, Francisco hadn't been in the courtroom for most of the death-penalty hearing. On the first day, his lawyers had asked that he be allowed to stay in his cell; he didn't want to hear the bad things they were going to say about his family members as they attempted to save his life. Of course, that meant he wouldn't have to hear from Brandy's family about the suffering he'd caused them, either. But he'd been back in the courtroom for the last two days of the hearing, listening to defense psychologists explain why he had joined a gang, explain his propensity for violence, and explain his inability to make good decisions while drunk and "under stress."

On the last day, before the closing arguments, Francisco had made his apology. Addressing the panel—Denver District Judge Robert Hyatt, Arapahoe County District Judge Deanna Hickman, and Villano—he said: "Your honors, I want to apologize to Angela Metzger, and Paul and Rose Vasquez, and say that I am deeply sorry for my participation in this crime. . . . She didn't do anything to deserve what happened. You didn't deserve this."

That was it. Then Sargent had begun his closing statement. "We would have to search a long time in the darkest reaches of our minds and imaginations to come up with a crime more depraved than this one," he told the courtroom. "We've seen hell in its most human form."

But that wasn't the point, Kaplan responded in his closing. "Who should live and who should die is not an easy question for a civilized society," he told the judges, urging them to make their decision "not just according to legal

concepts, but moral concepts." Then he ended his remarks
by recalling the Columbine shootings a month earlier. A
civilized society, he said, needed to ask questions about
what events preceded "something this horrible . . . whether
Brandy DuVall or Columbine, and what might have been
done to prevent either one."

This was the first time he'd had to argue whether a client
should live or die, Kaplan said, "and I'm not quite sure
how to sit down. Tomorrow it will be too late." He asked
the judges to try to understand the forces that created Francisco "and, hopefully, to understand is to forgive."

Then Sargent got the last word. "Mr. Kaplan ended with
a point that I think deserves some comment," he said. "Can
we explain? Can we understand Mr. Martinez?

"To understand does not mean to excuse. We can hope
to understand and to explain what combination of forces
make Francisco Martinez the man he is. But when we're
done with that, when we're done explaining who he is, the
question is, so what? What do we make of it? Do we excuse him?"

As Sargent spoke, twenty-five-year-old Francisco kept
his eyes averted. He no longer looked like the cocky gang-
banger who'd smirked at his murder trial, but like a man
who realized he'd reached the end of the line.

"Whatever combination of forces brought Francisco
Martinez to be the man he is," Sargent continued, "he is an
absolutely dangerous man. . . . All you've got to do is listen to him if you want to know what makes him tick, what
he is about."

Walking over to a blackboard where the defense had
created a time line charting Francisco's unhappy childhood
through his monstrous adulthood, Sargent pointed to several photographs of the defendant as an infant and a boy.
"I have sympathy for this child of one or eight who may
have seen more than any child should be exposed to," he
said. "That he failed to learn, failed to change his behav-

ior, is not our fault. He has to be held accountable for those decisions he made."

Then the prosecutor pulled out a book written by psychiatrist Willard Gatlin, in which he lamented the aftermath of the murder of a young woman named Bonnie Garland. " 'When one person kills another,' " Sargent quoted Gatlin, " 'there is an immediate revulsion at the nature of the crime. But in a time so short as to seem indecent to the members of the family, the dead person ceases to exist as an identifiable figure.

" 'To those individuals in the community of goodwill and empathy, warmth and compassion, only one of the key actors in the drama remains with whom to commiserate, and that is always the criminal. The dead person ceases to be part of everyday reality. She ceases to exist. She is only a figure in a historic event. And we inevitably turn away from the past towards the ongoing reality, and the ongoing reality is the criminal.

" 'He usurps the compassion that is justly the victim's, and he will steal the victim's constituency along with her life.

" 'Don't let that happen. He does not deserve your sympathy. He does not deserve your compassion. He doesn't deserve your mercy. And most of all, he does not deserve your leniency.' "

Sargent closed the book and picked up a photograph of Brandy. He held it up as he approached the judges. "Your compassion," he told them, "should be justly reserved for this fourteen-year-old girl. This little girl whose life he stole.

"And," he said, turning to face the spectator benches behind the prosecution table, "for the family he left behind because of his actions. Imagine the pain that they feel every day. As painful as it was to listen to them in the few minutes they described what her loss has been to them and how they feel . . . how that tears them apart. . . . Imagine how they live with that every single day, and will until they die.

"Those are the people who deserve your compassion, your goodwill," Sargent said, and pointed at Francisco. "Not this man. There is no other choice but to give him the ultimate punishment, and that is the sentence of death."

For a moment, the courtroom was absolutely silent. Then a sob escaped from Brandy's mother—a terrible reminder that for some, this would never be over.

The courtroom was packed again on May 27 when the judges announced their verdict. They had accepted all five aggravators, while agreeing to just the one catch-all mitigator that "this defendant did endure a difficult, disturbing and unsettled childhood."

They'd easily determined that the aggravators outweighed the mitigators, and so had proceeded to the fourth step. "In nearly fifty years of collective judicial experience, this panel has never dealt with a more shocking display of conscienceless depravity than that of the defendant," the judges wrote in their sentencing order. "While the panel acknowledges that many aspects of the defendant's childhood were very disturbing to this panel, nothing in that childhood adequately explains the man he has become."

Then Villano pronounced the verdict: "It is the judgment, sentence and warrant of the Court that the defendant, Francisco Martinez, Jr., be delivered to the executive director of the Colorado Department of Corrections to suffer the penalty of death by lethal injection."

After court was adjourned, DA Thomas said quietly, "This is society's way of defending itself."

For public consumption, Kaplan had commented previously that the death penalty should be reserved only for the worst of the worst. But that wasn't really where he stood. "I don't think anyone deserves to die," he said after the verdict was read. "This whole event started with an act of violence, and now it's ending with an act of violence."

But not all defense lawyers were upset by the verdict. "If our society is going to have a death penalty," attorney Scott Robinson told a reporter, "it needs to be imposed in appropriate cases, and certainly the facts in the DuVall murder are pretty horrendous."

Craig Silverman, who'd helped put Frank Rodriguez on death row, had run against Denver District Attorney Ritter in 1996 by criticizing his former boss for not being aggressive enough in pursuing the death penalty. Now in private practice, Silverman noted that Francisco Martinez fit the profile of the men already on death row. "This verdict is completely consistent with the people who have traditionally been sentenced to death in Colorado," he told the *Rocky Mountain News*. "Most of them were convicted of kidnapping, raping, torturing and murdering an innocent woman. . . . Killing multiple people will get you there, too."

"Apparently, judges are making the distinction between the crime and the defendant and the facts," legal analyst Andrew Cohen told the *Denver Post*. "If only one of every four is going to render a death verdict, it seems there are safeguards in place. Judges don't seem to be rushing defendants to death."

Angela Metzger didn't care about the legal community's debate. "This doesn't lessen my pain, no," Brandy's mother said. "It would be nice if any of these sentencings and all these years—even the death penalty—would bring Brandy back, but that can't happen."

She hadn't supported the death penalty before her daughter's murder, and she'd been ambivalent when the district attorney decided to pursue it for Danny Martinez and Francisco Martinez. She did not plan to attend the latter's execution. "It's nothing I want to see," she said. "It would not bring me any kind of satisfaction to see anyone else die. I'm not like that. I don't think we'd find any joy in watching a man die, even if he did kill my daughter."

So death row had a new tenant. But in the four cases they'd considered so far, the panels of judges had acted much more like juries than anyone had predicted.

Next up would be Lucas Salmon. A panel of judges would consider a type of testimony that no juries had ever heard. It was called a proportionality review and allowed the character and crimes of the defendant to be compared with the character and crimes of men already on death row. The proportionality review demanded a judgment call of where a particular killer fit on murderers' row: above or below the death-penalty bar.

# FOURTEEN

## "THIS IS WHAT
## I HAVE LEFT."

*June 16, 1999*

"Obviously, I'll never get to be the mother of the bride. I'll never be a mom again, never be called 'Mom.'"

Peggy Luiszer paused and drew a deep breath on the witness stand. It was the eighth day of Lucas Salmon's death-penalty hearing; tomorrow would be closing arguments, and then the three judges would decide whether he lived or died.

While she had testified at Salmon's trial, that was mostly to answer yes or no to questions about the night her daughter was murdered and to identify her jewelry. Today, she was trying to tell the judges how the death of Jacine had affected her. But how could she explain the unexplainable in a way that conveys the true depths of her despair?

The defense lawyers had argued that Jacine's family shouldn't be allowed to take the stand during the sentencing hearing. Such emotional testimony, say from the mother of the victim, might unfairly sway the judges, they claimed. But the prosecutors had pointed out that a victims' rights statute allowed it. The defense lawyers lost the argument.

As she spoke, Peggy's eyes skipped from the judges to Dan Zook to Lucas Salmon. For the first time since his trial began, he wasn't looking down at the floor or doodling on his legal pad. He was sitting up and watching her. The feeling of his eyes upon her made her skin crawl.

She had waited 778 days to say something to him. The prosecutors had told her to focus on her loss, but she wanted to tell him—tell him so that he really understood and would be haunted by it for the rest of his life—how much she hated his stinking guts.

After Salmon's trial concluded in February and she'd answered questions for the press, Peggy and Bob headed to the jury waiting room, where they hugged the jurors, many of whom were in tears. They told her that they'd agreed on his guilt almost as soon as they began deliberating, but decided that they should sleep on such an important decision. The next morning when they returned, they took another vote and the outcome was the same. Guilty. Guilty. Twelve votes for Guilty.

They said they had not believed any of the defense psychologists and felt the experts were only saying what they'd been paid to say. In an unusual move for a jury, but an indication of how strong their feelings were about the verdict, they'd signed a statement saying they believed that Salmon was "an active partner" in the crime. They hoped it would be considered by the judges who would decide his fate.

Public sentiment in Colorado Springs was to hang them high. After the conviction, the *Gazette* editorialized that the legislature had created the three-judge panels in the hopes that they would be "less susceptible than juries to the entreaties of attorneys, especially defense attorneys, and more systematic in determining whether the aggravating factors that warrant a death sentence are applicable. We hope so." But, the paper noted, so far the panels had produced three life sentences and one death penalty, further frustrating the public, which had "overwhelmingly and consistently supported the death penalty for years. . . . Its faith in the justice system, and ours, hinges on whether ultimate justice is carried out whenever it is so richly deserved."

In the days leading up to the death-penalty hearing, the press examined the issues surrounding the death penalty from just about every vantage point: from the living conditions on death row compared to those in the general prison population, to the comparative costs. Taking into account an average of ten years' worth of appeals if sentenced to death, the press figured the additional cost of his incarceration and legal fees to be about $350,000 to $400,000; on the other hand, if Salmon was sentenced to life and lived be seventy-five years old, his incarceration costs would top $1 million.

A pane of three judges would now decide which it would be. Following Heydt's resignation, another judge from El Paso County, Peter Booth, had been appointed. But another issue cropped up regarding the second judge, Frasher. Salmon's defense attorneys had moved to have him replaced because he had once worked with Woldt's attorney, Doug Wilson, in the public defender's office in Pueblo. They voiced the concern that because Woldt's attorneys' strategy would essentially be the same as theirs had been (blame the other guy) Frasher might lean toward his former colleague's client.

However, the prosecution argued that he should stay. There were concerns in the district attorney's office because Frasher had once been a public defender, most of whom were philosophically opposed to the death penalty. However, as a jurist he'd received fairly high marks in a survey of prosecutors, defense lawyers, defendants, victims, and jurors, though there were a few complaints that he was arrogant and sometimes rude in court. He also had a reputation as a fairly conservative judge who handed down tough sentences. If he was removed, whoever replaced him might be worse from their point of view. In fact, when his appointment to the Salmon panel was announced, one defense attorney in Pueblo who'd practiced in Frasher's court predicted, "He'll kill the guy."

Frasher remained on the panel and with Booth accepted the challenge of reading the 3,000-page transcript of the trail, representing ten days of testimony from witnesses. But Peggy and Bob continued to have their doubts about him, which only increased after the hearing began and they observed his behavior in the courtroom. He seemed uninterested, frequently looked at his watch as though he were missing his tee time at the golf course, yawned, or sat looking off at the wall or ceiling while twirling a pencil.

The hearing had gone pretty much like the trial. Dave Young had opened again for the prosecution with Salmon's confession:

"I told George to lift her head up by the hair, and to cover her mouth. I then made my attack." Six minutes of video projected onto a large screen showed the battered, nude body of Jacine lying on her stomach, facedown in a pool of blood, as the soundtrack of Salmon talking to the psychologists played over speaker into the courtroom. "It was surreal to me, an amazing disembodying feeling. I could feel the knife going into her."

During the openings, Peggy sat in the hallway outside the courtroom. There was no part she wanted to see or hear. Both fathers, Bob Luiszer and Bob Salmon, were present but were overwhelmed by the horrific video. Luiszer looked down at the floor and covered his ears with his hands. Salmon, who suffered from a hearing impairment, removed the headset he'd worn throughout his son's trial and stared at his lap.

"Jacine was the type of person your son or daughter would be friends with," Young said. "Her death caused pain and suffering to many people."

Young said the state would prove "beyond a reasonable doubt" the existence of six aggravating factors spelled out by the law: that Salmon "intentionally killed a kidnapped person"; that he was a party to a conspiracy to kill someone; that the murderers lay in wait and "ambushed" the victim; that the murder was committed to conceal another felony—in this case sexual assault; and that she'd been killed so that she could not identify them.

The last aggravating factor was the big one, the one that had pushed juries into voting for the death penalty in the past. Young said the prosecution would also prove the aggravating factor that the murder was "especially heinous, cruel and depraved" and committed in a "conscienceless or pitiless manner which was unnecessarily torturous to the victim."

Speaking to that last aggravating factor, Young noted that when Salmon and Woldt finally succeeded in killing Jacine, they'd exchanged high fives. Pointing a finger at the defendant who kept his head down and drew on his legal pad, the prosecutor concluded, "It is a horror of this crime that looms large in our conscience and calls for the death penalty. This is the man who committed this crime. The only appropriate punishment is the maximum penalty."

Robert Pepin, the president of the Colorado Criminal Defense Bar who had replaced Enwall, opened for the defense, saying his side would be calling witnesses to testify that Salmon was a nonviolent, caring individual until he fell under the sway of the much more evil George Woldt. Some of those witnesses would be psychologists who would attest that Salmon had a dependent personality disorder that made him so desperate to keep Woldt's friendship that he participated in the rape and murder.

"If it weren't for George Woldt, Lucas Salmon wouldn't be involved in this," Pepin said.

Salmon was not the leader in Jacine's murder, the attorney said. "He is a strange, lonely, immature, odd person, but he hadn't done a thing to hurt anyone before this. . . . He was captured by George Woldt, who made him his own."

Under Woldt's control, his client did not have a firm grasp of right or wrong. "This is not a 'woe is poor Lucas' argument," Pepin said, "but he was lost in this world. He was under unusual duress."

Apparently forgetting the high fives the two exchanged after Jacine's death, Pepin told the judges, "There is nothing that suggests there was a particular joy in her killing. There were no shouts of glee and no particular effort to humiliate her."

The experts' testimony, Salmon's age at the time of the murder (twenty-one), and his general immaturity would be offered as mitigators, he said. Another mitigator was that Salmon had "cooperated" with the police after his initial denial.

"He was told he didn't have to talk, and he did," Pepin said. "He was told he could get a lawyer anytime, and he didn't. He went with the police to show them the body."

Pepin then made a curious comment. Bad as the crime was, he said, Lucas Salmon did not "fit the profile" of the killers on death row; the defense would be calling a witness to demonstrate that, too.

"He needs to be taken away," Pepin said, "and spend the rest of his life in prison. Nothing can ease the pain that she died so young and so horribly.

His client should "spend every single remaining day of his life behind bars, but he should not be executed."

After Pepin finished, prosecutor Zook called the El Paso

County coroner to the stand to testify about Jacine's wounds—the pain, and fear, and suffering they had caused. And then Zook surprised everyone by announcing that he was resting his case. The judges had what they needed; there was little more the prosecution could add.

The remaining days of the hearing featured testimony by Salmon's friends and family, but mostly was taken up by another battle of the psychologists. The former described a completely different young man from the one who had raped and killed Jacine. His brother, Micah, testified, "He was a gentle person then and now. He was a nice, kind, quiet person."

Woldt was the problem, Micah said. "Lucas was jealous of George being a ladies' man and meeting women. He admired George's freedom."

The former girlfriend Salmon dated at the end of 1997 and early 1998, Christina, said she'd liked Salmon from the first time she met him. "He spoke German," she said. "He had a sarcastic sense of humor. I was happy when he characterized me as his girlfriend.

"He was consoling and so respectful of my boundaries. He enjoyed making out, but he was the most respectful guy I have ever dated."

Lucas's friends said that he never seemed to quite fit in. However, they acknowledged on cross-examination that they never thought of him as being anything more than another out-of-step teenager. They also conceded that he'd played in a rock-and-roll band, could be friendly and outgoing, and used his considerable intellect to engage in conversations and debates, especially on matters of religion.

As promised, the defense called its experts to testify about Salmon's psychological makeup. At Salmon's trial, Cleaver had told the jury that her client's dependent personality disorder made it impossible for him to "deliberate" the murder of Jacine. The jury had rejected that contention, but the defense still hoped that the judges would accept it as mitigating.

Colorado Springs psychologist Alice Brill said her examination revealed Salmon had "problems with reality and a high level of anxiety," but he did not fit neatly into any one psychological category. "He's passive and doesn't have a clear identity," she said "He's confused, has no direction, and can't find his way in life."

Wilfred Van Gorp, a professor of psychology at New York University and Cornell Medical Center in NYC, testified that Salmon suffered from an "introverted personality disorder" and was easily influenced by strong-willed people. "Lucas Salmon felt the friendship between he and George Woldt would be threatened if he didn't go through with the plan."

Berton Dragten, another Colorado Springs psychologist who said he'd interviewed Salmon twenty-one times since his conviction, said, "I see him as emotionally immature and dependent, a person who seeks the approval of others.

"He did not have the ego, strength or self-esteem to resist Woldt's influence in taking part in the crime." However, on cross-examination Dragten admitted that Salmon knew what he was doing was wrong and that there would be penalties for his actions.

Thomas Thompson, a neuropsychologist from New Mexico, said Salmon was immature. The defendant's thinking was "not orderly" and his social skills "impoverished." That all led to him falling "under the spell" of George Woldt.

The defense's star expert, Meloy, took the stand again to essentially reiterate what he'd told the jury: Woldt put Salmon under "unusual and substantial duress," important wording, as it mirrored one of the legal mitigators the defense was trying to get the judges to accept. By the time he stepped down from the stand, Meloy had racked up $70,000 for his examinations and testimony.

The prosecution had countered the defense experts with experts of their own, who again testified that none of the personality problems or "thinking disorders" described by their counterparts—even if they existed—took away from the fact that Salmon knew that was he was doing that night was wrong, and went ahead anyway. Nor was he simply a brainwashed follower. In instance after instance, they pointed out where Salmon had been an equal partner and, indeed, had taken a lead role in the stabbing of Jacine.

Colorado Springs psychiatrist Daniel Kinsey said Salmon was not suffering from an antisocial personality disorder, normally considered dangerous, nor was he under the control of Woldt. "He recognized emotions in himself and others. I don't think there is an adequate explanation for this crime. I don't see any mental illness."

The prosecution also called former coworkers and acquaintances to the stand to combat the image of Salmon as the introverted loser, painting him instead as self-assured and sexually aggressive. One woman from his father's business testified that they'd had normal conversations until the day he put his hand under her dress. "I wanted to be his friend but he wanted to get together to have sex," she said. "One day he thought we were laughing at him and he said, 'I'll have both you bitches fired.' "

Often during the defense case, especially when one of the experts testified about what a "victim" Salmon had been, or when one of his friends or family members described the sweet and good-natured young man they knew, Peggy and Bob had inserted the earplugs or cupped their hands over their ears. They were not in the courtroom, however, when Salmon's parents took the stand. They understood the other family was also suffering, they just didn't want to hear any apologies for his actions.

The Salmons told the panel they loved their son, but did not ask that his life be spared. Bob Salmon blamed himself in part but also said his son had always been a little strange.

"I was too busy to really dwell on everything that could happen to him," he said. "He was the sweetest, most unselfish, compliant child, but Lucas has always been different. He was slower to learn things. He sometimes wore his clothes inside out or backwards, didn't tie his shoes or comb his hair.

"Back then you thought it was cute, but he didn't quite get it. He looked like an unmade bed. You thought he would outgrow it but he didn't. . . . To know Lucas is to know that there is something horribly wrong here."

Lucas was picked on in school, his father said. Even when he got to college, he never fit in. "He wasn't popular. He's severely troubled. He doesn't think like other people. He had very strange and bizarre perceptions of what is real."

However, having said all that, Bob Salmon told the judges that he hoped that whatever decision they reached, he hoped it would "bring some closure for Jacine's family and friends. . . . I recognize that their loss is complete. Our loss can't be compared to theirs.

"I guess I don't envy your decision. I love my son. But I have to tell you that Jacine's family is my primary concern. I have to tell you that whatever's best for them is my desire."

Salmon's mother, Gail Keller, told the judges that Lucas was bright but had never "lived up to his potential."

"I'm not here today to make any excuses for my son. I want to express my deepest sympathy to Jacine's mother. I'm so sorry. She's been on my mind and in my prayers since this happened.

"I believe in a God who punishes sin. I love my son, but I hate what he did. I pray for all of you. I know it's a very difficult thing. His family will honor any decision that is made as a just decision.

"I never, never could have imagined this . . . that my son could be convicted of rape and murder and be facing the death penalty. I just ask that you come to this decision carefully and honestly. I'll be praying for you."

After the Salmons testified, and over the prosecution's objections, Judge Parrish allowed the defense to call defense attorney Ingrid Defranco to the stand to present a "proportionality review" that compared Salmon to the other men already on death row. Until this point, judges serving on death-penalty panels had considered much the same evidence that juries had. Even their decisions had mirrored past jury decisions. For instance, as stated previously, although the option was on the books, no jury had ever sent a defendant to death row for a first-degree felony-murder conviction. Nor had the panels that decided the fates of Robert Riggan and Jacques Richardson. But now, the Salmon defense team was offering evidence that no Colorado death-penalty jury had ever been asked to contemplate.

Always in the past, a proportionality review had been reserved for an appellate court trying to determine whether a defendant had been fairly sentenced. Gary Davis, through his attorneys, had asked the Colorado Supreme Court for a proportionality review—a comparison of crimes and criminals to determine if his death sentence for the 1987 murder of Virginia May was appropriate. In that case, the court had ruled that a proportionality review was not constitutionally required and determined that there was "no defect" in the state law. In pretrial motions in other cases, defense attorneys had asked that such information be allowed in front of a jury, but trial courts had denied those motions as well. Now all that had changed.

When Defranco took the stand to testify for Salmon's defense, she presented a chart comparing killers like Davis, Frank Rodriguez, Robert Harlan, Nathan Dunlap, and Francisco "Pancho" Martinez, the only man sent to death row by a panel, as well as the crimes they'd committed, to Lucas Salmon and the murder of Jacine Gielinski.

According to Defranco, Salmon was younger than any of those defendants, had not committed other crimes, and therefore did not "fit the profile" of the other men on death row. The defense strategy of a proportionality review had caught the prosecution by surprise. They had nothing to counter it, except the hope that the judges would see that the defense was comparing apples to oranges.

After the defense rested, Jacine's parents were allowed to speak, although they were limited in the scope of their comments. According to Judge Parrish's interpretation of the Colorado Victim's Rights Law, which allows victims or their families to address the court and the defendant, the family could not make recommendations as to what sentence they thought was fair.

Peggy Luiszer went first. She carried Jacine's favorite flowers, daisies, the photograph of her daughter that she'd kept on her lap throughout the trial, and a square bronze urn containing Jacine's ashes.

Before Jacine's death, when she'd learned about murderers like Gary Davis and Nathan Dunlap, and heard about their crimes, she'd thought that they didn't deserve to live and that the death penalty was a fitting punishment. But she'd never given capital punishment much thought beyond that.

Then Jacine was murdered, and Peggy had been forced to think about capital punishment. To be honest, she wasn't sure that life in prison was a better deal than the death penalty. But the law allowing executions was on the books, and if two men deserved to die, she thought they were Lucas Salmon and George Woldt.

So she didn't understand the rationale behind the proportionality review. How could the defense compare one murderer to another? So what if Salmon was young? He was over eighteen, the legal age for executions. Besides, Jacine had been young, too. And so what if this was his first offense? It was a horrible one.

But all she was allowed to do was speak on behalf of her daughter. Jacine was a good person, she told the panel, someone who'd always been willing to help others, whether it was teaching a child to kick a soccer ball or gathering clothes to give to homeless shelters.

"After twenty-two years of being a mom, this is all I have left," she said. "Obviously, I'll never get to be the mother of the bride. I'll never be a mom again, never be called 'Mom.'"

Peggy paused, tried to hold back the tears, couldn't, and went on. "I just miss her awful much. It's unexplainable. I can't tell you how I feel. There's a hole in my heart. It's like an amputation. It's just never going to come back."

As she spoke, Salmon continued to watch her or turned to read the transcript of her testimony as it appeared on a monitor in front of the defense table. Behind him, his father closed his eyes.

Before she started she was afraid that she would falter, but now the words came tumbling out, including words of regret. "After she died, we asked to come see her," she said. "But the coroner and doctor advised us not to. So we didn't get to say good-bye. It was terrible. Absolutely terrible."

Her life, her marriage, and her future had all been changed forever for the worse, Peggy testified. "This has been our life. Wherever we go, it always comes up. Everyone keeps saying how strong we are now. But we're not strong. It's just the way our life is now."

"At night I go to bed and see their faces, Salmon's and Woldt's faces, and I don't want anybody to touch me. I don't know how rape victims survive.

"Everyone says it's supposed to get better as time goes

on. But it hasn't. It just hasn't. . . . This has hurt so many people on both sides. It hurt the Salmon family, too."

Peggy spoke for fifty minutes. Throughout the courtroom people—spectators, jurors, families and friends, and lawyers—wept openly as Jacine's mother exposed her broken heart. At last there was nothing much more for her to say, except, "I just wish she was here. . . . I'll never forgive him for what he's done to me and to her."

Returning to her seat, Peggy buried her face in her hands and sobbed. Her husband put his arms around her shoulders, but he couldn't stay there long, as he was called next to the stand. All he carried with him were memories of the girl who promised that he could escort her down the aisle on her wedding day.

"It's finally our chance to speak, after listening to the defense talk about Salmon and Woldt and say nothing about Jacine," Bob Luiszer said bitterly, "as if she didn't exist."

His voice quavered and his breath often came in short gasps as he offered snapshot memories of the flower girl at his wedding, the young woman who'd cared for a biological father who had never given her much of anything as he was dying, and the unquenchable competitive fire that drove her. "She wasn't always the best player, but boy, she put her heart in it," he said and tried to smile. "She accepted everybody. She had close friends among teachers, coaches, everybody.

"I felt she was my own daughter. I would have done anything for her. I would have died for her. She had a smile that warmed anybody's heart."

When the horrible news came that night back in April 1997, Bob said, his wife began crying and screaming "as if she was feeling Jacine's pain as she was raped and murdered."

Bob, too, acknowledged that nothing would ever be the same. "Our marriage is shaky at times now. I pray ours will last. . . . My sex drive is gone. All I can think about is what happened that night to Jacine. I can't imagine how she felt.

"We couldn't bear the thought of the way she was, her body violated. We had her cremated. We saved some stuff for Jacine but we can't bear to look at it. We've gone through a lot of therapy. It's affected my job. I just sit there and stare. This is my reality."

Bob turned to look at the judges, each one in the face, as tears poured down his own cheeks. "I'm not looking for revenge," he said. "I'm looking for punishment that fits the crime. Lucas Salmon will have the comfort of family and friends. Jacine didn't have that chance. She was by herself and alone."

The next day, the final day of the hearing, Lucas Salmon stood at the defense table and spoke for the first time. The traditional apology was called allocution and was allowed without the prosecution being able to cross-examine him.

Throughout the trial and the hearing, Salmon had certainly played the role asked of him by his defense attorneys. He sat quiet as a mouse, doodling on a legal pad—the inept, immature, social misfit living in a fantasy world as the "adults" around him argued over his fate. But now he spoke clearly, almost eloquently, and with a strong, certain voice.

Salmon said he wished he'd pleaded guilty from the beginning and not let his attorneys talk him into a trial. He hated himself for what he had done.

"It seems pretty disingenuous to apologize now for something I could have stopped two years ago," he said. "If I could give up my life to bring Jacine back, I'd do that, but we all know that can't be done.

"Just as no member of my family asked for leniency, neither will I."

Neither did prosecutor Dan Zook when he gave his closing arguments. He went over the evidence and how it proved the aggravating factors. As he reviewed the details of the murder, the Luiszers dropped their heads and covered their ears.

"Being raped by one man is an extreme horror, but two people?" Zook said. "Doesn't that qualify as cruel and heinous? Doesn't that add horror and torture? The defendant did what only can be described as evil.

"There was often a place where he could have stopped. Where the voice of reason and humanity gives you the chance to stop."

Instead, the time they took to attack and then consider what to do next only made Jacine's torment "prolonged and remorseless." Then Salmon and Woldt high-fived each other "to celebrate what they did. And this," he said, showing the photographs of Jacine's bloody, battered body, "is what's left."

Zook concluded his thirty-minute closing, "Isn't life so precious . . . that society has the right to exact the highest penalty for a crime so random, vicious, cruel and heinous?"

After the prosecutor took his seat, Cleaver delivered the defense closing. She stressed that Woldt was the one who'd come up with the idea and that Salmon had been under duress, afraid of losing his friend. "An oddball . . . friendless, but harmless."

She recounted the testimony of her experts that Salmon was wholly under the influence of Woldt, "a psychopath and sexual sadist."

"But for the acts of another, he would not have committed this crime," Cleaver said. "Lucas Salmon is mentally ill. Do we execute the mentally ill in Colorado?

"He did a horrible thing and a terrible thing, but he is not a horrible and terrible person. I wonder what more violence can accomplish here. I know there are people in Colorado who have compassion and mercy and understanding."

Cleaver sat and Zook rose again for rebuttal. Because

the state has the greater burden of proving the facts beyond a reasonable doubt, the prosecution gets the last word. They are not allowed to make a new argument, only rebut what the defense said, and now Zook countered Cleaver assertions by reading from Salmon's confession.

" 'We both agreed it was something we would like to do,' " he read, then looked up at the judges. "Does this sound like duress?"

Then, finally, it was over. Outside the courtroom, the Luiszers told the press that they were not impressed by Salmon's apology.

"It's too little and too late for signs of remorse," Bob said. "His saying he's sorry doesn't make it okay. I don't forgive him."

Peggy said that while she felt Lucas Salmon was sincere, "he should have said so right after the murder, not waited two years." Now, it didn't matter. "Apology not accepted. It never will be," she said.

## June 24, 1999

Once more, the courtroom was packed. The atmosphere so tense that every little sound seemed magnified, every emotion on the brink of breaking loose like an avalanche. The judges had deliberated for a week, but now they were ready to pronounce Salmon's fate.

Before reading their verdict, Judge Parrish sternly warned against any outbursts. "This is an emotional time for everybody here, a solemn time and a serious time," he said.

Parrish glanced around the courtroom as if looking to see if anyone was about to disobey his order. Then he proceeded. "I asked the judges and myself to make certain they had made their decision with legal and intellectual honesty, and I'm convinced each of us has."

Peggy Luiszer sat quietly, lost in thought about another

tragedy. That morning as they drove down to Colorado Springs for the umpteenth time, they'd passed through Castle Rock where just two days earlier, a man named Simon J. Gonzales took his three young daughters—Rebecca, ten, Katheryn, eight, and Leslie, seven—to a fast-food restaurant. He then went to a store, bought a gun, and shot the girls to death inside his truck. That night, with their bodies still inside the vehicle, he drove to the parking lot outside the police department and, after firing several shots at the building, died in a hail of gunfire. He left a note saying he'd killed his daughters to get even with his estranged wife.

Peggy didn't understand how Gonzales could have taken the lives of his three precious children. She'd only had one child herself, a beautiful, vibrant daughter, and would have given anything to have her back. But there was no real answer to why Gonzales did such a horrible thing, just as there had been no real answer to why Salmon and Woldt had done such a horrible thing.

The judges had no answer either. In their written opinion, the panel noted up front that their decision was not a comment on the guilt or innocence of Woldt, who had yet to be tried. There was no getting around mentioning the co-defendant, however, as "Salmon's involvement is inextricably linked to Woldt's alleged involvement."

The panel agreed that the prosecution had proved most of its aggravating factors, including that the murder had been "especially heinous, cruel and depraved," and that the "acts were done in a conscienceless or pitiless manner which was unnecessarily torturous to the victim."

The judges' decision continued: "While it borders on the absurd to speak of murders in terms of their being senseless, it is noted that the more common reasons people kill each other are not apparent in this case—for example, greed or revenge. This murder was senseless to the degree that it was for the purpose of carrying out a twisted fantasy causing enormous and unquantifiable pain and damage to others for momentary gratification."

As mitigators, the judges accepted Salmon's age and lack of maturity. And while he had lived in a religious family, attended Bible study and a Christian college and so knew that what he was doing was wrong, they said, under Woldt's "considerable domination," his ability to conform his conduct to the requirement of the law was "significantly impaired." The judges noted that Salmon's life before the murder stood in "stark contrast" to what he did to Jacine Gielinski, and also allowed that he had cooperated with the police, at least after he was caught.

When it came to the third step in the process, the judges said there was no doubt that the aggravators far outweighed the mitigators. "The horror of Jacine Gielinski's death is virtually incomprehensible, and it is the judgment of the panel that this aggravating factor alone outweighs the mitigation found to be present in this case," they determined. That meant that Salmon fell "within the legislatively defined category of persons eligible for the death penalty."

There was only one more step, the fourth step, during which the judges had to decide whether, all things considered, Salmon "deserved" to die. But here they could not agree.

Judge Frasher's was the dissenting vote that saved Lucas Salmon's life. At the start of the hearing, Cleaver had tried to have Frasher removed from the panel, arguing that the former public defender had a conflict of interest because he had worked with one of Woldt's lawyers, Doug Wilson. But now he was the man who saved her client.

Frasher noted that the "presumptive sentence"—unless proved otherwise—was a life sentence. "I am unaware of any modern historical precedent in the State of Colorado for the execution of an individual with the characteristics of Lucas Salmon," he said. "The imposition of the death penalty on Lucas Salmon in this case would substantially lower the threshold for the imposition of the sentence of death in the state.

"It is human instinct to want to strike out at the perpetrator—to strike out at Lucas Salmon, to smite him dead as a symbolic act of retribution and vengeance for Jacine Gielinski and her family. Additionally, there is an emotional temptation to feel that the imposition of a sentence less than death demeans the value of Jacine Gielinski's life and the profound tragedy of her death or trivializes the depth of the loss sustained by her family and friends.

"As tempting as it may be," he continued, "I am not permitted, nor should I be permitted, the luxury of seeking vengeance out of the righteous emotionality which understandably surrounds this case. It is my conclusion that I am not convinced beyond a reasonable doubt that the execution of Lucas Salmon is necessary and appropriate."

So in the end, it was the proportionality review that had swayed one judge. And one judge was all the defense needed, as the Danny Martinez case had shown.

Judges Booth and Parrish disagreed with Frasher. Even if the crime was Woldt's idea, "Lucas Salmon willingly signed on and, in time, fully embraced the horror," Judge Booth wrote. "He never argued against it. Never suggested that they keep this in the realm of fantasy. Salmon's previous lifestyle was respectable, his service to others laudable, but his crimes were horrific.

"That nobody has been sentenced to death in the past twenty years in this state who has Salmon's characteristics is not surprising," Booth said. "Salmon is unique."

Arguing that Salmon didn't deserve the death penalty because he didn't fit the profile of other men on death row ignored all the aggravating factors, Judge Parrish said, "especially the horror of the crime itself in the calculus of the propriety of the death sentence in this case. The loss to the family and friends of Jacine Gielinski is enormous. Whatever action is taken by this panel, the death and manner of death of Ms. Gielinski will never be comprehensible.

"For this sentencer, the only adequate response beyond a reasonable doubt, in light of the circumstances of this case, is a measure of justice in fair and equivalent proportion to the actions of the defendant. He should be sentenced to death."

The decision was not read aloud in the courtroom. All Parrish said was that "as this is not the unanimous conclusion of the panel, by operation of law, he is sentenced to life in prison without the possibility of parole."

Neither Lucas Salmon nor the Luiszers reacted emotionally to the announcement. Bob Salmon stood and reached over the barrier to hug Lauren Cleaver, breaking into loud sobs. Friends of Jacine raced from the courtroom, also crying.

However, not until she was outside the courtroom did Peggy allow her eyes to fill with tears. Even then she spoke matter-of-factly. "We'll live with the decision. Eventually justice will be done. I can't imagine being twenty-three years old and living to die in jail. He's not going to make fifty years in prison.

"I'm done with the case now. It's out of my mind. But I don't forgive him, and it isn't going to weigh heavy on my soul for not forgiving him. He'll get his in prison, I have no doubt."

Bob Salmon also addressed the media outside the courtroom. Wiping away his tears with a tissue, he said, "I think there is some value for Lucas to wake up every morning for the next fifty years knowing what he has done."

Looking over at the Luiszers, he added, "I just hope that this gives them a chance for, perhaps, closure."


Afterward, the Luiszers and other family members, friends, and some members of the press went to a restaurant across the street. They'd grabbed copies of the judges' thirty-nine-page opinion and learned of Frasher's dissenting vote, though they were not surprised.

Day after day, they'd watched his demeanor. He rarely took notes or seemed to pay much attention to the witnesses. He never participated in the discussions when the lawyers raised objections, or asked for a conference before the judges over legal points. Worse, he seemed to have made his mind up before the hearing even began, and that the only question for him was how he was going to explain his reasons.

So they had braced themselves for the inevitable conclusion. At the restaurant, the Luiszers and their supporters gathered in front of a television screen to listen to the noon news about the judges' decision. When Frasher's face appeared on the screen, Peggy reacted not with words but by raising her hand and extending her middle finger.

# FIFTEEN

# "TO THE END . . ."

The reaction to Judge Frasher and his decision roared in fast and furious. The judge and his colleagues on the panel declined to comment, noting that there was a second trial and a potential death-penalty hearing still to come. But it seemed that just about everyone else had something to say.

"He just didn't seem involved at all," Bob Luiszer told the press. "Everyone could see it. We were just wishing his mind was there. But knowing he had practiced with Doug Wilson for eight years, it's no wonder he took the defendant's side."

District Attorney Smith praised her prosecution team, pointing out that for two years they had sacrificed their personal lives—skipping vacations, working long unpaid hours. She then took the unusual step of criticizing a judge, saying Frasher's decision demeaned the value of Jacine's life and her family's loss. "Lucas Salmon has been given the gift of life, a gift he took from Jacine Gielinski by torture and for his own pleasure, a gift he does not deserve," she said.

"We do have judges who do not believe in the death penalty," she said. "There is an obligation under the law for any judge who believes he could not in good conscience follow the law in a case to recuse himself.

"Judge Frasher's opinion contains an extensive discussion of how 'meaningful' a life sentence is. It sounds as if this judge, a former public defender, is opposed to the death penalty in principle as it is written. Two judges agreed that death was the appropriate penalty."

Former Colorado Springs police detective Pat Crouch, who'd taken Salmon's confession, said to the *Gazette*, "You've got to ask yourself where the justice is. The DAs met the burden of proof. Why haven't the judges?"

The *Gazette* took informal polls around the city, whose residents far and away thought Salmon should have received the death penalty. The reporter talked to students and faculty on the University of Colorado campus with the same results. "He'll be fed and clothed with a place to sleep; he'll be a ward of the state," Nina Gomez, a communications professor who had Jacine in several classes, told the newspaper. "This punishment does not fit the crime."

A reporter went over to the Foothills Elementary School and talked to parents who were watching their children on the playground. They, too, voiced their frustration and disgust with the justice system, some of them noting that their faith in the system had been eroding ever since a more famous case captured the nation's attention. "I am not surprised," one such woman said. "Ever since O.J., I'm not surprised by anything."

State Senator Ray Powers, the Republican from Colorado Springs who sponsored the bill creating the death-penalty panels, lashed out at Frasher, saying he ignored the facts in the case. "I think it's very difficult to explain to the public how this could have happened," he said. "If this case, as much as I know about it, doesn't qualify for the death penalty, I don't know what case will.

"My thought was that judges would base it on the facts, and not emotion or philosophy. This judge has done a disservice to our state and the victim's family and friends."

*Gazette* columnist Ralph Routon chastised Frasher. "Jacine Gielinski and her parents deserved three judges who cared enough to have an open mind and pay attention. . . . James Frasher didn't care. He took the easy way out, and then drove back to Pueblo. We can only hope, some day, he has to face Peggy and Bob Luiszer."

The newspaper also ran an editorial, noting that within hours of the decision its offices had been flooded with e-mails, letters and telephone calls registering "indignation, disgust and disbelief." The newspaper followed suit: "If Salmon's repugnant crimes don't merit the death penalty in a society where most people support capital punishment, then pray tell what does?"

The decision, according to the editorial, would further call into question the efficacy of the new death-penalty panels, which had meted out the ultimate penalty once in five tries. "It is troubling to contemplate whether the jury in the Salmon trial itself would have done any worse if it had weighed upon his punishment. It might even have done better."

Even the newspaper's editorial cartoonist, Chuck Asay, weighed in after the decision. His commentary was drawn on two panels. One depicted two men high-fiving each other over a body on the ground and the caption read: APRIL 29, 1997. NEWS ITEM—LUCAS SALMON TESTIFIED ON TAPE HE AND GEORGE WOLDT EXCHANGED HIGH FIVES WHEN THEY FINALLY SUCCEEDED IN KILLING JACINE GIELINSKI. The second panel, dated June 24, 1999, showed the Salmon defense lawyers—one of them obviously Lauren Cleaver—high-fiving each other over the fallen body of Justice, with her sword on the ground next to a tipped-over scale of justice.

Defense attorneys were quick to come to Frasher's support. Cleaver called Smith's accusations "outrageous." She further angered Jacine's family and supporters by calling his decision "a triumph for the justice system. I think this is an important case. I am very proud of the judge who refused to recognize vengeance as a valid form of government."

While everyone else was sympathizing with Jacine's family, she said that the proceedings had not been easy on the defendant's family or Salmon himself.

"Bob sobbed in my arms," she said of her client's father. "It's been a very tough time for them. They're very strong in their beliefs in personal responsibility and I think, in many ways, they felt like if the law accorded the death penalty, they would understand that.

"And Lucas wasn't as nervous as everyone would think. He really doesn't get it. I'm sure he's happy. But he's afraid to go to prison, as you can imagine."

Those who thought Salmon would have it easy in prison, she said, were wrong. "I think Lucas will be at the bottom of the totem pole as far as prison life."

Other defense attorneys praised Frasher. One who knew him in Pueblo said that while the judge's "mannerisms" made him appear uninterested, "he really doesn't miss much." The lawyer said he'd seen Frasher at a party and the judge had talked about the overwhelming amount of evidence he'd pored through to prepare for the hearing.

Defense lawyer and death-penalty critic David Lane noted that the U.S. Supreme Court held that whether or not to hand down a death sentence was a "profoundly moral" and individual decision. "We had a judge who decided that in Colorado, we don't execute people with mental illness that rises to this level."

Phil Cherner, vice president of the Colorado Criminal Defense Bar, told the *Rocky Mountain News:* "The legislature has seen fit to give this awesome task to three-judge panels. I can't imagine a decision that would be more difficult. We have a trial, a lengthy sentencing hearing, the judges come up with a decision, and then some DA in the Springs pops off and says they don't understand why he didn't get the death penalty. That's what we pay judges to do. Sometimes, Miss DA, you're going to lose."

The debate raged into the summer. Senator Powers said he was going to introduce a bill in the next legislative session to change the state's death-penalty system once again. If passed, his bill would have let the trial judge decide the sentence, as he initially had wanted to do back in 1995.

Too many judges were philosophically opposed to the death penalty for the current plan to work, he said. "A lot of them were defense attorneys," he added. "The judge from Pueblo was a defense attorney, which made it hard for him, when he'd been arguing against it for years."

Defense attorney Kaplan responded by saying that Colorado's law should never have been changed in the first place. Powers's latest proposal "irritates me to no end," he said. "Who died and made him God? Justice should not be determined on the whims of a politician or on the whims of any individual."

If anything, the state should return to allowing twelve jurors to decide death-penalty cases, he said. Prosecutors "didn't like jurors deciding because they thought it was too awesome a decision for an average citizen to make," he added. "But guess what? Judges find it a pretty awesome decision also."

While the lawyers and politicians took shots at each other on the front pages of the newspapers, hundreds of Colorado Springs residents voiced their opinion in the letters to the editor pages of their local newspaper: "If consciously and deliberately prowling the streets in search of prey, a young woman chose at random, stalking her, patiently waiting for the right moment to strike, capturing her and taking her to a secluded lair to be gang-raped, beaten and stabbed repeatedly to death, then dumping her naked, mutilated body at an elementary school doesn't warrant the death penalty, then what does Judge James Frasher think does?" Bill Schaffner wrote.

"This has seriously shaken my faith in the justice system," wrote Chee Woo Leong. "If judges can abdicate the duty of the judiciary to seek redress and justice through all means available—up to and including execution—then we have no justice available through government."

"Once again, we see a case of total incompetence by our judicial system," wrote Bob Rose. "Lucas Salmon gets to live in prison, while another murder victim lies in her grave. . . . There is not justice when you can see the facts, yet have not the courage to carry out the sentence deserved."

"Well, the justice (or lack of justice) system strikes again," wrote J.H. Anderson. "First there was O.J. Simpson and now there's Lucas Salmon."

"All you murderers out there come to Colorado and commit your crimes," wrote Daryl J. Muratori. "Let's feel sorry for the criminal and give no consideration to the victims. I am leaving this demented state and country and could not be happier. We have lowered ourselves about as low as you can go as far as most of our politicians and judicial policies go, and I have had enough."

"James Frasher, you do not deserve to be called judge because it is obvious that you are anything but," wrote Ron Lett. "You, sir, are totally spineless and incapable of carrying out the duties of a judge, and in my humble opinion, should resign immediately."

"If it is this easy for Lucas Salmon to get off after what he did," wrote Jennifer Dreiling, who said she was afraid now to leave home for college, "how do I know that he didn't talk someone else into doing the same thing, and that he won't choose me or someone else? . . . . Thank you so much, Judge Frasher."

Occasionally, someone wrote in support. "No one, especially the state, should ever put a price tag on the sanctity of life," wrote Bill Whitman, the director for Catholic Community Services. "It is irrelevant if it does indeed cost more money to put an offender in prison for life than to sentence that person to die."

"Because of Judge Frasher's decision, Lucas Salmon will live on," wrote Don Wonders, an acquaintance of Jacine's. "But Jacine, for those who knew her, can only be the scent of a flower they cannot see, the echo of a tune they cannot hear, the glimpse of a paradise they can never visit. I sincerely hope that all of us will think of her more than just occasionally and that her name and memory will never be lost in the careless flow of time."

In July, state officials announced that the Salmon murder trial had cost more than $1.25 million, the costliest of the five death-penalty cases argued in front of the three-judge panels. Of that, $310,422 went to Salmon's lawyers and another $187,076 went to the defense investigators. More than $786,000 was for expenses, including $27,500 for mental exams, $12,500 for witness fees and travel, $10,000 for trial transcripts, and a whopping $400,000 for expert witnesses. Of the last category, the defense's star expert, J.R. Meloy, billed the taxpayers the most: $70,000.

So far, more than $2.5 million had been spent on prosecuting and defending Robert Riggan, Jacques Richardson, Danny Martinez, Francisco Martinez, and Lucas Salmon, as well as several other defendants who'd never gotten as far as a death-penalty hearing for one reason or another. The impact wasn't just economic; resources were strained as well. When judges were appointed to death-penalty panels, their dockets had to be shifted to other judges for the duration of the panel.

Defense attorneys said they'd warned legislators that prosecutors eager to seek the death penalty would put more defendants before those three-judge panels, adding to the state's expenses. In turn, El Paso County District Attorney Smith, who also served as president of the

Colorado District Attorney's Council, blamed rising costs on defense attorneys, claiming they were trying to get rid of the death sentence by making death-penalty cases cost-prohibitive. When a man's life was at stake, defense attorneys countered, they had the moral responsibility to incur any cost necessary to make the state prove its case.

Also in July, Judge Parrish tacked an additional 184 years onto the twenty-three-year-old Salmon's sentence for his other crimes such as the rape of Jacine and the attack on Amber Gonzales. It was the last of the judge's involvement in the case.

He was scheduled to preside over Woldt's trial, too. But Woldt's defense attorneys, Wilson and Brake, demanded that he remove himself, saying that his voting in favor of the death penalty for Salmon would preclude him for remaining impartial for Woldt's trial. Moreover, they accused him of consistently ruling in the prosecution's favor, as well as being rude, including interrupting them before they could finish their arguments, criticizing them in open court, and accusing them of "creating problems."

Parrish decided to step down to minimize the grounds for appeal, should Woldt be convicted. "I believe that I would in fact be able to separate out matters," he said at a hearing on the issue, "but I believe there is an appearance that a judge would find it impossible to do that."

Wilson later told the press, "It was the appropriate decision." But District Attorney Smith was not so pleased. "I'm sorry that someone who was so familiar with the case is changing, because generally that results in some delays," she said.

However, Wilson may have recalled the old saying about being careful for what you wish—it may come true. Two weeks later the easygoing and tolerant Judge Parrish was replaced by El Paso District Judge Richard Hall. The new judge was a no-nonsense sort of jurist who was tough on lawyers, no matter which side of the aisle they were on. He was known to cut off wordy attorneys if he felt they were wasting his time, and to hand down tough sentences.

Wilson had even accepted lengthier prison sentences in plea bargains for clients in the past rather than take his chances in Hall's court. However, the judge's reputation did not stop the lawyer from immediately renewing his demand that the trial be moved away from El Paso County because of all the publicity.

Near the end of August, Hall announced that he was setting Woldt's trial date for February 2000. It seemed a long ways off to Peggy Luiszer. "It's been forever," she said. "It's going to be three years by the time this is done. That's amazing to me."

The Luiszers had just met with Colorado Governor Bill Owens to voice their displeasure over the Salmon decision and the long delays. "We just let him know how ridiculous the whole court system is," Peggy told the *Gazette*. "He knew all about the case. He was very caring. He even got teary-eyed."

She noted that the delay would prevent her from seeking a full-time job for that length of time because she would have to take another three weeks off in February to attend the trial, and then more time at the death-penalty hearing if he was convicted. Her husband, Bob, had used up all of his vacation time for 1999 attending hearings and the trial.

A week later, Hall listened to the lawyers make their arguments for and against moving the trial. Brake contended that the intense media coverage of the Salmon trial and death-penalty hearing, followed by the anger expressed by the community after the decision, meant her client could not get a fair trial in Colorado Springs. She blamed attorneys on both sides—Salmon's defense attorneys for portraying Woldt as a "sexual masochist" and the mastermind of the crime, and the prosecutors for making "disparaging and prejudicial" statements following the sentencing which, she added, made them too "emotionally involved" to try Woldt fairly.

"The community is drowning in opinions and feelings that will have no basis in fact in Mr. Woldt's trial," Brake said. "The community is infected with passions about this case. . . . I think the public here is numb to what the law is and is not."

Young countered, "This crime happened in this community, and this community has the right to try this case."

After the lawyers had their say, Hall didn't waste any time. He said the trial would go forward in Colorado Springs. However, he said, he might rethink his decision if it became impossible to seat a jury that could be fair.

Having lost one battle, Wilson was ready to start another. Now he accused the prosecutors of reneging on a year-old promise to seek nothing more severe than a life sentence for Woldt if Salmon got life.

The prosecutors knew from long experience with Wilson that the defense attorney would say just about anything, even accuse the district attorney's office of all sorts of illegalities and questionable ethics, if it served his purposes. But they felt this accusation was below the belt. But Wilson insisted that it was true, and Hall decided to have another hearing and this time put the lawyers on the stand under oath.

Wilson testified that back when the prosecution was seeking to continue Woldt's trial so that they could find an expert of their own to counter the defense's medical expert, Zook promised he would not seek his client's death if Salmon was sentenced to life. What's more, he said, the prosecutor offered to consider a plea deal for Woldt based upon mitigating medical evidence, even if Salmon received the death penalty. He said the conversation occurred during a break as they waited for Parrish to return to the courtroom during a hearing.

"I said to Zook on the break: You better not fuck me on this," Wilson said. "He smiled. I smiled. We sat down."

Wilson said that when he asked Zook to put the offer down in writing, the prosecutor declined, saying he didn't want the Salmon defense team to learn of the deal. The defense attorney added that he didn't push the issue or discuss the promise with Parrish because he didn't want to mess up the potential deal for Woldt.

Zook testified that the entire conversation never took place. The only discussion he said he had with Wilson during that hearing was on an entirely different matter. No one at the district attorney's office believed that the conversation had happened, either. No one else heard the offer, and they were all present during the hearing. For another thing, they all knew that Zook didn't have the authority to make such an offer without first getting District Attorney Smith to sign off on it, and any offer of this magnitude would have been in writing.

Someone was lying. This wasn't a matter of a misunderstanding about what was said. Before Salmon's trial, Cleaver had asked Wilson—on the record—if his client Woldt had received any promises or deals "whatsoever" if he was tried second. He told her and Judge Parrish that there were no promises or deals. But then he turned around and told Judge Hall that Zook had made this promise. It couldn't be both ways. In the end, Judge Hall tried to be diplomatic about it, but he sided with the prosecution. "This is not a conclusion that one side was lying or doing anything inappropriate," he said. "This is a real good example of why things need to be on the record so we don't have these types of disputes later. I am simply not persuaded that a promise existed."

The same day that story appeared in the *Gazette*, it as well as other newspapers around the state also carried a new story, about the Columbine shootings. The story stated that the young gunmen, Harris and Klebold, might have been stopped if school officials had at their disposal FBI profiling strategies to identify potential threats.

Attorney General Janet Reno said the Justice Department would sink some money into educating school officials and the community to be aware of certain personality traits and behaviors, such as fantasies about committing violent acts, "low tolerance for frustration and poor coping skills," failed love relationships, alienation, intolerance, and "inappropriate humor." School officials and parents would learn under the new program to be on the watch for their children gravitating toward negative role models such as Hitler or Satan and "unusual interest in sensational violence."

"We will be in a position to help those children who show a propensity for violence, before they scar themselves and others forever," Reno said. "And we will be in a position to protect innocent school children before they become senseless victims."

In the meantime, another death penalty hearing was beginning in Denver that would test the three-judge panels in an entirely new way that no one could have foreseen.

On June 30, 1998, William Lee "Cody" Neal went to a building-supply store, where he purchased, among other things, eyebolts, duct tape, rope, and a seven-pound maul (half ax, half sledgehammer). He then returned to a townhouse on West Chenango Drive outside Morrison, where he'd lived since July 1996 with forty-four-year-old Rebecca Holberton.

A consummate liar, Neal, forty-two, who'd hinted to friends and acquaintances both that he was a bounty hunter and a hit man for the mob, owed Holberton, a divorcee who worked for US West, more than $70,000. Now she wanted the money back, she told friends, as a prelude for getting Neal out of her life. She was already renovating the townhouse, which had butcher paper taped over the windows and just plywood flooring in the living and dining rooms.

After he returned from the store, Neal sat Holberton in a chair in the living room, telling her he had "a surprise" for her. He placed a briefcase on her lap, intimating that it contained her missing money, and then put a blanket over her head. Then he crushed Holberton's skull with the blunt side of the maul.

On July 3, Neal brought another divorced woman, Candace Walters, forty-eight, whom he'd conned into loaning him about $6,000, to the townhouse. At the urging of her daughter, Holly, Walters had been trying to learn more about the "mystery man" Neal played to the hilt. But Walters, who worked as a waitress and needed her money, also half believed his tales about the large amount of money he was about to receive; Neal had even convinced her to sell her car in anticipation of the car she'd receive, along with her money, when they would go to Las Vegas to collect his funds. But first, he said, he had "a surprise" for her, too.

Neal sat Walters in the living room. She refused to put her head under the blanket (she didn't want to muss her hair) but Neal still managed to sneak up on her, striking her several times in the head with the ax side of the maul. He then urinated on her corpse, placed a plastic bag over her head, wrapped her in a blanket, and put the body by the fireplace—not far from where Holberton's body was wrapped in plastic bags.

Using money obtained with Walters's debit card, Neal took a girlfriend and her roommate, twenty-one-year-old "Suzanne," out for a night on the town.

On July 5, Neal picked up Suzanne, who'd promised to do a job for him: accompanying him to Las Vegas to sign some papers with his attorneys. But first, he said, he had "a surprise" to show her at the townhouse.

Once inside, Neal forced Suzanne onto a mattress on the

floor, bound her, spread-eagled, with her wrists and ankles tied to four eyebolts he'd screwed into the floor, and cut her clothes off with a knife. To further terrorize her, he placed a piece of skull, bloody hair still attached, on Suzanne's naked stomach, showed her Walters's leg, and kicked a plastic-wrapped mound to demonstrate that there was another body there as well. Then he covered Suzanne with a blanket and, warning her not to make a sound, or "others" would come into the room to rape and kill her, left the townhouse.

Next, Neal picked up Angela Fite, a twenty-eight-year-old mother of two who was trying to escape an abusive marriage when she met Neal. Her "rescuer" brought her back to the townhouse, which she believed was the "surprise" home he'd promised for her and her children. But now Neal duct-taped Fite to a chair facing the mattress on the ground. "Welcome to my mortuary," he said, showing her the bodies of Holberton and Walters.

Then Neal pulled back the blanket to reveal Suzanne. "We're not going to get out of here alive, are we?" Fite said, looking at the other woman. Still, Neal took his time, even giving Fite a cigarette before announcing that he had to go feed his cat. He came back with the maul and struck Fite repeatedly—at least six times—as Suzanne watched in horror.

Neal picked Fite's cigarette off the floor and finished it. Then he untied Suzanne and, holding a pistol to her head, forced her to perform oral sex. After that, he made her return to the mattress, where he raped her. The next morning, Neal took Suzanne to her apartment. He'd told her he'd let her live as his "witness" if she cooperated. And there, for several days, Neal held Suzanne, his girlfriend, and a male friend of the women, who'd declined to leave once he saw that they were in trouble, at gunpoint. He made Suzanne tell the others about what she'd seen at his "mortuary" and recorded a rambling confession.

On Saturday, July 8, Neal left the three hostages, giving them his pager number and explicit instructions regarding how they were to contact the police. If they didn't follow those instructions, he warned, he might return to kill them.

Even as Neal was making his arrangements, the bodies of the three murdered women were discovered. Holberton's coworkers had grown concerned when she didn't show up for work and had asked the Jefferson County Sheriff's Office to conduct a welfare check. A deputy went to the townhouse and, failing to get an answer at the front door, went around to the back, where a sliding glass door led into the dining room.

The deputy opened the door a crack and called out. Getting no answer, he opened the door a little farther but stopped before entering. "I was overwhelmed by a sense of evil," the deputy later testified. "It was just one of those scenes where you know you just don't want to be there. . . . A wave of evil hit me. It looked like a torture chamber where somebody had suffered." The deputy called for help.

It was early evening by the time the detectives were ready to page Neal and try to get him to give himself up. When Neal drove Holberton's SUV into the parking lot of a Target store, he was taken down at gunpoint. A handgun and shotgun, along with items belonging to his victims, were found in the vehicle he'd been driving.

Neal didn't want any lawyers. He wanted to represent himself, *pro se,* which was his right under Colorado law. Claiming he desired to spare his victims and their families the ordeal of a trial, he said he would plead guilty to rape, robbery, and kidnapping, as well as three charges of first-degree murder after deliberation, which he knew would expose him to a potential death-penalty hearing. Neal even gave videotaped interviews to sheriff's investigators, waiving his right to have an attorney present. He confessed to members of the media, too, saying, among other things, that he'd killed the women to avoid having his thefts exposed.

By February 1999, Neal had succeeded in firing the public defenders appointed to represent him, although he agreed to accept private defense attorney Randy Canney as advisory counsel. And on February 25, acting as his own attorney, Neal pleaded guilty "without a doubt" to the thirteen counts he faced, including the three first-degree-murder charges.

During the hour-long hearing, Judge Thomas Woodford repeatedly asked Neal if he would reconsider and allow an attorney to represent him. Neal refused. The judge asked Neal if he understood that his guilty plea carried only two possible sentences: life in prison without parole or death by lethal injection. He'd been examined by a court-appointed psychiatrist, Neal told the judge, and "he didn't see any reason why I was not competent."

After the hearing, DA Thomas announced that his office would seek the death penalty, an announcement that met with immediate recriminations from defense attorneys. Going for the death penalty when a defendant was representing himself was "state-sanctioned suicide," said attorney David Lane.

"This is a total farce," public defender Jim Aber said. "Seeking the death penalty against a person not represented by counsel is like trying to kill an unarmed man. There is no morality or justice in this."

But prosecutors pointed out that declining to seek the death penalty for alleged murderers who chose to represent themselves could, in effect, negate the death penalty as a possible sentence. All a defendant would have to do in order to avoid being sentenced to death was demand to defend himself.

Thomas said he would have preferred that Neal have a lawyer. In deciding to represent himself, Neal almost guaranteed that appellate lawyers would be able to argue that he'd had incompetent counsel; if an appeals court agreed, then Jefferson County would have to go through the death-penalty hearing, and possibly an entire trial, all over again.

Even though Neal didn't want a lawyer, Canney continued to try to act as one. He had wanted to be a criminal defense lawyer all his life; he liked the idea of fighting for the underdog. His first obligation was to make the prosecution prove its case, but he felt the job went further than that. It was up to him to present his client as a human being, not a monster.

That's what he'd tried to do with Frank Vigil, his first client tried for first-degree murder. It wasn't a death-penalty case, although two of Vigil's co-defendants, Danny Martinez and Francisco "Pancho" Martinez, had faced the panels, but he'd still felt the weight of having the young man's life in his hands. It hadn't been easy talking with Vigil's mother, knowing that he couldn't offer much hope that she'd ever have her son, then only seventeen, back home again. And it wasn't easy trying to explain his client's role in the crime while fourteen-year-old Brandy DuVall's family was sitting in court, listening to every word.

Now he had to stand by while Neal refused to do anything to help himself. Canney believed that Neal was insane and had been when he'd committed the crimes. Just days before the death-penalty hearing was scheduled to begin, the attorney appealed to Judge Woodford, requesting that Neal be tested again for mental competency. At the hearing, Canney even called Neal's sister, Sharon, the one family member still talking to him, who over a speaker-phone testified that her brother would go "from being rational to incoherent in the same conversation" and talked about being "a prophet of God." But Woodford denied Canney's motions, saying Neal had showed no signs of mental disease in any of his multiple court appearances.

So on September 20, 1999, William Lee "Cody" Neal

shuffled into the courtroom in the standard-issue Halloween-orange jumpsuit, white T-shirt and socks, and blue slippers. Hunched over as he waited for the deputy to unlock the handcuffs behind him, he glanced at the spectator gallery.

If looks could kill, Neal would have crumpled immediately to the floor. The families and friends of his victims filled three rows behind the prosecution table and even spilled over to the other side. The one victim who'd survived his rampage, a pretty, young blonde, leaned against her mother's protective shoulder.

There wasn't enough space in the courtroom for everyone who wanted to watch the hearing. The victims' friends and families had been seated first. The first row on the other side, immediately behind the defense table, was kept clear by the deputies in charge of court security, as much for Neal's safety as anything else. The second row was reserved for Neal's family, of which no members were present, as well as Neal's supporters, of which there were few, and associates and colleagues of the defense counsel, including Jim Aber, the chief deputy state public defender.

Neal sat down next to Canney, his advisory counsel. In front of him on the defense table were arranged a dictionary, yellow legal pads for notes, a neat row of pens, and a television monitor.

Those assembled in the courtroom rose as the three judges—Jefferson County presiding judge Thomas Woodford as well as Frank Martinez and William Meyer, the last two from Denver, entered and took their seats at the enlarged dais built just for death-penalty hearings. In the preceding five months, Jefferson County had already had three such hearings. First had come Robert Lee Riggan, Jr., who'd been spared in April. Then Daniel "Bang" Martinez, Jr., who had been spared in May. In June, at the third hearing, Francisco "Pancho" Martinez, Jr., had been sentenced to death. Few in the courtroom expected Neal to escape the same fate.

Now Chief Deputy District Attorney Charles Tingle rose to deliver the prosecution's opening statements. At the table behind him were Deputy District Attorney Chris Bachmeyer and the lead investigator in the case, Jose Aceves.

Rebecca Holberton, Candace Walters, and Angela Fite were all vulnerable in one way or another, Tingle began. "[They were] in search of happiness, and he preyed upon each one of them. He promised to rescue them emotionally and financially. But he was a phony. A master manipulator . . . and he sucked them in with his lies and deceit."

Since there had been no trial, Neal's case hadn't been as physically demanding as some, but it had involved a lot more than Tingle's regular duties. He'd had more contact with Neal than anyone except for Aceves. As a *pro se* defendant, Neal had the right to discuss legal matters with the prosecutor, and he took full advantage of his cell-phone privileges, calling Tingle four or five times a week. To keep things running smoothly, and to stave off potential appeals, Tingle had made sure that Neal's requests were met.

In his fifteen years as a prosecutor, the forty-year-old Tingle had never run into anyone like Neal. The defendant was extremely intelligent, at least in his niche as a pathological liar and sociopath. He was also very meticulous, putting together a stack of case law regarding the death penalty in the United States that was eighteen inches high. From their conversations, it was clear that Neal had read every page of it, as well as the thousands and thousands of pages of discovery. And if there was something he couldn't read or a clarification he needed, Neal would stay after Tingle until he got what he wanted.

Of course, given the methodical way Neal had gone about the business of murdering three women and raping a fourth, his organizational skills shouldn't have come as a surprise. If there was one thing that stood out about the murders, beyond their horrific brutality, it was the incredible, multilayered web of lies that Neal had spun to snare his victims.

One of Tingle's greatest fears was that Neal would be underestimated by the courts, by his jailers, and even by the prosecutors. So Tingle had decided to consider anything that came out of Neal's mouth, no matter how seemingly innocent, as an attempt to manipulate them.

In their dealings, Neal had always been courteous and respectful, ingratiatingly so. It made Tingle's skin crawl to hear the defendant talk as though they were on the same team. But then, he'd seen for himself what Neal had done: Tingle had walked through the townhouse while the bodies were still there. He'd prosecuted more than a dozen murder cases, all with their own crime scenes, but none came close to Neal's carnage. To even look at Neal without revulsion, Tingle had to separate in his mind the ax murderer from the jailhouse lawyer.

The forty-one-year-old Bachmeyer had spent the past couple of years working domestic-violence cases. Her first impression of Neal was that he had an almost desperate need to be liked. But then she felt his behavior toward her go beyond friendliness to flirting, testing how she would respond as a woman. Her response was that he gave her the creeps. It bothered her that to the public, Neal's victims might appear gullible, even witless, for believing his outlandish stories and going off to the slaughter like sheep. She knew that the victims were intelligent, caring women. They hadn't engaged in behavior that put them at risk— they didn't hang out with gangs, they weren't prostitutes or drug addicts, and they didn't go out with strangers. Their only fault was that they were too trusting.

In court this morning, she and Tingle had noticed something different about Neal: the killer and rapist was wearing a new gold wedding band. A few days before the trial, a local jeweler had alerted Tingle that Neal was trying to buy a set of rings; apparently he was going to marry his new girlfriend, a trust-fund baby in Phoenix who sent him money regularly and had even been up to visit him in jail.

Incredibly, Neal was still able to cast his spells, even behind bars. Ted Bundy, the serial killer executed in 1989 whose exploits were favored reading material for Neal, had married while on death row, but at least that woman had been able to convince herself that her groom was innocent. With Neal's confession, no such fantasy was possible. Tingle wondered if the "wedding" was just another ploy to manipulate the judges, as well as a way to continue to control some poor woman.

In the final analysis, Tingle believed that Neal's demand to represent himself was a control issue. He simply had to be in control of everything: in control of the women, their money, their emotions, and their lives. He'd tied his rape victim to a bed to control her. Now he was exercising the ultimate control—over the decision of whether he lived or died.

After Tingle finished his opening statement, Neal stood and shuffled over to the lectern. The freedom to move across the courtroom was part of a deal he'd worked out in order to be his own lawyer, but the deputies came a couple of steps closer, just in case. Before he could start speaking, Woodford issued a warning. While opening statements were not considered evidence in any trial, just an outline of what each side intended to present, whatever Neal said could be used against him. He'd retained his right to remain silent, the judge reminded him.

Neal adjusted the microphone. It was "September 20, 1999, Monday morning, a day that's much more to some, much less to others," he said. It was Yom Kippur, the Day of Atonement, a "special day" for "reconciliation, forgiveness . . . peace."

From the victims' side of the courtroom came angry murmurs, but Neal continued. "This is one of the most horrendous things I ever heard of," he said of his own crimes. "How could someone do what I have done? I wish I could say I was innocent. There is no excuse for this crime. I can't wash my hands enough for this."

He was guilty as charged. "Mr. Tingle is an honorable man, and he speaks the truth," Neal said. "He has been honest with me and did not exaggerate anything. I would not change what he said, except maybe to fill in some blanks." And by doing so, he added, he would be the voice for "three wonderful, trusting, beautiful women."

He had been molested as a child, Neal said, an excuse that led him to point the blame at others while he "served only Satan." But now he was a changed man, a man who'd recently reaffirmed his "belief in the Lord, my God." He wanted to live so that he could "zealously" serve Jesus in prison.

"Even a wretched life means something," he implored the judges. "Even a wretched life can change. I do not want to die, for I know I've turned around."

However, if the judges decided he should die, Neal said, "I will submit fully . . . remembering special moments" with his victims.

In his opening, Tingle hadn't really outlined the aggravators the state would try to prove. So now Neal did it for him. The crime was "especially heinous, cruel and depraved," he said. "That's an accurate assessment."

He'd killed two or more people by "lying in wait." True. He'd "intentionally" killed two or more people with "universal malice and extreme indifference to the value of human life." True. He'd killed a kidnapped person. True. He'd killed to prevent prosecution. True: "That's what precipitated the whole thing." And he'd killed for monetary gain. "Yes," he concluded, "all of the aggravating factors are present."

As for mitigators, Neal said, there were only three, starting with his age. Although he was forty-two at the time of the crime, his troubled past had left him "a child . . . hiding and stalking . . . scared of being punished for what he had been doing and what he had become." As a result, he could not "appreciate the wrongfulness of his conduct," he said, then added, "I knew that what I was going to do was wrong and chose to do it anyway." Only halfheartedly, he contended that he might have been under "unusual and substantial duress" at the time of the crimes. "I've been through a lot of tough times in my life, but I don't see it."

After Neal's opening, the hearing moved quickly. Tingle and Bachmeyer presented the evidence of the crimes. Neal's rape victim took the stand and bravely recounted the horrors of her ordeal. Through it all, Neal sat listening, declining to cross-examine the witnesses, while his counsel, Canney, sat silently stewing. When it came time to present his case for mitigation, Neal called only a few witnesses, including Byron Plumley, an adjunct professor of religion at Regis University, who testified that Neal's conversion seemed genuine.

On September 29, 1999, the three judges returned with their verdict. In their deliberations, they had determined that the state had proved all of its aggravators. Then they'd rejected all of Neal's mitigators. More than that, they'd rejected everything Neal had to say for himself.

They didn't believe that he'd been sexually assaulted. They doubted his remorse: "William Neal is so self-absorbed that his capacity for remorse is questionable," they determined. Even his religious conversion "is suspect given the timing.

"William Neal claims to be a changed man and, therefore, requests mercy. William Neal cannot point to the past as a basis for mercy but asks the panel to trust him in his promise toward the future. This panel is unwilling to do so. The panel relies upon the past as the best predictor of the future. William Neal's plea rings hollow in light of his past deceits and evil deeds."

Judge Anderson read the verdict as Neal stared straight ahead. The "only penalty for the brutal, needless killing visited upon these kind and lovely ladies," the judge pronounced, "is death."

A few minutes later, Canney stood in the hallway outside the courtroom. "I don't know if Cody is so wrought with guilt that he felt he had to represent himself," he told reporters. "It may be part of his mental illness."

The victims' families gathered downstairs. "This brings some closure, but it does not bring back my mom, Angela, or Rebecca," Holly Walters said.

"This is not going to be over for us for a very, very long time," said Wayne Fite, Angela's father.

Both said they planned to attend Neal's execution. "To the end," added Wayne. "To the end," echoed Holly.

Now, when Woldt's defense attorneys again prepared to raise the issue of a proportionality review, and determine where on the spectrum of killers their client stood, they would have one more apple to compare to Woldt's clockwork orange.

# SIXTEEN

# "HE DID A VERY
# EVIL THING."

*February 3, 2000*

"There's going to be ample evidence to show Mr. Woldt was the ringleader. He had this idea years before and recruited Mr. Salmon." Deputy District Attorney Gordon Denison turned toward the defense table where his counterpart, Andrew Heher, was waiting to retort.

As the prosecution team's appellate attorney, Denison wasn't well known to the public, unlike the other attorneys in the case—Zook and Young for the prosecution and Doug Wilson and Terri Brake for the defense. His was a world of motions and countermotions and brief arguments in front of the judge, out of the limelight but no less important.

If he didn't do his job right, the Salmon and Woldt cases might come back to haunt the prosecutors on appeal. Now, with jury selection for Woldt's trial just a few days away, he was fighting a defense motion that might upset the entire prosecution strategy to send the defendant to death row.

In Salmon's trial, the prosecutors had contended that

both killers played an equal part in the abduction, rape, and murder of Jacine Gielinski, and even that at certain stages, such as who was the first to stab her, Salmon had been the leader. However, the strategy in Woldt's trial would be to essentially portray him the same way Salmon's lawyers had: as the sexual sadist who'd created the fantasy and then masterminded turning it into reality.

Woldt's defense team, however, was now calling foul with Heher arguing that they shouldn't now be able to "change their story. . . . They made their choice. If they flip-flop and suggest Mr. Woldt is more culpable and should be sentenced to death because he was the ring-leader, that should be absolutely forbidden."

Denison shook his head. The older he got, he observed society becoming more at ease with the abdication of personal responsibility. During Salmon's trial and sentencing hearing, the defense lawyers had argued what the press had labeled the "devil made me do it" defense. It was all Woldt's fault—Lucas Salmon would have never raped and murdered a young woman without his evil partner. He was immature. He was teased. He knew right from wrong but was incapable of exercising free will because he was worried about losing Woldt's friendship.

And here came Woldt's defense team. This killer wasn't responsible for his actions, either. His behavior was due to a tiny, and not uncommon, calcium deposit in his brain. He'd been pressured into raping and murdering Jacine because of Salmon's incessant complaints about being a virgin. He hated his mother and his father hit him.

It was always someone else's fault. In the wake of the Columbine shootings, the so-called experts in human behavior even blamed the media with its bloody video games, misogynist rap music, and violent movies. Salmon and Woldt had watched A Clockwork Orange and the film had somehow (at least according to Salmon) inspired them to stalk young women for the purpose of raping and killing them.

Now, Heher was complaining because the prosecution wanted to present evidence that suggested Woldt actually *was* responsible for planning and carrying out the murder of a lovely young woman. And it made him angry.

Denison had the appearance of a mild-mannered librarian, but he was tougher than he looked both physically (he was an avid runner and had completed several marathons) and professionally. As an appeals specialist, he was what is known in the legal community as a lawyer's lawyer. His oftentimes unsung job was to know the technicalities of the law inside and out. It was his job to know the precedent-setting cases and the most recent decisions by courts high and low, as well as steer the prosecution clear of mistakes that might result in a mistrial or a conviction being overturned. Andrew Heher was his counterpart on the other side.

Denison had come late to his career in the public sector. For twenty years, he'd served in the army as a lawyer and judge. The only part he didn't really like about the military system was that in his early years he had had to alternate between working as a defense lawyer and a prosecutor. It was good training, but his passion was for prosecuting criminals. The bad acts of human beings against other human beings angered him, and he saw prosecution as bringing some justice to the world.

He spent the last years of his army career as a military judge where he had a reputation as a hanging judge. Lawyers working for the defense hated him, but when they were playing the part of prosecutor, they loved him. Near the end of his career, he was transferred to Fort Carson, the large army post south of Colorado Springs. He, his wife, Suzanne, and their three daughters fell in love with the area and decided to remain there when he retired from the military. They enjoyed both the scenery and the small-town, family-oriented feel of Colorado Springs.

Denison was pleased that he soon had a job with the district attorney's office. The office reflected the conservative nature of Colorado Springs and surrounding El Paso County, which were compatible with his own outlook. The El Paso office was proud of its reputation of being tough on crime, as reflected in the statistics that showed they were loath to deal in plea agreements for the sake of avoiding trials.

However, Denison soon learned that there were aspects to civilian justice that rankled him. He wasn't used to the shenanigans and theatrics allowed in civilian courts. Military judges would not have tolerated much of it, and if they did, they wouldn't have bought into it. Something else that struck him about civilian law was the amount of recidivism. The military courts cracked down hard on criminal activity. One strike and the accused was going to do time. A second strike, and the culprit was gone. There were no third strikes. But in El Paso County, he saw the same names come up time and again.

Since starting at the district attorney's office, Denison had worn a number of different hats, including that of trial lawyer. He didn't like plea bargains, either, and his record for trying twenty-three felony cases in a year still stood. At one point, Denison headed up the office's drug prosecutions. He'd enjoyed that in part because he got to go along with the police on raids and stakeouts. And he'd handled his share of murder cases.

One of them involved a rare case of a teenager killing his parents. On the morning of December 17, 1992, a fifteen-year-old named Jacob Ind and his friend, Gabriel Adams, murdered Ind's mother, Pamela Jordan, and stepfather, Kermode Jordan. Ind, who was said to have dabbled in Satanism prior to the murder, hired Adams to do the murder. But his friend botched the job by creeping into the house in the early hours and shooting but not killing the Jordans, and Ind had to finish them off with his father's .357 handgun.

The pair, each of them blaming the other, were tried separately by Denison and Bill Aspinwall. Allegations of emotional and sexual abuse by the Jordans of Jacob and his brother, Charles, surfaced at Jacob's trial, as the defense lawyers tried to argue that the killings were done in self-defense. However, the prosecutors, bothered by the fact that Jacob had never shown the slightest bit of remorse, countered that Jacob was not in imminent danger and could have left the home.

Both Ind and Adams were each convicted of two counts of first-degree murder after deliberation. Due to their ages, they were not eligible for a death-penalty hearing and were sentenced to two consecutive terms of life in prison without parole, making them the youngest prisoners in Colorado with life sentences. Ind, who did not testify during his trial, spoke out at his sentencing, contending that the justice system was not interested in what had caused him to kill his parents. "The system sucks big, fat, sweaty toe," he said.

If the allegations of sexual abuse were true, Denison understood that there might be an explanation, if not an excuse, for the Jordan murders. But once again, it was always someone else's fault.

The crimes and the reasons that defense attorneys thought that they should be excused was simply incomprehensible to Denison. But no crime he'd ever prosecuted, or even heard of, could compare to the depravity of what had happened to Jacine Gielinski.

The first time he read the confessions by Salmon and Woldt, his blood had boiled. Perhaps it was because he had daughters in the same age range who'd driven alone at night down the same roads Jacine had traveled. Maybe because every time he drove north to Denver from his home

he had to pass the apartments where she had lived and the
road her killers had turned down to drive to the elementary
school. Maybe it was all of those things, but Jacine's murder haunted him and it made him sick to his stomach to
hear the defense lawyers lay the blame on anything but
their clients' own sick fantasies and desires.

As he told friends in his annual Christmas letter in 1998,
the case had become "an obsession for me. . . . It has been
the greatest challenge and will become (hopefully) the
ultimate accomplishment of my prosecutorial career.

"Yet, amidst the challenge and excitement, I live each
day with the suffering of Jacine and her parents and am
saddened by man's ability to inflict such pain on his fellow
man."

Nearly three years had passed since Jacine's death.
Three years and hundreds of motions from the defense
attorneys, arguments that their clients' rights had been
abused by some technicality, even making demands that
because of some alleged infraction by the police or prosecutors, the charges should be thrown out. As if Salmon and
Woldt should simply be allowed to walk away after what
they'd done to Jacine. The defense attorney would consider
that "winning."

Many of the defense motions were silly and easily countered, though that, too, took time and resources. Others
challenges were more serious, such as the attempt to keep
a key piece of evidence out of the Woldt trial: the testimony of Derrick Ayers, the former friend of Woldt who'd
told police about their venture into the mountains and the
defendant's idea to attack a couple with large rocks. The
testimony would show that Woldt had been trying to recruit someone to help fulfill his fantasy of rape and
murder for years. And it was important to combat the expected defense tactic of claiming that it was Salmon's
constant complaints about needing a sexual partner that
had pressured Woldt into going along with the plan.

The legal problem was that Ayers was dead. Although he had a record of petty crimes, most of them traffic related, Ayers had turned out to be a pretty decent sort. He'd agreed to have his statement videotaped and remain in the area. Back then, the police had taped him just in case he decided to disappear, but making the record turned out to be a stroke of good fortune after Ayers was killed in a freak hiking accident when he fell off a cliff.

Woldt's defense attorneys argued that the videotaped testimony should not be allowed because they would not be able to cross-examine the witness. However, Denison had pointed out that there were precedents for using taped confessions and testimony from defendants and witnesses who, for one reason or another, later decided not to testify or had died or disappeared. Also, Ayers's former girlfriend, Lisa, would be called to the stand to corroborate at least the most damning portion of her boyfriend's contentions—the rocks she'd found in her car after the pair's trip to the mountains.

With all the legal machinations and delays, Denison felt sorry for the Luiszers. Not only had they lost their only child, but then the justice system had dragged them down a long, tortuous road, and it still wasn't over. Despite all the lawyerly attempts to remain objective, he'd grown to like them and considered them friends. He'd gone out with them to dinner and they called each other before Bronco games. He saw how the heart had been ripped out of two people and how the system he worked for had made them victims as well. When he looked at his own daughters, he could imagine how devastated he'd feel if something that horrible had happened to one of them. But he knew the reality had to be infinitely worse.

It made him all that much more determined to do the best he could, including winning battles like the current one over whether the prosecutors could present the case that Woldt was the leader in the rape and murder of Jacine.

The prosecution wasn't changing stories, he told Judge Hall, just the emphasis. "It isn't a different legal theory," he said. "It's a different way of reacting to the evidence."

Judge Hall agreed. The prosecution would present its case as planned.

Despite a gag order prohibiting the lawyers for either side from commenting to the press, defense attorney Doug Wilson held regular press conferences. The swiftness with which the jury in the Salmon trial had reached its verdict (about an hour) indicated that he had a problem, because Woldt's defense was going to be essentially the same: blame the other guy and claim his client had some sort of mental disorder that had prevented him from "deliberating," the word that would ring in a death-sentence hearing.

The prosecution had the same ammunition: the detailed verbal and written confessions, the physical evidence, the bombshell of Salmon's videotaped statement to the psychologists contending that Woldt masterminded the crimes, and Ayers's statement.

Then there was the added problem of the media coverage, which had rekindled the community's anger, as well as the general knowledge that Salmon had already been convicted. If it came to a sentencing hearing, Wilson and Brake could argue that if the pair were equally guilty, then they should suffer the same fate—life in prison. However, they were aware there was also the potential for a backlash from frustration with the Salmon sentence that could come back at Woldt.

The defense attorneys were used to being seen as the bad guys. The press and the public accused them of being obstructionists and playing games, coddling killers and ignoring the victims' rights. But Wilson saw it as trying to save a man's life—that a state-sanctioned execution was not morally superior to murder.

About six feet tall, heavy set and balding, Wilson came from a background that hardly suggested that he would become a defense lawyer known for stopping at nothing to save the lives of murderers. As he would later tell the *Gazette*, he'd grown up in Ohio in a conservative Republican, middle-class family. However, the apple had rolled quite a distance from the tree. After a family vacation to Colorado when he was a boy, he had announced that when he grew up he was going to return to the state as a lawyer to "defend poor people."

He told the newspaper that he'd learned as a thirteen-year-old to distrust the government on May 4, 1970, when the Ohio National Guard opened fire on college students, killing four who were protesting the Vietnam War at Kent State University. He was further influenced by the book *To Kill a Mockingbird*, identifying with the defense lawyer's heroic, and unpopular, defense of a black man accused of rape in a southern town.

Love him (as did those who worked with or for him in the public defenders' office), or hate him (like the families of his clients' victims), Wilson walked the talk. He and his wife had agreed not to have children so that he could devote his time to representing those too poor to afford an attorney, especially those facing state execution.

He even carried a card in his wallet that stated: "I am opposed to the death penalty. If my death is the result of a crime, I do not want any person accused of the crime to face the death penalty. Please advise the court and all attorneys of this. I wish this card to be considered during any hearing in which the victim of a crime is allowed to speak."

Wilson certainly had not changed his spots while representing Woldt. He and Brake had even won a few of their motions, such as suppressing reports from the jail that Woldt liked to talk to other inmates about raping women. Wilson also complained a few days before jury selection was to start that the prosecution had not given him enough advance notice to deal with the proposed testimony of an inmate who claimed that Woldt had been faking his mental illness. Hall agreed, excluding the testimony from the trial, but said the inmate could testify if there was a sentencing phase.

The main thing was that Wilson and Brake had managed to delay the trial for nearly three years. It hadn't worked as far as getting the Luiszers and the district attorney's office to throw in the towel. However, they could hope that the pool of potential jurors had either forgotten the details of the crime or weren't even living in Colorado Springs when Jacine was murdered or Salmon was tried.

In the weeks leading up to the trial, Wilson ignored the gag order to try a little damage control by talking to the media. That included discussing the "medical evidence" of the calcium deposit that affected his client's ability to deliberate or control his behavior on the night of the murder.

"How sick do you have to be?" he asked the press rhetorically. "That'll be the jury's decision. I believe that our experts have told us, he's a pretty sick boy mentally."

Wilson had also complained long and often both in court and out that his client could not get a fair trial in El Paso County, especially after the Salmon trial. "Everything that came out in court was that Woldt was the bad guy," he told the *Gazette*. "It was 'blame us' time. We had to sit here for two months getting attacked and we couldn't do anything."

The defense lawyer said no one was trying to say Woldt wasn't guilty of murder. But "our guy isn't the Svengali that they painted him to be. . . . It's hard to deny that he did it with those confessions out there that they made. It's not a whodunit. It's a why it was done. A normal person could not do this.

"We're presenting a defense that deals with the question of deliberation."

* * *

The opening statements had followed the same general pattern as in the Salmon trial. Prosecutor Dave Young read from Woldt's confession, there was the same brief glimpse of Jacine when she was alive, but with the added material about the witnesses who would testify that Woldt had planned to fulfill his fantasy "for years."

Brake had opened for the defense as Woldt listened as though he were a college student hearing a mildly interesting university lecture. Mannerisms others had noted in his past, such as his habit of sniffing things he handled or came near, seemed to have accelerated or, as more cynical observers thought, he was acting to help his lawyers' arguments that he was mentally ill. He also walked with a curious stiff gait—the deputies in charge of security called it "the Woldt walk"—his hands hanging straight down to his sides rather than swinging back and forth with his steps. And when he looked at something to one side or another, he turned his whole body, rather than just his head.

Pointing to her client, Brake said he was only "joking" when he'd talked to Salmon and other friends about kidnapping and raping a woman. He'd been under pressure from two sides: his wife, Bonnie, to get rid of their houseguest, and Salmon, who harassed him constantly about finding him a sexual partner.

Then in April 1997, the defense lawyer said, Woldt's brain "malfunctioned" and he went into a "catatonic, dreamlike state" in which the joke became a reality. The malfunction, she said, was caused by an abnormal, calcified growth in his brain, which along with an obsessive-compulsive personality disorder made him incapable of using deliberation or controlling himself when Salmon insisted that they kill Jacine Gielinski.

Peggy and Bob had skipped the opening statements.

Neither wished to hear a lawyer again talk about one of their daughter's killers as if he were somehow the victim.

But once again, Peggy was called to the stand to tearfully identify her daughter's jewelry and relive the night she and her husband got the telephone call that changed their world and who they were forever—forevermore the parents of a murder victim.

Sometimes she wondered if she would have the strength to go on. She was grateful for the cards and letters of support she received from friends and from strangers, many of them still expressing their own struggles to deal with Jacine's death. But it was hers and Bob's burden to relive the murder over and over, even if they still had never heard all of the horrible details. She'd told the press, "After a while you just get numb to it." But that wasn't really true. It still twisted in her gut like a hot knife, and for that she often blamed Doug Wilson.

She hated him. He represented everything that was wrong with the justice system to her. It was all just a big game about losing and winning. To her, the defense attorneys seemed to enjoy listening to themselves talk and pretend that what they were saying made any sense. And she thought that Wilson was the worst of the lot. He dressed like a slob, as if he couldn't be bothered to show respect for the proceedings. At first she thought that maybe it was because he didn't make much money, but she'd learned that he made more than the prosecutors, who always dressed well. But worse than his physical appearance and gamesmanship, it seemed that he took every opportunity to make life even more miserable for her and Bob than it already was, even when that seemed impossible.

Terri Brake had done her part to keep the wounds open. The defense lawyer had even contacted (through another lawyer) a mutual friend of the Luiszers to ask her to intercede and get them to request that the district attorney not pursue the death penalty. The friend hung up and called Peggy, who thought that the defense team had sunk about as far as it could go. But she was wrong there, too.

During jury selection, Wilson had filed a motion to prohibit the Luiszers and their supporters from wearing the one-inch purple ribbons created in memory of Jacine for her memorial services. Nor did he want Peggy to carry the photograph of Jacine she'd brought with her for every hearing and Salmon's trial. He also asked the judge to stop them from inserting earplugs during the worst of the testimony or from leaving the courtroom when the crime scene or autopsy photographs were shown. The ribbons, the photograph, and the earplugs and exits might "inflame the jury . . . and undermine Woldt's presumption of innocence."

Gordon Denison had filed a countermotion defending the family's rights. U.S. case law and Colorado statutes protected crime victims' rights inside the courtroom, he wrote. That meant "spectators must be permitted to wear what they wish, including earplugs, carry what they desire, and come and go as they please."

Denison wrote it was unlikely that the jurors would even notice the ribbons or, if they did, know the significance. He noted that the jury forewoman in the Salmon trial told the prosecutors that they did not see the ribbons or pay attention to what the Luiszers were doing.

After Wilson filed his motion, Peggy had angrily addressed the media outside the courtroom. "He just doesn't want us in the courtroom," she said. "If his goal was to really upset us, he's succeeded. I think he's just doing it to tick us off."

At a hearing on the issue two days later, she'd fought the tears as she directed her ire at Wilson, who sat stone-faced at the defense table. "He's being mean and vindictive," she said. "We've gone through hell for the past three years, and he's trying to put us through more."

Wilson shrugged it off. All the prosecutors had to do

was agree to sentence Woldt to life in prison, he said. "We would like nothing more than to have the same sentence Lucas Salmon got, and we'd end this case today and end the Luiszers' pain."

Peggy and Bob thought Wilson's response was typical and sincerely doubted that he cared what they wore or did in the courtroom. The real purpose for his legal maneuvering was to beat them down and make them give up. It also showed how little he understood about what Jacine's death meant to them, as if their pain would end just because the trials would be over. Their pain would last for the rest of their lives. What they wanted was justice for Jacine.

Hall compromised. He decided that the jurors wouldn't notice the one-inch ribbons and the Luiszers could continue to use their earplugs so long as they didn't intentionally call attention to themselves when inserting or removing them. They could also enter and leave the courtroom, but he urged them to do so between witnesses so as not to pull the jurors' concentration away from the testimony. However, Peggy would only be allowed to carry the photograph of Jacine after the jury returned with its verdict, he said.

When the news of Wilson's latest motion was reported in the *Gazette,* the community again reacted with outrage.

"I just can't believe the justice system here in Colorado Springs would allow the defense team for George Woldt to even contemplate the idea of forcing these poor parents to take control of their emotions during this trial," a reader wrote.

"So what's next? Maybe they shouldn't cry either? Why is it that the accused has more rights than the victim or the parents of the victim?"

It was something Peggy and Bob Luiszer had often wondered themselves.

* * *

Terribly hurt by the loss of their daughter, the Luiszers took no joy in the pain of the other parents who sat on the defense side of the courtroom. Peggy had been contacted by Bob Salmon, who seemed haunted by guilt as he told her about his son's life in prison. "His father said Lucas wishes he'd done what he wanted to do and pleaded guilty and asked for the death penalty," she told the *Gazette*. "He's wishing he could just kill himself. . . . That gives me the willies."

Peggy had not forgiven Salmon after he apologized. But she'd felt he was sincere, at least until he was brought to court at the start of Woldt's trial to testify against his former friend and he refused.

The prosecutors had thought that there was a chance he would take the stand. They'd offered him complete immunity so that nothing he said could later be used against him if his case was overturned on appeal. He'd seemed genuinely remorseful when he apologized to the Luiszers at his death-penalty hearing saying he would give his own life if it could have brought Jacine back. But then that was when the issue was whether the judges would spare his life.

With the Woldt jury out of the courtroom, Salmon had been brought in, wearing shackles and seated in the jury box. He'd looked at the floor the entire time, shaking his head and mumbling "No" when asked by Hall if he would testify. He never looked at Woldt, who also stared straight ahead, as if his former partner in crime didn't exist.

Young requested that Hall force Salmon to testify. The convicted killer could reveal, he said, whether Woldt was suffering from a "brain malfunction" the night Jacine was murdered. "Mr. Salmon is the only surviving witness as to what happened to Jacine Gielinski, and he was with Mr. Woldt the whole time."

However, Jessica West, one of the new set of lawyers handling Salmon's appeals, said her client feared that his testimony might be used against him despite the prosecution's assurances. He was also worried that other prisoners would hear that he was a snitch and harm him in prison.

Hall cited Salmon for contempt of court and added six months to his life sentence plus the 184 years for his other crimes. He was led out one door, the jury was brought in another, and the trial of George Woldt, who was neatly dressed, with every hair in place, continued.


The women who'd witnessed the abduction were called again to the stand, the memories still vivid.

The Morman missionaries testified about hearing the woman screaming for help and watching her be dragged across the parking lot. Margaret Zarate recounted seeing the dark-haired man, who she identified in court as George Woldt, hitting the woman in the face as he straddled her in the backseat. And then her terror as he looked at her three times.

Then the police officers took the stand. Gregory Wilhelmi revisited the scene of the abduction and then later told of finding the bloody clothes and bloody knife in the trunk of Salmon's car.

Tom Heath recalled how after the knife was discovered and Salmon confessed, Woldt had asked to speak to him privately. The defendant had said that when the young woman pulled up next to them at the stoplight, Salmon had said, "She's the one." But that they had both decided after the rape that, because she had seen their faces, they could not let her go.

After they'd taken turns raping her, stabbing her, and packing mud in her vagina, they'd driven around discussing their chances of still getting into heaven. Salmon, according to Woldt, accused him of making him participate because Woldt had talked so much about it. "He said they'd been following girls for about a week," Heath testified.

Woldt had been emotional and "shaking" when first confronted, Heath said. But as soon as he started to talk about the crime, he became calm and "very unemotional." The only time he showed anything else was when he interrupted his recounting of the rape and murder to ask what was going to happen to his wife. When told that she would be all right, he calmed right down. "After that, it was like telling a story," the officer testified. "There was no emotion at all."

Woldt's lack of emotion was also noted on the stand by Detective Terry Bjorndahl, who recounted his interviews with the defendant on the morning following the murder. Throughout the interviews, the detective said, Woldt's demeanor was matter-of-fact, lacking in emotion, which he thought was "amazing under the circumstances."

He said Woldt told him that Salmon had indicated that they should follow the girl at the traffic light and the defendant said he replied, "Yeah, we'll get you one." They'd been following young women, Woldt told him, because Salmon was a virgin. The defendant said they'd followed at least four or five other women in the weeks leading up to Jacine's murder.

"Mr. Woldt seemed articulate, well-spoken, very in control," Bjorndahl testified. He was also quite willing to write out his statement on paper, which the detective read parts of to the jury.

" 'She was still breathing so Lucas handed me the knife,' " the detective read as the jurors followed a transcription of the words on a projector screen. " 'I cut her throat as well. I quickly handed the knife back to Lucas and he said that he was going to stab it into her heart.

" 'I gave Lucas back the knife and he stabs her another time in the chest, I believe. By this point I was so terrified that my whole body was shaking because she was still alive.' "

The police officers were followed to the stand by a parade of crime-scene technicians. When one began to describe for the jury what they were seeing in the gruesome photographs projected on a screen, George Woldt showed emotion for the first time in three years. With Jacine's battered, bloody body before him, he turned away and began to cry. His lawyers had to ask the judge to excuse the jury so that their client could compose himself.

This time, the judge did not allow the prosecution to show the crime-scene videotape that had reduced Salmon's defense attorney, Lauren Cleaver, to tears. Hall said it unnecessarily duplicated the crime-scene photographs.

However, the prosecution won the right to use Salmon's statements against Woldt. Heher protested the evidence, saying that Salmon's confession was self-serving and contradicted Woldt's own confession. Among his points: Salmon claimed the abduction, rape, and murder of a young woman were planned as much as a month earlier after watching *A Clockwork Orange*, but Woldt contended it was not planned in advance; Salmon said Amber Gonzales was struck intentionally, while Woldt claimed it was an accident; they disagreed over who saw Jacine first and whose idea it was to kill her.

But Zook said the prosecution needed the statements to cross-examine the defense's mental health experts, as well as Woldt's own self-serving confession. The judge sided with the prosecution.

Laura Shugart, the barmaid at the pool hall, appeared, as did Amber Gonzales, each pointing to the defendant as the man they recognized from their encounters with him on April 29, 1997.

Then the jury heard from the dead when the videotape of Derrick Ayers was played. He told them how he and Woldt had been best friends and spent a lot of time together in the spring and summer of 1996. Woldt had frequently talked about raping a woman, which Ayers had at first chalked up to guy talk. He began to wonder, however, when Woldt started pointing to certain women and suggesting, "She would make a good target."

There was no more wondering after the evening they drove up into the mountains and Woldt collected bowling ball–sized rocks and suggested they use them to attack a couple parked in a sports car. They would kill the man and rape the woman before also killing her, his friend said.

Woldt referred to women as "bitches" and told him that he preferred to have sex with women who would put up a fight and "it was no fun getting it from somebody that would just give it up." Ayers said he warned his girlfriend, Lisa, to get her sister away from Woldt and told her the truth about the rocks in the car. He was not surprised when the police found him in Seattle and he learned about the charges against Woldt.

Ayers's dramatic testimony was backed up by his former girlfriend, Lisa. She never liked Woldt and thought he was strange the way he was constantly "sniffing" things. He'd even sniffed her grandmother while they were all dining at a restaurant. "She was pretty put off by it."

She also recalled how her then-boyfriend had at first spent a lot of time with Woldt, but then began to express concerns about his "weird ideas." The concerns increased when she found the rocks in her car and he eventually told her the truth about why they were there. Woldt, she said, used to like to watch violent movies and joke before going out with Ayers, "Let's go rape some chicks and beat up some punks."

On cross-examination, Brake intimated that the sniffing was part of a mental illness, obsessive-compulsive disorder, that he might have inherited from his mother. Otherwise, his comments about raping women and beating up men were "never meant to be taken seriously."

The prosecution ended its case by calling Dr. David Bowerman, the El Paso County Coroner, to recount the wounds suffered by Jacine Gielinski and give the official

cause of death. "A stab wound to the chest which penetrated into the heart and as a result she died from internal
hemorrhaging in the heart."

As the jury viewed the photographs Bowerman used to
illustrate his points, some turned away in horror and revulsion. If any one noticed that Peggy and Bob Luiszer
were not in the courtroom, no one said anything.

Afterward, Peggy told the *Littleton Independent* she was
glad the second trial was under way. "It'll be over soon.
This has been going on for a long time." She still had a
ways to go.

Throughout the trial, the members of the press had frequently commented on how nice the Luiszers were. One
story the press didn't know had to do with Derrick Ayers.
The Luiszers had met him at one of the pretrial hearings
before his death and thanked him for his cooperation.

Not long afterward, they'd learned Ayers was staying at
a homeless shelter because he couldn't afford any place
else. When she saw him again, Peggy told him to call her
if he ever got into a "big jam" and needed help. He never
called and then they heard he'd died.

The sad thing was that he'd died a pauper and no one
had come forward to pay for a funeral, not until the Luiszers donated the money so that the former "best friend" of
one of their daughter's killers would have a decent burial
in a marked grave.

As promised in their opening, the defense presented experts who testified that a calcium growth near the
thalamus had affected Woldt's ability to reason and to control his behavior. The growth, along with two personality
disorders, obsessive-compulsive and "dissociative state,"
meant Woldt did not know what he was doing, according
to the defense's main witness, Dr. Rayna Rogers, a psychiatrist and frequent defense expert.

It was Rogers whom Salmon's defense expert, Meloy, had ridiculed as "outrageous" and had "switched the names" in her report that accused Salmon of being the instigator and leader. And for once, the prosecutors and the Luiszers agreed with him. They thought that what she had to say was outrageous, even though they were aware of the report she'd filed after examining Woldt nearly two years earlier.

Rogers described Woldt as "slavish" in his willingness to "place the needs of others above his own. . . . He is so preoccupied with pleasing others that he generally cannot defy anyone else or express his displeasure." This led him to give in to Salmon's demands to help find a woman to rape, especially after Woldt's wife insisted that he make their houseguest leave.

"One night George and Lucas watched Stanley Kubrick's *A Clockwork Orange* together. Lucas became particularly excited by the rape scenes and began to suggest to George that they go and do 'the old in and out.'" Woldt, she said, saw these comments as "jokes," and began to play a "game" together with Salmon in which the two would drive around in one of their cars pretending to be searching for a woman on whom to perform "the old in and out."

The "game" progressed to the point of following some women in their cars for a distance, according to Rogers. The women were chose for the "game" at random. When one of the men spotted an attractive young woman, he would say, "Let's follow her!" The game progressed to the point of carrying a kitchen knife in the car as part of the fantasy.

In addition, she said, Lucas repeatedly implored George to accompany him to pornography shops where they could watch movies. Woldt recalled that Salmon was particularly fond of films that involved rape or sexual abuse of women. George did not watch those films with Lucas but rather went into a different viewing room to watch movies that were not sexually violent.

On April 29, 1997, Woldt and Salmon were driving around the Garden of the Gods playing the "following game." Salmon spotted a young woman jogging along the road and suggested that George run into her with his car so they could "drag her inside."

Woldt explained that in prior escapades they had discussed such a maneuver as part of the "in and out" fantasy. When Salmon actually suggested it, however, Woldt laughed at the "joke" and continued driving. The woman ran out of sight so Woldt drove around the park twice more "pretending to look for her as part of the game." On the third pass around, Woldt accidentally collided with the young woman around a blind curve.

He immediately stopped got out and ran to see if she was all right, according to Rogers. He offered to drive her to her vehicle or to the hospital, but the woman declined, stating that her father was a park ranger and they lived nearby.

After playing several games of pool that night, the two men departed. In the car on the way home, Salmon began crying about not having a girlfriend. George felt guilty about kicking Lucas out and felt pity for his inept friend's sexual failure. George tried to cheer him up with a sexually suggestive joke when suddenly Lucas exclaimed, "There's one . . . follow her!" He had spotted Jacine Gielinski driving home.

As the two men abducted the young woman and then took her to the elementary school to rape her, Rogers testified that at that point Woldt "snapped" into a dissociative state, an almost out-of-body experience in which he didn't know what he was doing. In fact, she said, in a statement that brought gasps from spectators throughout the courtroom, his perception was so altered that he believed that he was the one being raped.

"He felt Jacine grabbed him, disrobed him, and mounted him," she said. "His main concern was to hurry home and confess his infidelity to his wife."

Lucas was merely sitting in the front seat watching what was happening, according to Rogers, when Woldt said, " 'What are you looking at?' because in his frantic and dissociated state of mind these were the only words that would come out. What he really means to say was 'please help me!' or something like it to get the woman to 'stop having sex with him.' " Woldt lay there and cried during intercourse, she said, and felt as if he was "being victimized."

According to Rogers, the next thing Woldt remembered was retrieving the knife, at Lucas's direction, from the glove compartment in which they had placed it earlier in the day. Still in "a state of bewilderment," Woldt found himself holding up the victim's head while Lucas "ran the knife across her throat." Lucas then told George to do the same, but George didn't feel he could do it and refused. Lucas pressured him until George took the knife and swiped it across her neck.

Salmon stabbed her in the chest and then handed the knife to Woldt, indicating he should do the same. "Although sickened and horrified," Woldt felt that the only way to "be away" from the situation was to take the knife. Seeing no other options, Woldt turned his head away and plunged the knife at the victim's chest.

According to Rogers, Salmon wanted to cut out the victim's genitals so that no semen could be retrieved for DNA testing. Woldt could not bear the thought of Salmon mutilating the woman's body, she said, and so was able to think of an alternative, the mud.

There was no indication of any formal thought disorder while speaking with Woldt, according to Rogers. "Nevertheless, over the months he has experienced several visual and auditory hallucinations of 'angels' visiting his cell. One time the 'angel' lay on his bunk, so Woldt took a sheet from the bed and slept on the cold cement floor so that the male angel on his bunk would be comfortable."

Those in the courtroom seemed stunned by Rogers's testimony. Woldt was the rape victim? He was so determined to please others that he'd unwillingly gone along with Salmon's plan to rape and murder Jacine Gielinski?

A visibly angry Dave Young cross-examined Rogers, asking her if Woldt didn't enjoy having sex with Jacine, "How was it that he had an erection and an orgasm?"

Rogers shrugged. Even brain-dead people can have erections and orgasms, she said. To which Young retorted to the defense's objections, "Are you saying he's brain-dead?"

The psychiatrist said she'd read Salmon's confession and even Woldt's earlier confession, in which he'd mentioned nothing about feeling like he was the rape victim or that it was all Salmon's idea to abandon "the game" and really rape and murder someone. But that hadn't changed her mind.

Young asked why Woldt placed the knife in the glove box of the car if he didn't intend to use it.

"It was part of the fantasy, a part of the game," Rogers said.

"Do you think rape and murder is a game?" Young retorted.

"Of course not," Rogers sniped back.

After Rogers's testimony the rest of the trial was anticlimactic. Bonnie Woldt testified that she loved her husband but he had an "unhealthy attachment" to Salmon, who constantly pestered him about finding a girlfriend. She also denied making statements to friends that her marriage and sex life with Woldt were violent, or that she'd overheard her husband and Salmon talking about imitating what they'd seen in *A Clockwork Orange*.

On rebuttal, the prosecution had presented their own experts who denied that the calcium deposit would have affected Woldt's behavior, at least not without causing other behavioral disturbances that would have been detected. In fact, one said there was strong evidence from tests to indicate that Woldt was faking his "mental illness."

In his closing argument, Dave Young hammered on the different stages at which Woldt had shown he was deliberating. He'd deliberated when he decided to follow Gielinski. Deliberated when he decided to rape her first. Deliberated again, for fifteen minutes, with Salmon as they tried to decide whether to kill Jacine, and then over the next hour or so, stopped what they were doing several times to deliberate over how to kill her. Then they'd deliberated when they shoved mud in her vagina to cover up evidence of the rape.

"There's no room for sympathy for this defendant," Young told the jurors. "He certainly didn't have sympathy for Jacine Gielinski."

Wilson countered that the case wasn't about what happened to Jacine but why it happened. "Why is George Woldt's brain malfunctioning?" he asked. "Why do the circuits not work?

"This case is about why George did not exercise good judgment. She was killed. We are sorry, but why do we get to that point?"

He said that the defense had promised in their opening statements to hold the prosecution to proving its burden beyond a reasonable doubt. Any hesitation the jurors now had was reasonable doubt, he said. Even the fact that the experts had disagreed was enough to show there was reasonable doubt.

Wilson reminded them of the expert who'd testified, "If I were a mad scientist, I could not think of a better place to put a lesion or a tone than in the center of George Woldt's thalamus."

But Zook came right back on rebuttal by saying the

brain-lesion theory "is just an excuse." He noted that Woldt had been trying to recruit others for years into raping and killing a woman "because he thought that it would be fun.

"His guilt is as permanent as Jacine Gielinski's death," Zook said. "All the king's horses and all the king's men . . . they can't save him. They can't excuse him."

*March 23, 2000*

Judge Richard Hall cleared his throat and prepared to read the verdict. In her seat, Peggy Luiszer clutched at the photograph of Jacine that she had not been allowed to bring into the trial, and she feared the worst.

After the Salmon jury reached its verdict so quickly, she had expected the same thing with the Woldt jury. To her, his guilt seemed even more apparent. But the jury had deliberated for more than three hours the day before and then went home for the night, then returned in the morning to deliberate for another hour. The delay did not bode well for her.

However, Hall soon relieved her of that notion. As Woldt sat staring straight ahead without any emotion and Peggy sobbed quietly, the judge read off the guilty verdicts. First-degree murder after deliberation. Guilty. Felony first-degree murder. Guilty. First-degree sexual assault. Guilty. Guilty. Guilty. George Woldt would face a death-penalty panel.

Soon afterward, the Luiszers met with the jurors, who told them that they never believed the defense theory about the brain lesion or psychological problems being responsible for Woldt's actions. They described Rayna Rogers's testimony and theories as "a joke."

They'd actually agreed on his guilt the day before, but wanted to sleep on it to be sure.

Now, the Luiszers were going to have to go through the whole process of a death-penalty hearing again. Asked if they were worried about a similar outcome as with Salmon, Peggy said she felt that Woldt was "definitely the more evil of the two."

"We just want three judges who will listen and apply the factors," she said. "If that happens, we can live with whatever they decide."

Whatever happened to Woldt in the future, she added, "I hope he has a really rotten time. He thinks he's cool. I hope he gets knocked down a couple of notches. . . . I think he deserves to die."

Six months later, so did a panel of judges—this time including Trial Judge Richard Hall and appointed Judges Douglas Anderson and Larry Schwartz, all of El Paso County.

Yet again, Jacine's family members had recounted their loss. Peggy Luiszer, clutching the urn containing her daughter's ashes, once again tried to explain to strangers who Jacine had been.

Except for the prosecutors, no one seemed to care that her whole world had been turned upside down. She couldn't bring herself to go back to work or even to travel alone very far from her home. She couldn't be alone with a man without feeling panic. When her husband touched her, all she could see was Salmon and Woldt on top of her daughter, doing the things they had done to Jacine. But how could she explain all of that to three judges? And even if she managed, would it matter?

Doug Wilson and Terri Brake argued that Woldt's life should be spared because he had suffered the brain lesion that had impaired his judgment. He also suffered from an obsessive-compulsive disorder stemming from his abusive childhood, they said.

They brought in several experts to testify, including Dr. Jonathan Pincus, a Washington, D.C., neurologist. He said he'd interviewed 150 to 200 convicted murderers, many of them on death row, and found that their crimes involved a combination of three factors: mental illness, physical and/or sexual abuse as a child, and neurological disorder. Woldt had all three, he testified.

As at Salmon's death-penalty hearing, the defense attorneys were allowed to introduce proportionality evidence. Rather than calling a witness, this time the defense had put together a large book comparing the cases of other men on death row. They argued that Salmon had been the leader in the crime and had inflicted the fatal blows. Since Salmon had received a life sentence, they told the judges, singling Woldt out for a harsher punishment would be unfair.

The prosecution had rebutted the brain-damage and personality-disorder testimony with its own experts. And this time, they were better prepared to counter the proportionality review with a review of their own, demonstrating how both Woldt and his crimes fit the profile of other killers on death row. While all the evidence pointed to the men being equally culpable in the crime, "It was Woldt's idea," they argued.

After the defense rested its case, Woldt had apologized. The smooth talker, the confident ladies' man, was gone, and he handled himself with far less dignity than had the friend he'd talked into helping carry out his terrible fantasy. Crying and sniffling, Woldt told the judges that he had become a Christian. If allowed to live, he said, he would "honor God, read the Bible, and help others."

"I don't want to die," he pleaded. "Everyone knows that I did a horrible thing." Then he turned to Jacine's family. "I'm sorry I took her away from you," he said. "I'm sorry for the last three and a half years. I don't know what I can say. 'Sorry,' it's not even good enough for me when I say this. Nothing I say, nothing I do is going to make this better. I'm sorry for what I did to you, I'm sorry."

Peggy and Bob Luiszer felt nothing but contempt for his apology. At least Salmon had sounded sincere. Woldt with all his sniveling simply sounded like the murderous coward he was.

In her closing arguments, defense attorney Brake said Woldt was "not an evil person; he did a very evil thing."

But Zook noted that the cruelty of the crime far outweighed any possible mitigating factors. "You know the evil he has done," he said. And then he repeated a line that prosecutor Eva Wilson had used six years earlier, when she'd asked a jury to sentence Nathan Dunlap to death: "If not this case, what case? If not now, when? And if not this defendant, who?"

On September 6, 2000, the judges answered those question as Peggy sighed and wept quietly. If she and Bob had known this would take three and a half years, they would not have asked the district attorney's office to pursue the death penalty, though they believed it was merited. But now these judges had handed down justice for all the pain Jacine had suffered, and for all the pain they had suffered.

"The panel was struck by the senseless brutality inflicted by Woldt and Salmon on Jacine Gielinski," the judges wrote in a sixty-two-page decision. "She was forced to suffer unspeakable pain and anguish during the time that she was held hostage. The kidnappers wholly ignored her pleas for mercy and the pitiful suffering she was enduring at their hands. It is obvious that Jacine Gielinski was merely a physical object to Woldt and Salmon, necessary to act out their mutual fantasy to kidnap, rape and kill, leaving no room for the least amount of human compassion for her plight.

"The fact that they apparently exchanged high fives at the conclusion of Jacine's killing speaks volumes of their lack of humanity toward her."

For the third time out of seven tries, a panel of judges had sentenced a man to die. In order to reach that decision, they'd determined that certain murderers were more deserving of the death penalty than others. Like Frank "Pancho" Martinez and Cody Neal, George Woldt was one of those murderers.

This time, District Attorney Smith had nothing but praise for the judges and for her prosecution team, on whose lives this case had taken an "enormous toll." The sentence, she said, "reaffirms that Colorado's death penalty will be used for these most heinous crimes. We do not rejoice in seeing another person die, but it is truly the only just punishment for someone like George Woldt, who was willing to rape, torture, and murder merely for the sport of killing."

She also praised her prosecution team for the enormous sacrifice of their personal lives. "But the most important members of this team have been Bob and Peggy Luiszer," and she pledged to fight Woldt's appeals process "to the end."

Wilson and Brake slipped out of the courtroom after the verdict was read and could not be reached. Bob Salmon, who had attended the trial and sentencing hearing said, "I just feel bad for the Luiszers. They truly had a great loss that can never be replaced.

"I think the sentence is fair. Quite frankly, if my son had received the death-sentence penalty, that would have been fair."

Bob Luiszer said he and his wife had no plans now except "to go on with our grieving process, which has kind of been interrupted, and to try to carry on some kind of normal life."

Peggy Luiszer praised the judges. "They saw the truth for what it was, and I think the judges made the right decision," she said. "I think they should have done it in Salmon's case, also, but that's over and done with.

"I hope he's scared to death and thinking about his daughter and son . . . and when the time comes for him to be put to death that he remembers how he treated Jacine and maybe how she felt that night."

Asked what she was going to do with the photograph of Jacine she'd carried all that time, she replied, "It goes back up on the shelf in the family room, where it was the first night when I got that call."

Then there was another question. Would she attend the execution? She didn't hesitate. "You bet."

# EPILOGUE
## A NEW NORMAL

A few days after Christmas 2002, Bob and Peggy Luiszer made the hated drive back down to Colorado Springs to bring his holiday cookies to the staff at the El Paso County District Attorney's Office. They had remained friends with the prosecutors, though mostly it was limited to holiday cards and the occasional telephone call.

There was another purpose to the visits as well, and that was to tell District Attorney Jeanne Smith "No more." They were through—the system opposed to the death penalty had beaten them down, and it finally won.

Earlier in the year, the U.S. Supreme Court had handed down a decision in an Arizona case that essentially said that the jury that convicted a killer also had to make the decision on whether he would live or die. At the time, Arizona law left it up to a single judge, but even states like Colorado that placed the burden on a panel of judges were affected.

A hearing took place in the fall at the Colorado Supreme Court with attorneys for the state attorney general's office arguing that the decision did not necessarily affect Colorado. The justices disagreed. They decided that the U.S. Supreme Court decision had also negated the death-penalty decisions for Francisco Martinez and George

Woldt. William "Cody" Neal's case would take further study as Neal had voluntarily waived his right to a jury trial and placed himself in the hands of the panel of judges.

Relatives for the victims attended the hearing. All they had been through—the countless hours sitting on hard wooden pews, listening to lawyers and witnesses talk about the brutal murders of their loved ones, testifying about the effects on their own lives—was all for naught.

A lawyer for the attorney general's office told Peggy that "we'll fight this all the way to the Supreme Court." But Peggy shook her head. "Not with us, you won't."


Nothing had stopped because of Woldt's sentencing, not even the defense tactics to hit the Luiszers again. A week after Woldt was sentenced to death, he and his attorneys refused to attend the sentencing hearing for the other convictions, including the assault and attempted kidnapping of Amber Gonzales. Wilson told the press that because Hall had already handed down the worst penalty, the judge would probably sentence Woldt to the maximum number of years. So, according to the lawyer, there was no reason for him, Brake, or their client to be present.

Wilson also said that he didn't want to subject himself or Woldt, who had been placed on a suicide watch, to "being confronted" by Gonzales. After arriving at his home in Pueblo the day of the sentencing, the lawyer had loaded his SUV, told his wife he was leaving for a bit, then went fly-fishing in a remote area of Colorado. He would later tell the *Gazette* that he was "devastated" and needed the time for a little soul-searching and reflection on the job he had done. Whatever conclusions he reached, they didn't include wanting to listen to Gonzales testify about the affects of the crime on her life.

Wilson would have gotten an earful. After the verdict, the now twenty-two-year-old Gonzales told the press that only recently had she been able to jog with her mother past the place in the Garden of the Gods where she'd been struck by the car.

"It's changed me a lot," she told the *Gazette*. "I've never really trusted strangers, but now I'm a little more leery of everyone. It took me a long time to begin to have a relationship, as far as a boyfriend. Even though nothing happened, I felt, in a way, I was violated."

Gonzales said she was haunted by what happened to Jacine. "When people talk about Jacine and what a wonderful person she was, I wish it didn't have to be her. I wish it didn't have to happen at all. It scares me to think that could have been me."

It scared other people, too. Gonzales's parents, Carol and Al, had attended the verdict and hugged Peggy Luiszer immediately afterward, then watched as she was swarmed by the media. "It could be us standing over there," Al Gonzales said. "Amber was their first target. We could have lost our daughter. We were lucky, very lucky. I just wish Jacine was that lucky."

The prosecutors tried to force Woldt and Wilson to attend the sentencing. Zook contended that Wilson was skipping it to give his client further grounds for appeal (his lawyer wasn't present to represent him). Denison argued that the Colorado Victim's Rights Act required that a defendant be present at the sentencing. However, Wilson asserted that the defendant and his lawyer had a constitutional right to attend, but it was not a requirement. The judge shrugged and said that if Wilson and his client had put it on record that they didn't want to attend, then that was their choice.

The defense table was empty when Gonzales took the stand and told her story. This time, Woldt received the same sentence as Salmon for the remaining crimes—184 years, should he escape his date with the state's execution chamber.

The murder of Jacine Gielinski had a ripple effect that touched many lives. Like with the Salmon case, many of the Woldt jurors attended the sentencing hearing, the judges' announcement of their decision, or both. Juror Jamie Tepley, who after the trial described psychiatrist Rayna Rogers's testimony as "a joke," said it was impossible for the jurors not to have been deeply affected by what they saw and heard. "There were some emotional times when I'd go home and bawl," said Tepley, who was about the same age as Gielinski.

"It could have been any one of our daughters," juror George Renaud, the father of a thirteen-year-old, told the *Gazette* as he wept outside the courtroom. He said he'd been sickened and frightened for his own children by the horrific evidence and brutality of the crime. The punishment fit the crime, he said. "Taking a life is not a game. For this case, the death penalty should take effect."

Not every spectator was as relieved by the judges' decision. Woldt's family didn't attend the sentencing hearing, except on the day they had testified on their son's behalf, and they weren't present for the decision. But they had friends in the courtroom, many of them from the Korean-American Christian community, who groaned and shook their heads when Hall said the decision was death.

Jimmy Son said he thought that the sentence would be overturned on appeal. "I hope society gives him a chance," he told the *Gazette*. "He was young and his background didn't make him fit in society. I hope God gives him forgiveness."

The Rev. Young Chull Lee was confident that God would. He'd been meeting with Woldt for two months to study the Bible and pray. "He has dedicated his life to repentance," Lee told the paper. "Deeply in his heart he says sorry to Gielinski's family and the Colorado Springs community."

\* \* \*

In February 2001, the proportionality review again came into play in a Colorado case that would reignite the fires of the death-penalty debate. Two years earlier, a hulking halfway-house inmate named Donta Page murdered a twenty-one-year-old woman named Peyton Tuthill.

Page beat, slashed, and raped Tuthill so brutally that imprints of her bloody head were left on the walls of her bedroom. Then he slit her throat with a knife he'd found in her kitchen, carefully wrapping the handle with a towel so as not to leave fingerprints, and when that didn't kill her, stabbed her twice in the chest. Page even interrupted his attack to go out to Tuthill's car to look for her purse before returning to rape her and finish her off. The jury convicted him of first-degree murder after deliberation.

At the death-penalty hearing, Page's lawyers trotted out a questionable accounting of their client's "abused" childhood, claimed he'd suffered brain damage as a result. He was immature (though not so immature as to be incapable of pulling off other armed robberies) and had reacted to Tuthill's appearance in her own home while he was robbing it with rage, but not deliberation. They admitted that the murder was brutal, but said it didn't rise to "the level of depravity" of the crimes committed by the other men on death row.

The very thought of comparing murders horrified the victim's mother, Pat Tuthill, as it had horrified Peggy Luiszer. How could these defense attorneys argue that what had happened to her daughter was somehow "less heinous" than what had happened to other victims? She wanted to scream: What else would Page have to have done to climb over some imaginary bar? Decapitate her instead of just cutting her throat? Dismember her rather than nearly slicing her thumbs off? How many more times did he have to stab her? How many more ways did he have to rape her? How much more of her blood did there have to be on the walls, the bed, the floor?

How could they rank murders?

But on March 2, 2001, the judges returned with their decision and did just that. They called Donta Page's crime "vile" and "repugnant," but they also spared his life. As a result of the proportionality review, they had determined that "imposing the death penalty on Donta Page would lower the bar for executions in the State of Colorado."

Their reasoning was, of course, a bunch of legal mumbo-jumbo. Each of the murders committed by the men on death row was different. Some stalked their victim; some did not. Some killed quickly; some dragged it on for some time. Rape was involved in some, but not in others. The judges had simply found an excuse.

In the days that followed, the judges' decision inspired yet another death-penalty debate at the legislature. Two members of the panel and one member of Salmon's panel had done what no jury had ever done, what no jury could have done because that information would not have been provided to them, and that was create a ranking of murderers.

Defense lawyers, who'd complained in 1995 when the death-penalty decision was taken away from juries, now praised the Page hearing judges. "I think they have given us a road map for how to search for justice in a death-penalty case," defense attorney Larry Pozner, who'd been the lawyer who tried to contact a friend of the Luiszers on behalf of Woldt's attorneys, told the *Denver Post*. "These judges have come up with the mechanism, the procedure. They have given us the book on what to do if you want to try to figure out who is going to be executed and who is going to go to prison for life."

District attorneys, however, slammed the judges' procedure as nothing more than smoke and mirrors, with no legal basis. Even prosecutor-turned–defense lawyer Craig Silverman, who'd been a Denver deputy district attorney prosecuting the Rodriguez brothers, said the decision set a "disastrous precedent . . . in effect, [prosecutors] will be trying seven or eight cases at the same time."

Adams County District Attorney Bob Grant, whose office had sent Robert Harlan to death row, complained that the danger of proportionality reviews was that only "twins" of the type of cases already on death row stood a chance of adding to the inmates there. "It would completely eviscerate the law," he said.

State Senator Ken Chlouber, a Republican from Leadville, wasn't taking any chances. Shortly after Page's sentencing, he introduced a bill that would change Colorado's death-penalty system, replacing the three-judge panel with a single judge, the trial judge.

Chlouber was more familiar with the death penalty than most lawmakers, having recently witnessed the Kansas execution of a man who had raped and murdered his elderly aunt. He said he was "disgusted" with the panel's decision to spare Page's life. "The public was outraged, and that's an understatement," he said. "There's nothing I can do about that case, but we can do something about the next trial."

Chlouber was supported in his efforts by Peggy Luiszer. Both Salmon and Woldt "deserved to die for their actions," she told the press. Had his trial judge made the death-penalty decision, Salmon would have landed on death row, too.

Chlouber's bill faced opposition from both sides, however. The Colorado District Attorneys' Council said it was too soon to abandon the existing system; the Colorado Bar Association said the measure would put "inappropriate pressure" on a single judge. The proposal met a quick death, as did another measure that would have returned the death-penalty decision to juries.

As with other cases before it, the Donta Page sentencings had shown that, for better or worse, judges were just as subjective and human in making their decisions as any twelve jurors. The difference was that judges were required by law to say how they'd reached that decision.

And in the end, it didn't matter. The U.S. Supreme Court decision placed the onus back onto the jurors. In February 2003, the Colorado Supreme Court ordered that Francisco Martinez, William Neal, and George Woldt be taken off death row and resentenced to life in prison.

After the Colorado Supreme Court overturned Woldt's death sentence, Peggy and Bob Luiszer no longer had the will to fight the system anymore. A few days after Christmas, Peggy made sure District Attorney Smith understood that if her office decided to appeal and go after Woldt again, "You'll have to do it without us."

The Luiszers no longer cared. They simply want to find a place in the world again. They remain married, but their marriage is a fragile thing, held together by friendship and memories more than anything to do with being a man and a woman.

Peggy grows angry with all the platitudes, and she has even lost some of her friends over it, especially when she hears people talk about "time healing all wounds" or that "God must have had some plan." The former simply isn't true; time does not heal *all* wounds. The latter sounds too much like Lucas Salmon explaining to the defense psychologist Meloy that there was nothing he could have done to prevent what happened to Jacine. "It was God's will for Jacine to die as bad as that sounds," Salmon told the psychologist. "It happened regardless of what I wanted. Everybody dies . . . it's not right to question God."

That is not the sort of God that the Luiszers can believe in, and nothing will ever be the same for them. They are the parents of a murder victim, and that makes them different.

The mother of one of Jacine's best friends, who had gotten married and named her first child after Jacine, called Peggy and told her not to contact her daughter anymore. Peggy has never been allowed to see the baby. "And I want to so much," she said, bursting into tears during a final interview for this book in January 2003.

Lucas Salmon and George Woldt stole more than Jacine's dignity and life. They took more than her smile and love from her family and friends. They also ripped apart the future of Peggy and Bob Luiszer. There would be no wedding bells, no happy hours holding a grandchild of their own. Now, there would be no visiting with Jacine and her friends as their children played, as she had once played in the small house near the little elementary school.

"There is no going 'back to normal,'" Bob Luiszer said with a sigh as his wife wept, sitting at the kitchen table holding the photograph of Jacine she'd carried to court. "There is only a 'new normal.' . . . We're the parents of a murder victim, and they never let you forget it."